הגדה של פסח

THE PASSOVER HAGGADAH

The Seder Night: An Exalted Evening

THE BERMAN EDITION

THE BERMAN EDITION

The Seder Night: An Exalted Evening

The Passover Haggadah
הגדה של פסח

With a commentary
based on the teachings of
RABBI JOSEPH B. SOLOVEITCHIK

Edited by
RABBI MENACHEM GENACK

OU PRESS
New York

Library of Congress Cataloging-in-Publication Data

Haggadah. English & Hebrew.
The seder night : an exalted evening : the Passover Haggadah : with a commentary based on the teachings of Rabbi Joseph B. Soloveitchik / edited by Menachem Genack.
p. cm.
"The Berman Edition."
Text of Haggadah in Hebrew with English translation; rubrics and commentary in English.
ISBN 978-1-60280-118-9
1. Haggadot – Texts. 2. Seder – Liturgy – Texts. 3. Judaism – Liturgy – Texts. 4. Haggadah. I. Genak, Menahem Dov ben Hayim Yitshak. II. Soloveitchik, Joseph Dov. III. Title.
BM674.643.G46 2009
296.4'5371–dc22

2008053716

Design and typesetting by Koren Publishing Services
Jacket design by Sara Jaskiel
Manufactured in the United States of America

Published by
OU Press
Orthodox Union
11 Broadway
New York, NY 10004

Distributed by
KTAV PUBLISHING HOUSE
527 Empire Blvd
Brooklyn, NY 11225
Website: www.ktav.com
Email: orders@ktav.com
Ph: (718) 972-5449 / Fax: (718) 972-6307

Print year 2018

This Haggadah is lovingly dedicated
to the memory of our parents

Rabbi Henoch and Sarah D. Berman

הרב חנוך בן מאיר
שרה דבורה בת אריה לייב

and to the memory of our brother

Meyer Berman

מאיר אבא בן הרב חנוך

Our parents, individually and jointly, taught all who knew them what it means to be an authentic עבדא דקודשא בריך הוא. Our brother, through his generosity of spirit that knew no bounds, genuinely heard נאקת בני ישראל and reacted in the only way he knew how.

Julius and Dorothy Berman
Tobias and Rosalie Berman

In Loving Memory of Our Parents

David and Ruth L. Balter

דוד זאב בן הרב שלמה
רחל בת חיים

dedicated by

Howard and Chaya Balter

In Honor of Our Parents

Rabbi Joseph and
Pepa Karasick עמו"ש

הרב יוסף בן יעקב
פעסיה בת יצחק

A constant source of inspiration and pride to their children, grandchildren and great-grandchildren

dedicated by

Benjamin and Bernice Mandel and Family
Mark and Linda Karasick and Family
George and Denise Karasick and Family

In Loving Memory of Our Parents

Joseph and Gwendolyn Straus

יוסף שמואל בן בנימין
גיננדל בת משה יעקב

dedicated by

Moshael and Zahava Straus
Daniel and Joyce Straus

In Loving Memory of Our Husband and Father

Rabbi Yitzchok Singer

הרב יצחק אהרן בן הרב אליהו

Rabbi of the Bialystoker Synagogue
and a renowned תלמיד חכם

In Loving Memory of
Our Brother-in-Law and Uncle

Rabbi Dovid Singer

הרב דוד בן הרב אליהו

Rabbi of First Congregation Anshe Sfard
and a scholar of great erudition

dedicated by

Rebetzin Bluma Singer
Baruch and Susan Singer
Eli and Rivki Singer
Nussie and Ruchy Singer
Yossi and Suri Singer
Sruly and Leah Singer

In Loving Memory of Our Parents

Abraham and Ruth Parkoff

אברהם בן יצחק דוב הכהן
רחל בלומא בת יהושע

In Honor of

Rabbi Steven Weil

dedicated by

Richard and Debra Parkoff

PREFACE

This volume consists of a compilation of insights and commentary on the Haggadah by the Rav, Rabbi Joseph B. Soloveitchik, *zt"l*. The Rav spoke publicly about the Haggadah in a variety of settings and genres throughout his decades of teaching. Many of his Talmudic classes and *yahrzeit shi'urim* in memory of his father, Rabbi Moshe Soloveitchik *zt"l*, focused on themes of *Halakha* and *lomdus* related to the Haggadah. His public lectures (including those in memory of his wife, Tonya) and his essays focused on more general themes. In addition, during the season of the *Pesaḥ* holiday, the Rav would often speak about the Haggadah in his *shi'ur*, reviewing it paragraph by paragraph and bringing alive to his students the contemporary meaning of the text's eternal message.

The sources for this work are three-fold in nature. First, we have quoted extensively, sometimes in slightly abridged form, from the Rav's written works. The majority of this material is from recently published works of the *MeOtsar HoRav* series of the Toras HoRav Foundation. Generations of readers will be in the Foundation's debt for preserving and disseminating the Rav's intellectual legacy. We are grateful to the Foundation's leaders, Dr. Atarah Twersky and Rabbi Aharon and Dr. Tovah Lichtenstein for their leadership, and we regret that Rabbi Yitzchak Twersky's untimely passing prevented him from seeing the fruits of the Foundation's labors. We also commend the Foundation's Editorial Publication Committee, Professor David Shatz, Dr. Joel B. Wolowelsky, and Rabbi Reuven Ziegler, for their untiring efforts. Selections from other published works are included with the permission of the respective publishers.

The other two sources for this Haggadah are *Kol ha-Rav*, which comes from the various tapes of the Rav's *shi'urim* that are in wide circulation, and *Reshimot*, which are my own lecture notes taken during decades of being privileged to experience the Rav's teachings first-hand.

In his published works, the Rav referred to biblical personalities and books of the Bible by their common English names. In his *shi'urim*, he would often use the Hebrew terms. We have adopted the former as the unified style for this work, although Rambam rather than Maimonides is used in the *Kol ha-Rav* and *Reshimot* annotations.

In bringing this Haggadah to fruition I was assisted by many friends, colleagues and former students, and I express grateful appreciation to all of them for their generous contribution of time, effort and learning.

First and foremost, I wish to especially thank my friend Dr. Joel Wolowelsky, whose initiative and involvement – from the initial conceptual stages, through the composition, organization and editing of material, and finally

to the details of publishing – were indispensable in bringing this project to a successful culmination. Absent his talent and industry, this volume would not have been published.

I offer thanks to Rabbi Simon Posner, my colleague at the Orthodox Union and friend from childhood, for his sage counsel and constant encouragement. His review of successive drafts of the entire manuscript, numerous editorial suggestions and overall guidance in all aspects of the project were invaluable.

Mr. David Olivestone, my colleague at the Orthodox Union, was in charge of the design features of the Haggadah, and I express my appreciation for his presenting us with this aesthetically pleasing volume.

Rabbi Hershel Schachter reviewed significant portions of the final manuscript and provided numerous helpful stylistic and substantive suggestions. Rabbis Arnold Lustiger and Michael Taubes also reviewed portions of the final manuscript and made helpful comments. Rabbi Reuven Ziegler provided important and valuable information. Many of my colleagues and former students assisted in the transcription and editing of the *Kol ha-Rav* and *Reshimot* annotations. This group included Rabbis Daniel Besser, Gad Buchbinder, Daniel Feldman, Moshe Genack, Chaim Yitzchak Genack, Eli Gersten, Avrohom Gordimer, David Hellman, Seth Mandel, Ephraim Meth, David Mintz, Yehuda Muehlgay, Avi Muschel, David Nachbar, Gavriel Price, Jacob Sasson, Kenneth Schiowitz, Ethan Schnall, David Shabtai, Tzvi Sinensky, Yigal Sklarin, Yaakov Werblowsky, Netanel Wiederblank, Eliyahu Wolf, and Michael Zylberman. In addition, Rabbi Yitzchak Lichtenstein, author of the wonderful *Si'aḥ ha-Grid* Haggadah, was a source of helpful information.

I acknowledge Bernard Scharfstein of KTAV Publishing House and thank him for his assistance and cooperation. I thank Matthew Miller, Raphael Freeman and Chaya Mendelson of Koren Publishing Services for their work on the design and typesetting. I extend thanks to Jewish Publication Society for granting permission to reprint excerpts from *Halakhic Man*. My appreciation also to Rabbi Steven Weil for his encouragement and support.

The Orthodox Union is an organization that holds the Rav's legacy in high esteem, and I express appreciation to Mr. Stephen Savitsky, President of the Orthodox Union, and Dr. Simcha Katz, Chairman of the Orthodox Union Kashrus Commission, for their enthusiastic and unflagging support. This Haggadah is a publication of the OU Press which was established by the Orthodox Union for the purpose of publishing significant works of lasting Jewish value. I know that the leadership of the Orthodox Union and the editors of the OU Press are gratified to make the Rav's thoughts on the Haggadah available to a wider audience.

We extend our profound thanks to Julius Berman for his astute advice and

critical support in fostering this project and so many other projects relating to the dissemination of the Rav's teachings. Mr. Berman, a prize student of the Rav, was the Rav's confidant and attorney, and the Rav had enormous confidence in his judgment, wisdom and loyalty. When a former student asked the Rav what position to take on a particular public policy issue, the Rav responded, "Check with Julius Berman; that is what I always do." Mr. Berman's consistent agenda, from the launching of Mesorah journal, to his role in the Toras HoRav Foundation and the publication of the Rav's thought through the OU Press, has been to make the Rav's teachings accessible to the multitudes in the Jewish community who thirst for them. A past president of the Orthodox Union, Mr. Berman serves as Chairman of the OU Press Commission. It is only fitting that this publication of the OU Press in the endeavor to disseminate the Rav's thought to the public be dedicated by Julie and his brother Teddy in memory of their parents and brother.

We are grateful as well for the assistance provided by the Balter, Karasick, Parkoff, Singer and Straus families, all of whom are devoted supporters of the ideals personified by the Rav.

Menachem Genack

Second Edition

The publication of the second edition of *The Seder Night: An Exalted Evening* has given us the opportunity to include commentary by the Rav on *Shir ha-Shirim*. I am grateful to Rabbis Simon Posner and Gil Student and Dr. Joel B. Wolowelsky for their help in preparing this addition.

M.G.

INTRODUCTION

The exalted evening of the *Seder* is characterized by the themes of the acceptance of God's sovereignty, the transmission of our tradition – the *Masorah* – and the dynamic and creative force of the *Torah she-be-al peh,* the Oral Law. The Rav expressed all these themes in his life's work. For decades, he taught the senior *shi'ur* at Yeshiva University's Rabbi Isaac Elchanan Theological Seminary, continued teaching his former students and thousands of others at lectures delivered under the auspices of the Rabbinical Council of America and public *shi'urim* given at the Moriah Synagogue in New York City, and served as the chief rabbinic figure in Boston where, with his beloved wife Tonya, he founded and continued to direct the Maimonides School. A rabbinic figure without peer and a seminal Jewish thinker of the twentieth century, the Rav was able to convey to all those who engaged in Torah study with him the immediacy and power of Torah and the experience of Torah as a living force.

For the Rav, the study of Torah was the ultimate path to accepting God's kingship. By infusing the Torah with new insights and fresh approaches, the Rav ensured that Torah would be a continuing source of life that enabled generations of students to experience the eternal connection that every Jew has with Torah, thereby effecting the transmission of the *Masorah.* Moses is called the "*Safra Rabbah de-Yisrael,* the great scribe of Israel," explained the Rav, because he not only wrote the Torah on parchment, but he also effectively inscribed the words of Torah on the hearts and minds of the Jewish people.

The Haggadah says that even though we are all scholars, we are obligated to recount the story of the Exodus and we all must view ourselves as though we personally experienced the momentous events of the Exodus. Rambam echoes this language when he discusses the *mizvah* of *Hakhel,* the commandment that the entire Jewish people assemble in Jerusalem once every seven years to hear the King of Israel read to them from the Torah. He writes, "Even converts who are unfamiliar with the language [of *Hakhel*] are obligated to listen, with fear and awe, joy and trembling, as the day it was given at Sinai. Even great scholars who know the entire Torah are required to listen with intense concentration, for the Torah established [the *mizvah* of *Hakhel*] to strengthen the true creed. One should view oneself as now being commanded and hearing it directly from the Almighty, for the King is a messenger to proclaim the words of God" (*Hilkhot Ḥagigah* 3:6). The Rav, with his majestic personality and towering intellect, was the epitome of the King proclaiming and transmitting God's teachings. Surely those who were privileged to be present at the Rav's *shi'urim* perceived his regal bearing and felt the immediacy of Torah as though they

were re-living the revelation at Sinai and receiving soaring words of Torah directly from the Almighty.

The Rav personified *Torah she-be-al peh*, its vitality and dynamism, its intellectual excitement and spiritual depth. He also embodied *Masorah*. As the King was at *Hakhel*, the Rav was the noble messenger of the Almighty whose entire being was a testament to the transmission, preservation and perpetuation of Torah. He would say that when giving the *shi'ur*, he felt that Hillel and Shammai, Abaye and Rava, Rashi and Tosafot, the Taz and Shakh were present in the room as he explicated the Gemara. Similarly, when sitting at his father's *Seder*, he felt that the Rambam and the Rashba, the Vilna Gaon and Rabbi Akiva Eiger, were invited guests, alive and vital, and active participants in the animated discourse around the *Seder* table. The Rav inspired his students to join him in this fellowship of learning.

The *Masorah*, however, can be preserved and transmitted to the next generation only if it is expressed intimately. It was to that endeavor that the Rav brought his extraordinary talents, his genius, integrity, eloquence, and his intense sense of mission and purpose. It was in large part because of his inspired leadership and brilliant pedagogy that we have a religious Jewish community in the United States that is integrated in contemporary society, yet committed to our ancient, glorious tradition, a community that not only observes the precepts of the Torah, but can also still hear the echo of Sinai which reverberates through the generations.

The core text of the Haggadah is an exegesis and interpretation of the Biblical passage of *Arammi Oved Avi* (Deut. 26:5–11), the declaration that a pilgrim landowner in the Land of Israel recites when he brings his *bikurim*, first fruits, as an offering to the Priest in the Temple. The Rav would often ask why those particular verses, which refer in summary fashion to the Exodus from Egypt, were chosen as the core of the Haggadah, as opposed to passages from the beginning of the Book of Exodus, in which the narrative of the events of the Exodus appears in much greater detail. His explanation touches on a fundamental aspect of the *mizvah* of retelling the story of the Exodus, and it too is a reflection of his life's mission.

The obligation of retelling the story of the Exodus on the night of the *Seder* is more than a recounting of historical events, he explained. Retelling the story of the Exodus must intrinsically encompass the *mizvah* of Torah study. The Mishnah (*Pesaḥim* 10:4) states, "*ve-doresh*, one 'expounds' from the verse *Arammi Oved Avi*." The word *ve-doresh* implies that one must engage in Torah study, interpreting the text of the Torah using the established exegetical methods to extrapolate details that are not readily apparent in the text. A mere reading of the Exodus narrative from the beginning of the Book of Exodus is not sufficient. Our Sages chose the *Arammi Oved Avi* passage as the central

text of the Haggadah precisely because its description of the Exodus is so succinct; it is a text that lends itself to study and interpretation. We answer the wise son, "you should also tell him the laws of the Passover." We are obligated to teach the wise son all the laws of the *Seder* night through the evening. The *Seder* night is not only about recounting the historical events. One must also engage in Torah study by discussing the actual laws pertaining to Passover as detailed in *Torah she-be-al peh*.

The Rav's teachings emphasized the centrality of Torah study to the *Seder* night. But the question remains: Why is Torah study so integral to this night? An understanding of this flows from the Rav's comments on the *miẓvah* of reciting the *Shema*, the quintessence of which is *kabbalat 'ol malkhut shamayim*, accepting the yoke of Heaven.

Rambam explains that a person is required to begin the *Shema* with the initial paragraph because that paragraph consists of three essential components – "the unity of God, the love of God, and the study of Torah which is the great principle upon which all else depends" (*Hilkhot Keri'at Shema* 1:2). While *keri'at Shema* is an independent *miẓvah*, it must intrinsically include Torah study, because without it there is a deficiency in *kabbalat 'ol malkhut shamayim*. Our *weltanschauung* is defined by Torah study, through which we glimpse God's infinite mind. That Torah study is intrinsic to the *miẓvah* of *keri'at Shema* is further demonstrated by the fact that *Ahavah Rabbah*, one of the blessings of the *Shema*, serves also as a *birkat ha-Torah*. (One who did not recite the blessings prior to Torah study fulfills his obligation by reciting *Ahavah Rabbah*.) Similarly, the Rav explained, we find a special *birkat ha-Torah* for the Haggadah, namely, *Barukh ha-Makom Barukh Hu*. The *Seder* night parallels the *miẓvah* of reciting the *Shema* in that they are both expressions of *kabbalat 'ol malkhut shamayim* that must come through the instrumentality of the cognitive act of Torah study.

Another essential element of the *Shema* consists in remembering the Exodus, which is expressed in the third paragraph of the *Shema*. The Rav's grandfather Rav Hayim points out that although it is a *miẓvah* to mention the Exodus, Rambam does not enumerate it as one of the 613 *miẓvot*. He explained that Rambam omits it because he considers it not an independent *miẓvah* but as subsumed under the *Shema*. Remembering the Exodus is an essential part of *keri'at Shema* because accepting the yoke of Heaven requires our belief in a God who is intimately involved in history and human events. That is why the *miẓvah* to believe in God states "I am God your Lord, *who took you out of the Land of Egypt*" (Deut. 5:6) for we affirm our belief in a God who cares about the creation and humanity; this is the principle of remembering the Exodus. On *Pesaḥ* night, the Jewish people accepted God as a master who would be involved in every aspect of their lives. "I and not an angel, I and not a seraph,

I and not a messenger." The redemption from Egypt was achieved by God's revealing Himself and being directly involved in history; and this divine revelation is the very basis of the Jews' knowledge of and faith in God.

Torah study is an integral part of the *Seder* night because both *Torah she-be-al peh* and the Haggadah are eternally fresh religious experiences in which one's entire personality becomes identified with and integrated into the experience. The *Seder* night is not simply the retelling of an event that occurred in antiquity, but the personal re-experiencing of the event. This concept, observed the Rav, is implicit in the very word "*Haggadah*," which can be seen from the phrase "*haggadat edut*," a declaration of testimony. One of the basic principles of the law of evidence is that hearsay, testimony known only to the witness through someone else, is not admissible evidence. In this vein, the Haggadah emphasizes that "a person is obligated to see himself as if he personally left Egypt." Accordingly, the *mizvah* of retelling the story of the Exodus cannot be a mere recounting of the chronicle of a historical event. It must be first-hand testimony, an acknowledgement of an event that is in the actual realm of experience of the testifying individual.

The Jew who brought his first fruits to the Temple keenly appreciated the contentment and tranquility he enjoyed. Yet this celebrating pilgrim must momentarily transform himself into a victim of the Egyptian slavery, as he declares in the first person, "The Egyptians afflicted us, and we cried out," praying to God for help, "and He took us out… and He brought us to this place." With his first-person pronouncement, the pilgrim relives the events of the Exodus. The *bikurim* declaration as the foundation of the Haggadah is most appropriate, since both the pilgrim bringing *bikurim* and the Jew on the *Seder* night are obligated to re-live and actually experience the Exodus. The sense of immediacy and relevance is a fundamental aspect of Torah study, and that is what the Rav challenged us to recreate at the *Seder.*

The *Torah she-be-al peh* enables each generation to uncover novel interpretations and applications. It is not static; rather, it constantly radiates new vistas that bring joy to those who study it. "The orders of God are upright, gladdening the heart" (Psalms 19:9). The Rav brought this to all who were privileged to study with him. Alas, it is impossible to fully capture this experience with the printed word – even when the text was penned by the *Safra Rabbah de-Yisrael* of the last century himself. But our hope is that this work will help readers gain a deeper appreciation of the Rav and his life's work.

Menachem Genack

הגדה של פסח

THE PASSOVER HAGGADAH

The Seder Night: An Exalted Evening

THE SEDER NIGHT: AN EXALTED EVENING

In my experiential – not intellectual – memory, two nights stand out as singular, as endowed with a unique and fascinating quality, exalted in their holiness and shining with a dazzling beauty: the night of the *Seder* and the night of *Kol Nidrei*. As a child I was fascinated, indeed entranced, by these two clear, moonlit nights, both wrapped in grandeur and majesty. I used to feel stimulated, aroused, inspired; illuminating vision heightened my senses, which were sharpened and liberated from all inhibitions. A strange silence, stillness, peace, quiet, and serenity enveloped me. I surrendered to a stream of inflowing joy and ecstasy.

I can still hear the solemn, sad, nostalgic melody of "*YaKNeHaZ*" – the mnemonic acronym for the order of the sections of the *Kiddush* and *Havdalah* – which I heard most probably at the age of seven, when my grandfather recited the *Kiddush* on a *Seder* night that happened to coincide with the end of the Sabbath. I still remember the finale of the blessing, "*ha-mavdil bein kodesh le-kodesh*, Who distinguishes between holy and holy." The melody gradually faded away – or, shall I say, was transposed into another melody, namely, one of silence. As a child, I used to brood for hours over the notion of "*ha-mavdil bein kodesh le-kodesh*" – two sanctities, one of the Sabbath and the other of the holiday. I liked both, I cherished every spark of holiness; I hated the everyday, the gray, the routine, the workaday dreariness. I always saw in my frail young mother, with her pale face, deeply set eyes, and aristocratic, gentle features, the personification of the Sabbath, of the Princess. I saw the holiday in all its glory represented by one of my uncles, an athlete, tall, dark and handsome. All these memories are at the root of my religious *Weltanschauung* and experience. Without them, I would miss the ecstasy accompanying religious observance and the depth and sweep of religious meditation and thinking. However naive and childish, these emotions and visions have always been, and still are, the wellspring of my colorful religious life.

On the night of the Exodus, the people met God, had a rendezvous with Him, and made His acquaintance for the first time. On *Pesaḥ* night, man, free, hopeful, and courageous, enhanced by fulfillment, exalted by his independence, surges forward, expands, grows, ready to accomplish all that is related to his blessedness and freedom. All selfishness renounced, he forgets himself, rising like the mighty river to do, to practice, and to immerse himself in *ḥesed*.

(*Festival of Freedom*)

סֵדֶר בְּדִיקַת חָמֵץ

אור לארבעה עשר בודקין את החמץ לאור הנר.
קודם שיבדוק מברך:

בָּרוּךְ אַתָּה יְיָ, אֱלֹהֵינוּ מֶלֶךְ הָעוֹלָם, אֲשֶׁר קִדְּשָׁנוּ בְּמִצְוֹתָיו, וְצִוָּנוּ עַל בִּעוּר חָמֵץ:

אחר הבדיקה מבטל החמץ ואומר:

כָּל חֲמִירָא וַחֲמִיעָא דְּאִכָּא בִּרְשׁוּתִי, דְּלָא חֲמִתֵּהּ וּדְלָא בִעַרְתֵּהּ וּדְלָא יְדַעְנָא לֵיהּ, לִבָּטֵיל וְלֶהֱוֵי הֶפְקֵר כְּעַפְרָא דְּאַרְעָא.

מי שאינו יודע ארמית, יאמר בלשון שהוא מבין.

סֵדֶר בִּעוּר חָמֵץ

ביום ארבעה עשר שחרית שורפים את החמץ.
אחר שריפת החמץ קודם שעה ששית יבטל את החמץ בליבו ויאמר:

כָּל חֲמִירָא וַחֲמִיעָא דְּאִכָּא בִּרְשׁוּתִי, דַּחֲזִיתֵהּ וּדְלָא חֲזִיתֵהּ, דַּחֲמִתֵּהּ וּדְלָא חֲמִתֵּה, דִּבְעַרְתֵּהּ וּדְלָא בִעַרְתֵּה, לִבָּטֵל וְלֶהֱוֵי הֶפְקֵר כְּעַפְרָא דְּאַרְעָא.

מי שאינו יודע ארמית, יאמר בלשון שהוא מבין.

BEDIKAT ḤAMEẒ –
SEARCHING FOR THE ḤAMEẒ

On the night of the fourteenth of Nisan, *we conduct the search for leaven. The search is done by candlelight.*

Before beginning the search, we light a candle and recite the following:

Blessed are You, Lord, our God, King of the universe, who has sanctified us with His commandments, and commanded us concerning the removal of leaven.

After the search has been completed, the following is recited:

Any type of leaven that may still be in my possession, that I have not seen or not removed, or that I do not know about, let it be nullified and shall be considered ownerless, like the dust of the earth.

BIUR ḤAMEẒ – BURNING THE ḤAMEẒ

On the morning of the fourteenth of Nisan, *all of the remaining leaven in the house is burned. After burning the leaven, prior to an hour before midday one is to nullify the leaven in his heart and recite the following:*

Any type of leaven that may still be in my possession, that I may or may not have seen, found or removed, let it be nullified and shall be considered ownerless, like the dust of the earth.

סֵדֶר עֵרוּב תַּבְשִׁילִין

אם חל ערב פסח ביום ד׳ בחו״ל עושים עירוב תבשילין.

לוקח מצה וכזית תבשיל, ומברך:

בָּרוּךְ אַתָּה יְיָ, אֱלֹהֵינוּ מֶלֶךְ הָעוֹלָם, אֲשֶׁר קִדְּשָׁנוּ בְּמִצְוֹתָיו, וְצִוָּנוּ עַל מִצְוַת עֵרוּב:

בַּהֲדֵין עֵרוּבָא יְהֵא שָׁרֵי לָנָא לְמֵיפָא וּלְבַשָּׁלָא וּלְאַטְמָנָא וּלְאַדְלָקָא שְׁרָגָא, וּלְמֶעְבַּד כָּל צָרְכָנָא, מִיּוֹמָא טָבָא לְשַׁבְּתָא, לָנוּ וּלְכָל יִשְׂרָאֵל הַדָּרִים בָּעִיר הַזֹּאת.

סֵדֶר הַדְלָקַת נֵרוֹת

בָּרוּךְ אַתָּה יְיָ, אֱלֹהֵינוּ מֶלֶךְ הָעוֹלָם, אֲשֶׁר קִדְּשָׁנוּ בְּמִצְוֹתָיו, וְצִוָּנוּ לְהַדְלִיק נֵר שֶׁל (בשבת: שֶׁל שַׁבָּת וְשֶׁל) יוֹם טוֹב.

בָּרוּךְ אַתָּה יְיָ, אֱלֹהֵינוּ מֶלֶךְ הָעוֹלָם, שֶׁהֶחֱיָנוּ וְקִיְּמָנוּ וְהִגִּיעָנוּ לַזְּמַן הַזֶּה.

הַדְלָקַת נֵרוֹת Rambam (*Hilkhot Shabbat* 5:3) states that one must light Shabbat candles before sunset while it is still day. This *halakhah* begs interpretation. Of course one is forbidden to light candles after sunset. Why must Rambam instruct us to light candles "while it is still day"?

Rambam (*Hilkhot Shabbat* 30:5) states that one must arrange his home before nightfall in honor of Shabbat – the candle lit, the table set, and one's bed prepared – because all these are honors for Shabbat. Vilna Gaon (*Be'ur ha-Gra, Oraḥ Ḥayyim* 529:1) explains the difference between delighting in Shabbat (*oneg Shabbat*) and honoring Shabbat (*kavod Shabbat*). *Oneg* refers to the acts that are performed on Shabbat proper to enhance the day, while *kavod* refers

EIRUV TAVSHILIN

When the first day of Pesaḥ falls on Thursday, an eiruv tavshilin should be prepared on Wednesday for it to be permissible to cook on Yom Tov for Shabbat. One should take some mazzah and a ka-zayit of any cooked food and set them aside. The following is recited:

Blessed are You, Lord, our God, King of the universe, who has sanctified us with His commandments and commanded us concerning the commandment of eiruv.

With this eiruv it shall be permitted for us to bake, cook, keep food warm, kindle flame and make all necessary preparations on Yom Tov for Shabbat for ourselves or for all Jews who live in this city.

CANDLE LIGHTING

On Friday night add the words in brackets:

Blessed are You, Lord, our God, King of the universe, who has sanctified us with His commandments and commanded us to light the [Shabbat and] Festival candles.

Blessed are You, Lord, our God, King of the universe, who has granted us life, sustained us, and enabled us to reach this occasion.

---

to those preparations that are performed before Shabbat in anticipation of the day. Since Rambam includes lighting candles in the category of *kavod Shabbat*, like all components of *kavod Shabbat* the lighting of candles must rightfully be performed on *erev Shabbat*. The requirement that candles be lit on *erev Shabbat* is not merely a consequence of the prohibition of lighting candles on Shabbat. This approach yields the following practical consequence. Although one is permitted to light a fire on *Yom Tov*, one must still honor *Yom Tov* by lighting candles before sunset. Just like all other matters that pertain to *kavod Yom Tov*, this, too, must be performed on *erev Yom Tov*.

(*Reshimot*)

סֵדֶר הַקְּעָרָה

The custom of the Ari z"l   לפי מנהג האר"י ז"ל

ג' מצות

Three Mazzot

ביצה   זרוע

Beizah   Zero'a

מרור

Maror

כרפס   חרוסת

Karpas   Haroset

חזרת

Hazeret

סֵדֶר הַקְּעָרָה The Talmud (*Pesaḥim* 114b) discusses the requirement to place *shenei tavshilin*, two cooked items, on the *Seder* plate, commemorating the *korban Pesaḥ* and the *ḥagigah* offering that were eaten when sacrifices were brought in the Temple. Rav Huna says that this requirement may be fulfilled by using beets and rice. According to Rav Yosef, one must use two different types of meat. Rambam (*Hilkhot Ḥamez u-Mazzah* 8:1) follows the opinion of Rav Yosef, while the popular custom is to place one item of meat and an egg on the *Seder* plate (see *Kesef Mishneh*, loc cit.).

The presence of the egg at the *Seder* also has another source. The first day of Passover always occurs on the same day of the week as *Tishah be-Av*, the day that marks the destruction of the Temple and the exile of the Jews (*Oraḥ Hayyim* 428:3). Accordingly, the custom is to eat an egg, a symbol of mourning, on the first night of *Pesaḥ* (see Rama, *Oraḥ Ḥayyim* 476:2). The egg, therefore, symbolizes both joy, the *ḥagigah*, and mourning, *Tishah be-Av*.

The *Beit ha-Levi* explains the correlation between the first day of Passover and *Tishah be-Av* as follows. Several midrashic sources indicate that the Exodus from Egypt was premature. The Jews were supposed to have been enslaved in

THE SEDER PLATE

The custom of the *Gra z"l* לפי מנהג הגר"א ז"ל

חרוסת Ḥaroset		מרור Maror
	ב' מצות Two Maẓẓot	
ביצה Beiẓah		זרוע Zero'a

Egypt for 400 years but were redeemed after only 210 years. After 210 years of exile, the Jews were in danger of completely losing their Jewish identity. Had they remained in Egypt any longer, they would have been hopelessly assimilated. The urgent need to redeem them without further delay explains why the Exodus occurred "*be-ḥipazon*, in haste" (Deut. 16:3). God, therefore, redeemed them prematurely, and the balance of their term of exile would have to be completed in future exiles. Thus, the redemption from Egypt was not a complete redemption, since it was the cause of the later exiles. It is, therefore, appropriate to eat an egg, an open expression of mourning, on the very night of redemption.

It is interesting to note that the terminology of *shenei tavshilin* occurs with respect to the laws both of Passover, when one is required to place *shenei tavshilin* on the plate, and of *Tish'ah be-Av*, when one may not eat *shenei tavshilin* in the meal preceding the *Tish'ah be-Av* fast. The similar terminology further points to the correlation between Passover and *Tish'ah be-Av*.

(*Reshimot*)

סֵדֶר לֵיל פֶּסַח

קַדֵּשׁ.

וּרְחַץ.

כַּרְפַּס.

יַחַץ.

מַגִּיד.

רָחְצָה.

מוֹצִיא. מַצָּה.

מָרוֹר.

כּוֹרֵךְ.

שֻׁלְחָן עוֹרֵךְ.

צָפוּן.

בָּרֵךְ.

הַלֵּל.

נִרְצָה.

סֵדֶר לֵיל פֶּסַח There is a logic and a structure not only to the *Maggid* section of the Haggadah, but also to the entire *Seder*. The Gemara emphasizes in several places the necessity of preserving the proper order of performance on *Pesaḥ* night. For example, the Gemara (*Pesaḥim* 114b–115a) asks what blessing should be made if one must eat *maror* before the *Maggid* section because there is no other vegetable for *karpas*. It is evident from the discussion that the fulfillment of the *miẓvah* of *maror* would not have occurred the first time it was eaten when it was eaten as *karpas*, but rather the second. If one could fulfill the *miẓvah* of *maror* at the first dipping, the whole discussion of the Gemara would be superfluous. Apparently, one may not eat *maror* before *maẓẓah*. According to Rashbam (*Pesaḥim* 114a), the sequential order of eating *maẓẓah* first and then *maror* is biblically mandated. This is based on the verse "*al maẓẓot u-merorim yo'kheluhu*, they shall eat it (the *korban Pesaḥ*) with unleavened bread and bitter herbs" (Num. 9:11), implying that the *maẓẓot* are eaten first, and then the *maror*. The requirement to maintain a sequence, however, is also applicable to the entire *Seder*.

In order to explain this, we must understand that each of the *miẓvot* of *Pesaḥ* night has two aspects, two *kiyumim*, two fulfillments. The *miẓvah* of *sipur Yeẓi'at Miẓrayim* is discharged in a twofold way – through the medium

THE ORDER OF THE SEDER

Kadesh	Recite *Kiddush*.
Urḥaẓ	Wash hands.
Karpas	Eat vegetable dipped in salt water.
Yaḥaẓ	Break the middle *maẓẓah* and hide the larger piece for the *Afikoman*.
Maggid	Recite the narrative of the *Pesaḥ* story.
Raḥẓah	Wash hands prior to eating *maẓẓah*.
Moẓi	Recite the "*Ha-moẓi*" *berakhah* on the *maẓẓot*.
Maẓẓah	Recite the "*Al akhilat maẓẓah*" *berakhah* and eat the *maẓẓot*.
Maror	Eat the bitter herbs.
Korekh	Eat the *maẓẓah* and bitter herbs together.
Shulḥan Orekh	Eat the meal.
Ẓafun	Eat the *Afikoman*.
Barekh	Recite Grace after Meals.
Hallel	Recite *Hallel*.
Nirẓah	Conclusion of the *Seder*.

---

of speech and through symbolic actions. A person who eats the *maẓẓah* and the *maror* before saying *Maggid* fulfills the *miẓvah* of eating *maẓẓah*, but does not fulfill the *miẓvah* of *sipur Yeẓi'at Miẓrayim* by means of eating *maẓẓah*. That is what the Gemara (*Pesaḥim* 115b) means by referring to *maẓẓah*, *leḥem oni* (Deut. 16:3), as "*leḥem she-onin alav devarim harbeh*, the bread over which we recite many things." Since eating *maẓẓah* is also part of *sipur*, we understand the need for *Seder*, for a particular order of performance.

(*Kol ha-Rav*)

The language utilized by Rambam in his introduction to the order of the *Pesaḥ Seder* is reminiscent of his introduction to the Temple service of *Yom Kippur*. In *Hilkhot Ḥameẓ u-Maẓẓah* (8:1), Rambam begins "*Seder*, the order, for the performance of the *miẓvot* on the night of the fifteenth is as follows." In *Hilkhot Avodat Yom ha-Kippurim* (4:1), Rambam begins, "*Seder*, the order, for the performances of the day is as follows." Just as following the order of the *Yom Kippur* service is essential for the proper performance of the *miẓvah*, so, too, following the order of the *Seder* is essential for the proper fulfillment

קַדֵּשׁ

מוזגים לו כוס ראשון ע"י אחר, נוטלו בשתי ידיו, מחזיקו ביד ימינו ומקדש

---

of the *mizvot* of this night of the fifteenth of Nisan. By following an order we demonstrate that all the parts of the *Seder* are interconnected and only collectively do they properly retell the story of *Yezi'at Mizrayim*. If, for instance, one were to consume the *mazzah* before reciting *Maggid*, the narrative would be deficient in that one would not have satisfied the facet of *lehem oni*, bread over which we are to recount the Exodus. Similarly, the *karpas* is intended to elicit the questions that will enable the *Maggid* discussion to proceed, and the failure to eat the *karpas* in its proper sequence would impair or forestall the *Maggid* section. Only through adherence to the prescribed order can we express the overarching principles and ideas that are intended to emerge from, and which are coordinated with, our actions on the *Seder* night.

(*Reshimot*)

קַדֵּשׁ A slave is relieved of *mizvot aseh she-ha-zeman geramah*, of intermittent commandments that depend upon time. This is because the slave lacks the time experience. While everything exists in time, only the human being is capable of experiencing time. God endowed man with time awareness, the ability to sense and feel time and the existential stream of selfhood. This time awareness or experience has three basic component parts. First, retrospection: without memory, there is no time. Second, the time experience includes exploration or close examination of things yet unborn and events not yet in existence. This means the anticipatory experience of events not yet in being. Third is appreciation or evaluation of the present moment as one's most precious possession.

No one is worthy of time awareness if retrospection is alien to him, if he is incapable of reliving, recovering and reproducing past experiences. Indeed, the *mizvah* of *sipur Yezi'at Mizrayim* does not exhaust itself in a historic review of bygone events that have vanished completely. It is more than that; it is a drama charged with emotion and tenseness, participating in the past. Past events which are not re-experienced belong not to history, but to archaeology. Archaeology involves past events that occurred once upon a time, disappeared, and – while they may be reproduced by memory – are not alive anymore. They are not re-experienced; there is no retrospection of the archaic. Memory is not just the storehouse for latent impressions; there is also the living memory, which reproduces and re-experiences the past.

KADESH

Each participant's cup is poured by someone else. He then takes the cup with both hands, holds it in his right hand, and recites Kiddush.

(There is, of course, a distinction between slaves and women regarding their respective exemptions from *mizvot aseh she-ha-zeman geramah*. Women live in and experience time. That is why, when a woman performs a *mizvah*, the act is as meaningful as that of a man. Thus many authorities have ruled that a woman recites a blessing before performance of a *mizvat aseh she-ha-zeman geramah*, whereas a slave does not.)

The Judaic philosophy of time comes to expression in the text of *Kiddush*. In physics, time is quantified, measured by the clock. But pure time, real time, cannot be quantified; it is pure quality. With *Kiddush*, we sanctify time and endow it with creativity and meaning. It is the first thing we do as free people at the *Seder*.

(*Festival of Freedom*)

The *Shulḥan Arukh* (*Oraḥ Ḥayyim* 472:1) rules i the *Kiddush* of the *Seder* night, unlike the *Kiddush* of Shabbat or other *yamim tovim*, cannot be recited until after nightfall. Magen Avraham explains that since *Kiddush* is the first of the *arba kosot*, the four cups of wine of the *Seder*, we cannot drink it until after nightfall when the *Seder* can begin. According to this explanation, a person could technically say *Kiddush* earlier, as long as he waited to drink the wine later, after dark. However, Taz disagrees and explains that just as the *mazzah* (like the *korban Pesaḥ*) can be eaten only after nightfall, so, too, the *Kiddush* can be said only at a time when one could eat the *mazzah*.

Rambam (*Hilkhot Ḥamez u-Mazzah* 7:10) explains that the obligation of the four cups of wine is rooted in the obligation upon each of us to make it appear as if we ourselves left Egypt; drinking the wine symbolizes our freedom. He rules that one must recite a specific *berakhah* for each cup: *Kiddush* for the first cup, the *Haggadah* (*asher ge'alanu*) for the second cup, the *Birkat ha-Mazon* for the third cup, and *Hallel* and *Birkat ha-Shir* for the fourth cup (*Hilkhot Ḥamez u-Mazzah* 7:10). Moreover, he rules (7:6–7) that besides the actual drinking, the *berakhot* of the four cups are also part of this *mizvah*. They, too, are a fulfillment of *sipur Yezi'at Mizrayim*, the *mizvah* of recounting our Exodus from Egypt.

The *Kiddush* of the *Seder* night is therefore unique, playing the dual role of fulfilling the regular requirement of *Kiddush* and of being the *berakhah* of

בשבת מתחילים כאן

יש מתחילים: וַיַּרְא אֱלֹהִים אֶת כָּל אֲשֶׁר עָשָׂה וְהִנֵּה טוֹב מְאֹד

וַיְהִי עֶרֶב וַיְהִי בֹקֶר יוֹם הַשִּׁשִּׁי: וַיְכֻלּוּ הַשָּׁמַיִם וְהָאָרֶץ וְכָל צְבָאָם. וַיְכַל אֱלֹהִים בַּיּוֹם הַשְּׁבִיעִי מְלַאכְתּוֹ אֲשֶׁר עָשָׂה וַיִּשְׁבֹּת בַּיּוֹם הַשְּׁבִיעִי מִכָּל מְלַאכְתּוֹ אֲשֶׁר עָשָׂה. וַיְבָרֶךְ אֱלֹהִים אֶת יוֹם הַשְּׁבִיעִי וַיְקַדֵּשׁ אוֹתוֹ כִּי בוֹ שָׁבַת מִכָּל מְלַאכְתּוֹ אֲשֶׁר בָּרָא אֱלֹהִים לַעֲשׂוֹת.

בחול מתחילים כאן:

סַבְרִי מָרָנָן וְרַבָּנָן וְרַבּוֹתַי בָּרוּךְ אַתָּה יְיָ, אֱלֹהֵינוּ מֶלֶךְ הָעוֹלָם, בּוֹרֵא פְּרִי הַגָּפֶן.

---

the first of the four cups. It is, therefore, not surprising that Rav Saadiah Gaon included a lengthy *piyut* detailing the Exodus in his version of the *Kiddush*, for the text is not only *Kiddush*, but also a fulfillment of *sipur Yeẓi'at Miẓrayim*.

Similarly, we can now understand the opinion of Taz. *Kiddush*, as the berakhah for the first cup of wine, is a fulfillment of *sipur Yeẓi'at Miẓrayim*, and therefore can be recited only after nightfall, like the other *miẓvot* of the night.

(*Reshimot*)

Rambam (*Hilkhot Ḥameẓ u-Maẓẓah*, 8:1) begins his explanation of the order for the *Seder* by stating that on the night of the fifteenth of Nisan, *mozegim kos*, a cup of wine is first poured for each individual and the blessing over it is then recited. *Mezigah* is the process of diluting, mixing, and pouring the wine according to each person's preferred strength and taste (*Hilkhot Ḥameẓ u-Maẓẓah* 7:9). Rambam's wording seems to imply that there is a requirement that the *mezigah* be done at night. *Mezigah* is thus not just a functional process to ensure that the wine is properly prepared, but also an integral component of the *miẓvah* of the four cups of wine. It is the step that transforms the ordinary cup of wine into a *kos shel berakhah*, a cup of blessing. Just as the blessing on the wine must be recited only at night, so, too, the preparation of the wine to be a *kos shel berakhah* should only be done at night. The centrality of *mezigah* can also be learned from the laws of *Birkat ha-Mazon*. In explaining the procedure for reciting *Birkat ha-Mazon* over a cup of wine, Rambam (*Hilkhot Berakhot* 7:15) instructs that the cup of wine should not be prepared until the second blessing is reached. Clearly, if *mezigah* were purely a practical consideration, there would not be laws associated with its performance. Rather we see that *mezigah* is an integral part of the *miẓvah* of the cup of wine. Additionally, we

On Friday night begin with the following paragraph:

Some begin: And God saw everything that He had made, and behold, it was very good

It was evening and it was morning The sixth day. The heavens and the earth and all their hosts were completed. On the seventh day God finished His work which He had made, and He rested on the seventh day from all His work which He had made. God blessed the seventh day and made it holy, for on it He rested from all His work which God had created and done.

On other nights begin here:

With your permission, gentlemen, my masters and my teachers. Blessed are You, Lord, our God, King of the universe, who creates the fruit of the vine.

---

see from the Mishnah (*Pesaḥim* 116a) that the *mezigah* of the second cup precipitates the asking of the Four Questions. The *Maggid* is recited only after the cup of wine is properly prepared and transformed into a *kos shel berakhah.*

(*Reshimot*)

וַיְכֻלּוּ הַשָּׁמַיִם וְהָאָרֶץ וְכָל צְבָאָם The scriptural text "And the heaven and the earth were finished, and all the host of them" (Gen. 2:1) – the Targum, the Aramaic translation of the Pentateuch, translates *va-yekhullu*, "were finished," as *ve-ishtakhlalu*, "were perfected" – is both a profound expression of the soul of the people and the most fervent desire of the man of God. This lofty, ontological idea illuminates the path of the eternal people. When a Jew on the Sabbath eve recites this passage as part of the *Kiddush*, the sanctification over wine, he testifies not only to the existence of a Creator but of man's obligation to become a partner with the Almighty in the continuation and perfection of the creation. Just as the Almighty constantly refined and improved the realm of existence during the six days of creation, so must man complete the creation and transform the domain of chaos and void into a perfect and beautiful reality.

(*Halakhic Man*)

בּוֹרֵא פְּרִי הַגָּפֶן One of the purposes of having the four cups of wine is to demonstrate *ḥerut*, freedom, and consequently the four cups should be drunk *be-derekh ḥerut*, in a manner that is expressive of freedom. One of the required elements of *derekh ḥerut* is that one should enjoy the wine one drinks. Someone

בָּרוּךְ אַתָּה יְיָ, אֱלֹהֵינוּ מֶלֶךְ הָעוֹלָם, אֲשֶׁר בָּחַר בָּנוּ מִכָּל־עָם, וְרוֹמְמָנוּ מִכָּל־לָשׁוֹן, וְקִדְּשָׁנוּ בְּמִצְוֹתָיו, וַתִּתֶּן־לָנוּ יְיָ אֱלֹהֵינוּ בְּאַהֲבָה (בשבת: שַׁבָּתוֹת לִמְנוּחָה וּ)מוֹעֲדִים לְשִׂמְחָה, חַגִּים וּזְמַנִּים לְשָׂשׂוֹן, אֶת־יוֹם (בשבת: הַשַּׁבָּת הַזֶּה, וְאֶת־יוֹם) חַג הַמַּצּוֹת הַזֶּה, זְמַן חֵרוּתֵנוּ, (בשבת: בְּאַהֲבָה,) מִקְרָא קֹדֶשׁ, זֵכֶר לִיצִיאַת מִצְרָיִם. כִּי בָנוּ בָחַרְתָּ וְאוֹתָנוּ קִדַּשְׁתָּ מִכָּל־הָעַמִּים. (בשבת: וְשַׁבָּת) וּמוֹעֲדֵי קָדְשֶׁךָ (בשבת: בְּאַהֲבָה וּבְרָצוֹן,) בְּשִׂמְחָה וּבְשָׂשׂוֹן הִנְחַלְתָּנוּ. בָּרוּךְ אַתָּה יְיָ, מְקַדֵּשׁ (בשבת: הַשַּׁבָּת וְ)יִשְׂרָאֵל וְהַזְּמַנִּים.

במוצאי שבת מוסיפים:

בָּרוּךְ אַתָּה יְיָ, אֱלֹהֵינוּ מֶלֶךְ הָעוֹלָם, בּוֹרֵא מְאוֹרֵי הָאֵשׁ:

בָּרוּךְ אַתָּה יְיָ, אֱלֹהֵינוּ מֶלֶךְ הָעוֹלָם, הַמַּבְדִּיל בֵּין קֹדֶשׁ לְחֹל, בֵּין אוֹר לְחֹשֶׁךְ, בֵּין יִשְׂרָאֵל לָעַמִּים, בֵּין יוֹם הַשְּׁבִיעִי לְשֵׁשֶׁת יְמֵי הַמַּעֲשֶׂה. בֵּין

---

who does not enjoy wine is better served by drinking grape juice. Regarding the permissibility of using grape juice, the Talmud states (*Bava Batra* 97b) that juice squeezed from a cluster of grapes may be used for *Kiddush*. Although, based upon this Gemara, grape juice could theoretically be used for all four cups at the *Seder*, there is a separate concern regarding the use of grape juice for *Kiddush*, which constitutes the first cup. Rambam (*Hilkhot Shabbat* 29:14) states that one is not permitted to recite *Kiddush* on wine that is not fit to be poured on the altar in the Temple, which includes cooked and sweetened wines. Since all contemporary grape juice is pasteurized, according to Rambam it would not be acceptable for *Kiddush*, as it constitutes cooked wine, which is unfit to be poured on the altar. Ravad disagrees with Rambam and points out that the Talmud Yerushalmi states that *konditon* (sweetened wine) may be used for the four cups, which appears inconsistent with Rambam's view that only wine which is fit to be poured on the altar may be used for *Kiddush*. Rambam apparently viewed the Yerushalmi's statement as not referring to *Kiddush*. It is best for a person who does not enjoy drinking wine to drink unsweetened non-*mevushal* (uncooked) wine for the first of the four cups at the *Seder* and grape juice for the remaining three cups.

(*Reshimot*)

אֲשֶׁר בָּחַר בָּנוּ We say in *Kiddush* that God has chosen us and concluded a unique covenant with us. This charismatic reality is the fourth aspect in the message

On Shabbat, add the words in brackets:

Blessed are You, Lord, our God, King of the universe, who has chosen us from among all people, and raised us above all tongues, and made us holy through His commandments. And You, Lord, our God, have given us in love [Sabbaths for rest and] festivals for happiness, feasts and festive seasons for rejoicing [this Sabbath-day and] the day of this Feast of Maẓẓot and this Festival of holy convocation, the Time of our Freedom [in love], a holy convocation, commemorating the departure from Egypt. For You have chosen us and sanctified us from all the nations, and You have given us as a heritage [Shabbat and] Your sacred holidays [in love and favor], in happiness and joy. Blessed are You, Lord, who sanctifies [the Shabbat and] Israel and the festive seasons.

On Saturday night add the following:

Blessed are You, Lord, our God, King of the universe, Creator of the light of fire.

Blessed are You, Lord, our God, King of the universe, who makes a distinction between sacred and profane, between light and darkness, between Israel and the nations, between the seventh day and

---

of redemption that God revealed to Moses: "I will take you to Me for a people, and I will be to you a God" (Ex. 6:7). Hence, the proclamation of our chosenness certainly belongs in the Haggadah.

(*Kol ha-Rav*)

בְּאַהֲבָה When *Pesaḥ* falls on Shabbat, the word "*be-ahavah*, with love" is added to *Kiddush* and the *Amidah* to describe God's bequest of Shabbat to the Jewish people. The endowment of Shabbat with the unique quality of *ahavah* is manifested in the sacrifices brought in the Temple. The *musaf* sacrifices brought on all the festivals invariably include a *ḥattat*, a sin offering. The *musaf* sacrifice brought on Shabbat, however, does not include a *ḥattat*. God wished to show His profound love of the Jewish people by omitting any suggestion of their sin, as it is written, "love covers up all sins" (Prov. 10:12).

(*Reshimot*)

קְדֻשַּׁת שַׁבָּת לִקְדֻשַּׁת יוֹם טוֹב הִבְדַּלְתָּ, וְאֶת־יוֹם הַשְּׁבִיעִי מִשֵּׁשֶׁת יְמֵי הַמַּעֲשֶׂה קִדַּשְׁתָּ. הִבְדַּלְתָּ וְקִדַּשְׁתָּ אֶת־עַמְּךָ יִשְׂרָאֵל בִּקְדֻשָּׁתֶךָ. בָּרוּךְ אַתָּה יְיָ, הַמַּבְדִּיל בֵּין קֹדֶשׁ לְקֹדֶשׁ:

בכל לילה מסיימים:

בָּרוּךְ אַתָּה יְיָ, אֱלֹהֵינוּ מֶלֶךְ הָעוֹלָם, שֶׁהֶחֱיָנוּ וְקִיְּמָנוּ וְהִגִּיעָנוּ לַזְּמַן הַזֶּה:

שותה את הכוס כולה ובדיעבד רובה בבת אחת בהסיבת שמאל, ואינו מברך אחריה.

הַמַּבְדִּיל The separation between light and darkness is perceptible and clear to everyone; even animals and birds feel the contrast between light and dark. The separation between sacred and profane is entirely different. The eye no longer sees the border between them; the senses cannot feel what is holy and what is mundane. We cannot notice it through superficial observation; for this we need a far view, a broad concept, and an especially deep intuition. The boundary between the sanctified and the ordinary is, after all, abstract; but one who is attentive can feel it.

Deep in the Jewish soul, no matter how sunk in sin it is, there is something holy and mysterious which cannot be erased or eliminated, and upon which there lies the seal of individuality and originality. But in order to perceive this separation, one must be capable of peering into the depths of the soul. In Egypt, the Almighty had to distinguish between Israel and the nations at a time when there was hardly any contrast between Jew and Egyptian. Only God, the knower of thoughts, He who distinguishes inner things, saw the difference. "God saw the children of Israel and God knew" (Ex. 2:25). He saw sanctity in the abyss of the Jewish soul, even though it was full of profanity and sin, and therefore He saved His people. What *Pesaḥ* expresses is the idea of separation even when superficially there is no reason to distinguish.

(*Kol ha-Rav*)

In *Birkhot ha-Shaḥar*, the group of blessings that commences the daily morning service, the first blessing, "*ha-noten la-sekhvi vinah*," expresses our thanks to God for having endowed the rooster with the intelligence to discern between day and night, and the second blessing, "*she-lo asani goy*," expresses our thanks to God for not having made us gentiles. Two themes expressed in the *Havdalah* service, the distinction between light and dark and between Israel and the other

the six work-days. You have made a distinction between the holiness of the Shabbat and the holiness of the festival, and You have sanctified the seventh day above the six work-days. You have set apart and made holy Your people Israel with Your holiness. Blessed are You, God, who makes a distinction between holy and holy.

On all nights, conclude with the following blessing:

Blessed are You, Lord, our God, King of the universe, who has granted us life, sustained us, and enabled us to reach this occasion.

Drink the wine while reclining to the left. It is preferable to drink the entire cup; but it is sufficient if one drinks most of the cup.

---

nations, reflect these two blessings in *Birkhot ha-Shaḥar*. That these blessings are so prominently positioned at the beginning of the morning service demonstrates that the capacity to make distinctions and to prescribe limits is an essential component of a religious philosophy and the halakhic system.

(*Reshimot*)

בְּהַסֵּיבָה The slave lives in fear. He is afraid not only of those who are stronger than he or of those who have jurisdiction over him; the slave is afraid of contradicting anyone, of antagonizing even a stranger. The fear might be unjustified, but this fear is the motivating force in his life. This is the reason, in my opinion, why the Sages introduced *haseivah*, leaning on one's left side, as the symbol of *ḥerut*, freedom. *Haseivah* symbolizes, first, complete relaxation, which in turn manifests relief from or abatement of tension and anxiety. Second, *haseivah* symbolizes the throwing-off of the mental shackles depriving man of freedom of movement. *Haseivah* is the reverse of erect posture, which demonstrates obedience and submissiveness. Soldiers standing erect symbolize the readiness to obey. *Haseivah* is indicative of disobedience, of a courageous stand, of refusing to take orders, of rejecting the authority of man. *Haseivah* means defiance. That is why *Ḥazal* said that if one's teacher is present, the student is relieved – indeed, enjoined – from *haseivah* (*Pesaḥim* 108a).

(*Festival of Freedom*)

וּרְחַץ

נוטל את ידיו לאכילת הכרפס שהוא דבר שטיבולו במשקה ואינו מברך על נטילת ידים.

כַּרְפַּס

לוקח מהכרפס פחות מכזית ומטבילו במי מלח או בחומץ ומברך בורא פרי האדמה, ויזהר לכוון בברכה זו לפטור גם את המרור, ואוכל בלא הסיבה. ויש ראשונים הסוברים דצריך לאכול כזית, וכן כתב הגר"א. ולדעה זו, לדעת הרמב"ם (פ"ז מהלכות חמץ ומצה ה"ח) אין צריך להסב, ואילו לדעת האבודרהם צריך להסב.

בָּרוּךְ אַתָּה יְיָ, אֱלֹהֵינוּ מֶלֶךְ הָעוֹלָם, בּוֹרֵא פְּרִי הָאֲדָמָה:

Haseivah requires leaning on something; merely tilting one's body to the left without actually leaning on the table, the arm of the chair, or some other object does not constitute *haseivah*. The Talmud (*Pesaḥim* 108a) records that Abbaye stated that the students would lean on each other to fulfill *haseivah*. Implicit in this statement is the idea that *haseivah* was fulfilled only because they were leaning on something, namely, each other. Therefore, a person whose chair has no armrest should rotate the chair so that when he faces the table, the back of the chair is on his left and perpendicular to the table, and he should then lean on the back of the chair. This was the *minhag* that was followed in Volozhin. (*Reshimot*)

"Even the poor person in Israel may not eat [on Passover eve] *ad she-yassev*, until he reclines." The Midrash (*Ex. Rabbah* 20:18) derives this requirement from the verse "*Va-yassev*, God led the people roundabout, by way of the wilderness at *Yam Suf*" (Ex. 13:18). The dictum of the Midrash is not simply a play on words. The Jews wandered in the wilderness before reaching the Promised Land, but they were still able to rejoice over having been saved from Egypt. They understood that although the route was circuitous, it led to their ultimate destination, the Land of Israel. Similarly, the poor man wanders in his own wilderness, struggling every day and worrying about his future.

URḤAẒ

Hands are washed prior to eating the karpas, without reciting the blessing.

KARPAS

Take less than a ka-zayit (the volume of one olive) of the karpas, dip it into salt-water or vinegar, and recite the following blessing, keeping in mind that it is also for the bitter herbs (of maror and korekh), to be eaten later on. Some are of the opinion that a ka-zayit should be eaten. There are different opinions as to whether one reclines:

Blessed are You, Lord, our God, King of the universe, who creates the fruit of the earth.

Nonetheless, he must rejoice over his redemption from Egypt, singing *Hallel*, drinking the four cups of wine and reclining. He too must perceive that, although often buffeted by harsh circumstances, he is an integral part of *Kelal Yisrael*, whose collective eschatological destiny will surely culminate in redemption.

(*Reshimot*)

כַּרְפַּס One narrates the story not only through speech, but through eating as well. *Sipur Yeẓi'at Miẓrayim* is a blend of storytelling, Torah teaching, and eating the symbolic food-items; it is a fusion of the spoken word and the physiological functions of eating and drinking. The practice of dipping relates to the aspect of *sipur* via the spoken word, because its purpose is to intrigue the children and to provoke them to ask a question. As we know, in olden times they used to dip vegetables only once, before the meal, and on Passover they used to dip twice – once the *karpas*, and the second time the *maror*. This arouses the curiosity of the child, because a child is usually sensitive to any departure from the routine. The Haggadah's mandate regarding the "child who does not know how to ask" – "*at petaḥ lo*, you prompt him" – means to stimulate his curiosity, to provoke him. The provocation itself is part of the *miẓvah* of *sipur Yeẓi'at Miẓrayim*. The *miẓvah* is not just to tell the story, because children do not listen if they are not interested.

(*Kol ha-Rav*)

יַחַץ

בוצע את המצה האמצעית לשתים, את הפרוסה הקטנה מניח בין שתי המצות השלמות, ואת הפרוסה הגדולה יתן לאחד מן המסובים לשומרה לאפיקומן.

מַגִּיד

יכוון לקיים מצות עשה מן התורה לספר בלילה הזה ביציאת מצרים.
מגלים את המצות ומגביהים את הקערה ואומרים בקול רם.

הָא לַחְמָא עַנְיָא, דִּי אֲכַלוּ אֲבָהָתַנָא בְּאַרְעָא דְמִצְרָיִם. כָּל דִּכְפִין יֵיתֵי וְיֵיכוֹל, כָּל דִּצְרִיךְ יֵיתֵי וְיִפְסַח. הָשַׁתָּא הָכָא, לַשָּׁנָה הַבָּאָה בְּאַרְעָא דְיִשְׂרָאֵל. הָשַׁתָּא עַבְדֵי, לַשָּׁנָה הַבָּאָה בְּנֵי חוֹרִין:

מַגִּיד Maimonides says that as we start the recital of *Maggid* over the second cup, we say, "*Bi-vehilu yaẓa'nu mi-Miẓrayim*, We departed from Egypt in a hurry." Does it make much difference whether the Jews departed from Egypt slowly or in a hurry? Yet, it is so important that Maimonides apparently made it the symbol of the great freedom of the Exodus. It refers to our acquisition of time-consciousness – the Exodus can happen now, and may not happen later. This sense of time was the shibboleth of our ancestors when they left Egypt. The first commandment they were given in Egypt, marking the commencement of their liberation, was to mark time: "This month shall be to you the beginning of months" (Ex. 12:2). *Bi-vehilu yaẓa'nu mi-Miẓrayim* – we have gained the consciousness of time, and hence we are free.

(*Festival of Freedom*)

הָא לַחְמָא עַנְיָא *Pesaḥ* is the holiday of solidarity. Not all the Jews in Egypt were slaves. Slavery was neither uniform nor homogeneous; there were various degrees of slavery. *Ḥazal* tell us that the tribe of Levi was never enslaved. The Jewish aristocracy, the people who were wealthy, those who paid high taxes, did not have to do physical labor. Still, there was unity of purpose, solidarity, and responsibility. Each one felt the pain of his neighbor, and that helped bring about the *ge'ullah*.

Therefore, on *Pesaḥ*, before we sit down to read the Haggadah, we declare, "This is the poor bread that our forefathers ate in the land of Egypt. Let all who are hungry enter and eat; let all who are in need come and celebrate the Passover." I interpret "in the land of Egypt" as referring to the period that they

YAḤAẒ

Take the middle maẓẓah and break it into two, one piece larger than the other.
The larger piece is set aside to serve as afikoman.
The smaller piece is put back between the two maẓẓot.

MAGID

One should have in mind to fulfill the positive biblical commandment
to tell the story on Pesaḥ night of the Exodus from Egypt.
The maẓẓot are uncovered and the seder plate raised.

This is the bread of affliction that our fathers ate in the land of Egypt. Let all who are hungry come and eat; let whoever is in need come and conduct the Seder of Passover. This year we are here, next year in the land of Israel. This year [we are] slaves; next year we will be free people.

---

were slaves. They not only ate this bread, but shared it with each other. One had a *maẓẓah*, while the other had none; the former split the *maẓẓah* in two and passed half to his unfortunate brother. Therefore, we eat the "poor bread" as does a pauper, *she-darko bi-perusah*, who eats a broken piece.

(*Festival of Freedom*)

כָּל דִכְפִין יֵיתֵי וְיֵיכֹל, כָּל דְצָרִיךְ יֵיתֵי וְיִפְסַח Though they initially might seem redundant, the two invitations we issue – "Let all who are hungry enter and eat; let all who are in need come and celebrate the Passover" – in reality are not. Whoever is in need of bread, *dikhfin*, is hungry. *Kol diẓrikh* refers to one who is alone, who has a lot of *maẓẓah* and wine but no home or family. There are indeed many ways to be included among the *kol diẓrikh*. The invitation to "all who are in need" is not *yeitei ve-yeikhol*, to eat with us; rather, it is to spend the *Pesaḥ* with us, *yeitei ve-yifsaḥ*, to celebrate with us. It is an invitation addressed to unfortunate and lonely people. They might be millionaires; it is completely irrelevant. Whoever is in need should come and celebrate.

Ha laḥma anya is the renewal of a pledge of solidarity among the Jewish people – solidarity between individual and individual, and between the individual and the Jewish community as a whole. It is a proclamation that we are one people, and we are ready to help each other. *Pesaḥ* night is a time of

מניחים את הקערה ומסלקים לקצה השולחן. מוזגים כוס שני, וכאן הבן שואל:

מַה נִּשְׁתַּנָּה הַלַּיְלָה הַזֶּה מִכָּל הַלֵּילוֹת:
שֶׁבְּכָל הַלֵּילוֹת אָנוּ אוֹכְלִין חָמֵץ וּמַצָּה, הַלַּיְלָה הַזֶּה כֻּלּוֹ מַצָּה:
שֶׁבְּכָל הַלֵּילוֹת אָנוּ אוֹכְלִין שְׁאָר יְרָקוֹת, הַלַּיְלָה הַזֶּה (כֻּלּוֹ) מָרוֹר:

---

sharing; without manifesting and demonstrating the sense of solidarity, responsibility, unity and readiness to share and to participate, the whole *Seder* becomes meaningless.

(*Festival of Freedom*)

מְסַלְּקִין הַקְּעָרָה The practice of removing the table (or, in modern times, the *Seder* plate) before the recitation of *Mah nishtannah* is prescribed in the Talmud (*Pesaḥim* 115b). However, it is not stated there at what point the table is returned. According to *Tosafot* (*Pesaḥim* 114a, s.v. *hevi'u*; see also *Oraḥ Ḥayyim* 473:7), this takes place immediately after *Mah nishtannah*, prior to *Avadim hayinu*. This is due to the requirement of *leḥem oni*, which, in the Talmud's interpretation (*Pesaḥim* 115b), is rendered "bread upon which many things are said (*leḥem she-onin alav devarim harbeh*)." This indicates that the recitation of the Haggadah must be performed in the presence of exposed *mazzot*. Rambam, however, rules that one does not bring the table back until just before "*Raban Gamli'el*." This approach would seem to be at odds with the requirement of *leḥem oni*. We may explain this by suggesting either that Rambam rules in accordance with one of the Talmud's alternative understandings of the phrase "*leḥem oni*," or that he recognizes an obligation to recite the Haggadah in the presence of *mazzot*, but only those parts of the Haggadah that specifically deal with interpreting the *mazzah*.

(*Reshimot*)

וְכָאן הַבֵּן שׁוֹאֵל The form of narration in the Haggadah avails itself of dialogue: one person asks and another responds. It is necessary to dramatize this narration because God reveals Himself to man if and when the latter searches for Him. If one does not inquire, if one expects God to reveal Himself without making an all-out effort to find Him, one will never meet God. "But from there you will seek the Lord and you shall find Him, if you search after Him with all your heart and all your soul." (Deut. 4:29).

Nachmanides, in his comments on the verse "His habitation you shall seek and there you shall come" (Deut. 12:5), says: "You should come to Me from distant lands, and you should keep inquiring where is the road leading to

The seder plate is moved aside, the second cup is poured, and the child asks:

Mah Nishtannah, How different this night is from all other nights:

On all nights we eat *ḥameẓ* or *maẓẓah*, and on this night only *maẓẓah*!

On all nights we eat any kind of vegetables, and on this night *maror*!

God's habitation." The searching for the sanctuary, the curiosity to know the location of the sanctuary, is itself redeeming and sanctifying! The curiosity hallows the pilgrimage and makes it meaningful. If one does not search for God, if a Jew does not keep in mind where is the road leading to the Temple, then he or she will never find the Temple.

On the first night of *Pesaḥ*, we tell the story of a long search by man for God, of God responding to the inquisitive search, of God taking man, who longs for Him, into His embrace. At the *Seder*, we try to stimulate the naive curiosity of the children and thereby make them God-searchers. The quest for God, along with the acceptance of the commandments, is the true spiritual liberation.

(*Festival of Freedom*)

It is impossible to foresee what kind of a question a child will ask. Quite simply, children's minds work differently from ours. Provoking children to ask and arousing their curiosity does not mean working with them for weeks before *Pesaḥ* to memorize a text. The *miẓvah* is that the child should ask spontaneously, not be coached in advance. Children have their own naive questions, formulated in their own way. It can be four questions or only one, depending upon the intelligence, curiosity, and precociousness of the child. The *Mah nishtannah*, according to Rambam (*Hilkhot Ḥameẓ u-Maẓẓah* 8:2), was not designed for the child; it is too difficult a text. Rather, the one who presides over the *Seder* says *Mah nishtannah*. This is the way my grandfather Rav Hayim used to do it. Because of Rambam's position, every member of the household – adults as well as children – would say *Mah nishtannah*, for we no longer follow the practice of having one person recite the Haggadah on behalf of everyone.

(*Kol ha-Rav*)

מַה נִּשְׁתַּנָּה *Mah nishtannah* can be understood as a single affirmative statement ("How different is this night from all other nights!") similar to the phrase "*Mah nora ha-makom ha-zeh*, how awesome is this place" (Gen. 28:17). Taken as an affirmative statement, *Mah nishtannah* is akin to the declaration made before performing a *miẓvah*: "*Hineni mukhan u-mezumman*, I am ready to

שֶׁבְּכָל הַלֵּילוֹת אֵין אָנוּ מַטְבִּילִין אֲפִלּוּ פַּעַם אֶחָת, הַלַּיְלָה הַזֶּה שְׁתֵּי פְּעָמִים:

שֶׁבְּכָל הַלֵּילוֹת אָנוּ אוֹכְלִין בֵּין יוֹשְׁבִין וּבֵין מְסֻבִּין, הַלַּיְלָה הַזֶּה כֻּלָּנוּ מְסֻבִּין:

מחזירים את הקערה למקומה ומגלים את המצות:

---

fulfill the *miẓvot* of *Pesaḥ, maẓẓah, maror*, and *sipur Yeẓi'at Miẓrayim*." It high-lights the fact that we do not just perform the *miẓvah* without experiencing its normative character and great importance. We declare that we are ready, with all our heart and soul and body, to fulfill the *miẓvah* with full awareness and to do God's will.

(*Kol ha-Rav*)

Rambam (*Hilkhot Ḥameẓ u-Maẓẓah* 7:1) links the verse regarding remember-ing the Exodus to a verse regarding remembering the Sabbath: "It is a positive *miẓvah* in the Torah to recount the miracles and wonders that were done on behalf of our ancestors in Egypt on the night of the fifteenth of Nisan, in ac-cordance with the biblical verse 'Remember the day on which you left Egypt' (Ex. 13:3); this is similar to the verse 'Remember the Sabbath day' (Ex. 20:8)." Rambam elsewhere emphasizes that the *miẓvah* of *Kiddush* is more than merely saying that the day is holy. Rather one must emphasize that the day is fundamentally different from the other days of the week: "We mention…the holiness of the [Sabbath] day and its greatness, and we contrast it with the other days [of the week]" (*Sefer ha-Miẓvot, Miẓvah* 155). The reason Rambam compares relating the story of the Exodus on the night of Passover to the *Kiddush* of Friday night is that there is a similar imperative to contrast the night of Passover with all other nights of the year. It is *Mah nishtannah* which serves this halakhic function. The recitation of *Mah nishtannah* is thus integral to the *miẓvah* of *sipur Yeẓi'at Miẓrayim*. The four statements specifically address the imperative to conceptually separate this night from other nights. The emphasis is upon *ha-laylah ha-zeh*, this night and its singularity. In the same manner that one declares the uniqueness of the Sabbath in *Kiddush*, we place emphasis upon the uniqueness of *Pesaḥ* night, because it results in the emer-gence of singular *miẓvot*.

The *Mah nishtannah* affirms the nature of the *kedushat ha-laylah*, the sanctity of the night, by enumerating the *miẓvot* related to this night, in contradistinction to all other nights: *maẓẓah, maror*, and telling the story of

On all nights we need not dip even once, on this night we do so twice!

On all nights we eat sitting upright or reclining, and on this night we all recline!

The seder plate is restored to its place and the maẓẓot are uncovered.

---

the Exodus, and the *korban Pesaḥ* (which, according to Rambam, in the time of the Temple, was reflected in a fifth statement on why only roasted meat is eaten this night). The dipping expresses the obligation of *ve-higgadta le-vinkha* by eliciting the child's questions, and the *haseivah* expresses the obligation to view oneself, *li-reʾot et aẓmo*, as having left Egypt.

(Reshimot)

הַלַּיְלָה הַזֶּה כֻּלָּנוּ מְסֻבִּין Rambam (*Hilkhot Ḥameẓ u-Maẓẓah* 7:8) writes that a son, even when in the presence of his father, is obligated in the *miẓvah* of *haseivah*, but a student in front of his *rebbe* should not recline unless he has specifically received permission to do so. It would appear that only a student is required to obtain the requisite permission before reclining.

While the requirement to display *mora* (awe) applies equally to parent and *rebbe*, the quality afforded to each is not parallel. The *miẓvah* of *mora* does not *per se* exempt the student from *haseivah*. Rambam (*Hilkhot Talmud Torah* 5:6) writes that a student should not recline in front of his *rebbe* but instead should sit as one does before a king. Indeed, the Talmud (*Pesaḥim* 108a) explains that the *mora* one must display to one's *rebbe* is comparable to the *mora* one is required to display toward God. The *miẓvah* of *mora* regarding parents, however, is not quite as expansive; it does not demand that a child not recline in their presence.

Meiri (*Pesaḥim* 108a) challenges this distinction, asserting that the *miẓvah* of *mora* applies equally to parent and *rebbe*. We can always assume, however, that parents are willing to forgo their honor and would prefer that their children fulfill the *miẓvah*. A son in the presence of his father who is also his *rebbe* would similarly be obligated in *haseivah* without requesting permission, because he can assume that his father forgoes his honor. However, Meiri would agree that if the father specifically demanded that the appropriate *kavod* be afforded to him, the son would be prohibited from performing *haseivah*.

(Reshimot)

עֲבָדִים הָיִינוּ לְפַרְעֹה בְּמִצְרָיִם (דברים ו׳, כ״א). וַיּוֹצִיאֵנוּ יְיָ אֱלֹהֵינוּ מִשָּׁם, בְּיָד
חֲזָקָה וּבִזְרֹעַ נְטוּיָה (דברים כ״ו, ח׳). וְאִלּוּ לֹא הוֹצִיא הַקָּדוֹשׁ בָּרוּךְ הוּא אֶת־

עֲבָדִים הָיִינוּ לְפַרְעֹה בְּמִצְרָיִם In Deuteronomy, the phrase *"Avadim hayinu le-Far'oh be-Mizrayim"* is the response to the question of the wise son: "What are the testimonies, statutes, and ordinances that the Lord our God commanded you?" The wise son's question does not address the story of the Egyptian Exodus alone; it includes the laws of Passover as expounded in both the *Torah she-bi-ketav* and *Torah she-be-al peh*, the oral and written laws. The night of Passover is first and foremost a night of Torah study.

The citations in the Haggadah from the Tosefta and the Mekhilta – the Oral Law – concentrate on the major laws of *sipur Yeẓi'at Miẓrayim* so that we will be able to fulfill the commandment of discussing the laws of *Pesaḥ*. Without discussing the laws, the Haggadah cannot begin. We start with "We were slaves" in order to stress that the source of everything is the Exodus from Egypt. Then straightaway we proceed to the laws of *sipur Yeẓi'at Miẓrayim*. (1) "Had the Almighty not redeemed our forefathers from Egypt" is the law that in every generation a person is obligated to see himself as if he personally left Egypt. It explains what we mean by saying that we, and not simply our forefathers, were slaves. (2) "Even if we were all wise" expresses the law that the obligation of *sipur Yeẓi'at Miẓrayim* must be kept even if we already know all the details. Furthermore, there is a *miẓvah* to add or innovate something in our *sipur*. (3) "Whoever elaborates on the story" expresses the element of the law that *sipur Yeẓi'at Miẓrayim* is a commandment that has no bounds. (4) The story about Rabbi Eliezer, Rabbi Joshua, and the sages in Bene-Berak teaches that *sipur* may last all night long, despite the opinion of Rabbi Eleazar ben Azariah that the paschal lamb may be eaten only until midnight. (5) "The Torah addressed itself to four children" teaches that there is a commandment of telling another person in general, and children in particular; that we must tailor the mode of *sipur* to the understanding of the child; that a child who does not acknowledge the requirement of fulfilling the commandments should not be told the story of the Exodus; that we must elicit the curiosity of the child so that he or she will ask questions on *Pesaḥ* night; and that clarification of the laws of *Pesaḥ* is an inherent part of the story of the Exodus. Finally, (6) we determine the timing of the *miẓvah* of *sipur* to be at a time when *maẓẓah* and bitter herbs are set before us. (Kol ha-Rav)

The telling of the Exodus story begins with *"Avadim hayinu,"* the initial response to the Four Questions. The first sentence of this response succinctly summarizes the entire story: "We were slaves to Pharoah in Egypt, and God

We were slaves to Pharaoh in Egypt (Deut. 6, 21), and the Lord, our God, took us out from there with a strong hand and with an outstretched arm (Deut. 26, 8). If the Holy One, blessed be He, had

---

took us out from there with a strong hand and an outstretched arm." Afterward, the Haggadah expands significantly in the relating of the story.

This format is a function of our obligation, on *Pesaḥ* night, to relive the experience of the Exodus as realistically as possible. When someone survives a dangerous adventure, he reports the experience in two stages. First, he quickly makes it clear to his loved ones that he is alive and well. Only afterwards, when that message is understood, does he tell the story in more detail. So too, at the *Seder*, the message is first conveyed in the brief style of a telegram stating "I am safe, details to follow." Once that message is transmitted, we are able to relate the story at a slower pace, with a more complete description. (*Reshimot*)

We were slaves to Pharaoh, not Pharaoh's slaves. The former would be only a juridic-social description; the Jews belonged to Pharaoh legally, but spiritually were free people with their own minds and an independent approach to reality. However, when we state that someone is "Pharaoh's slave," we identify his whole personality with Pharaoh. Serving Pharaoh is not just incidental; it is the whole purpose of his life. Pharaoh's Egyptian slaves are called "*avdei Far'oh*" (Gen 50:7; Ex. 10:7, 11:3). Our service to the Almighty is not something foreign and incidental, but rather something indispensable to our existence, something intrinsic and inseparable from our ontological awareness. That is why the term "*eved Hashem*, God's servant" is used in the Bible. We are just servants of God, and nothing else.

The Jews in Egypt were slaves only in a political-economic sense. Had they been slaves existentially, had they lost their love of freedom and their spiritual heritage, had they been "Pharaoh's slaves" and not just "slaves to Pharaoh," they never would have been liberated. They would have lost their personality and their quest for freedom. For the Jews, slavery was extrinsic, not intrinsic. It did not destroy their inner personality. Even in the crucible of slavery and oppression, the Jews had not forfeited their dignity and sense of loyalty. They remained the children of the patriarchs, hoping and praying for a better future. Since slavery had not corrupted them fully, and since they remained spiritually free, the great miracle of the Exodus took place.

Moses had doubts about the Jews' eligibility for freedom. He thought of them as slaves, especially after his very unpleasant experience with the two Hebrew slaves who were fighting. Moses was in despair, wondering whether the Jews were worthy of redemption. Therefore, God presented him with the

אֲבוֹתֵינוּ מִמִּצְרַיִם, הֲרֵי אָנוּ וּבָנֵינוּ וּבְנֵי בָנֵינוּ, מְשֻׁעְבָּדִים הָיִינוּ לְפַרְעֹה בְּמִצְרָיִם. וַאֲפִלּוּ כֻּלָּנוּ חֲכָמִים, כֻּלָּנוּ נְבוֹנִים, כֻּלָּנוּ זְקֵנִים, כֻּלָּנוּ יוֹדְעִים אֶת־

---

very strange revelation of the burning bush. In its middle was a fire, while its outside was cold and dark. From the outside , it looked just like any other thorn bush in the desert; but inside that bush, in its hidden center, there was a fire burning. The ecstasy of the Jews for God, their commitment to His path, had never been extinguished in Egypt. It was rather invisible, covered up. God told him, "*Ra'oh ra'iti*, I have surely seen the wretchedness of My people who are in Egypt" (Ex. 3:7). Our Sages say, "*Atah ro'eh re'iyah aḥat*" – meaning, you see only My people in Egypt – "*va-Ani ro'eh shetei re'iyot*" – whereas I penetrate into the depths (*Ex. Rabbah* 3). And once we penetrate into the depth of a Jew, no matter how repugnant his exterior, no matter how subservient he is to the taskmaster, we will find him questing for freedom and searching for God. Within every Jew, there is a burning bush. The Jew himself has never become Pharaoh's slave, but only a slave to Pharaoh. "We were slaves to Pharaoh in Egypt," but we remained free, even during the time of oppression.

(*Kol ha-Rav*)

Why does the Haggadah specify that "We were slaves to Pharaoh in Egypt"? Does it make any difference whether we were slaves to Pharaoh or to someone else? Apparently it is important. There are two types of relationship between master and slave. Sometimes a slave is owned by an individual, and sometimes the slave is the property of the state.

Both forms of bondage are degrading, but there is a distinction between private and public bondage. When owned by an individual, a slave may attain a position of power in the master's household. The best example is Joseph, who had Potiphar's complete trust. However, if the slave is the property of a cold, merciless, cruel corporate state, then no personal relationship is imaginable, no friendship or sympathy will ever be aroused, no personal contact developed. Usually the slaves of the state lose their identity; no matter how long the prisoner stays in jail, he is as new to the warden as he was the first day. The same impersonal, indifferent, cruel relationship persists from day to day, week to week, year to year. There is not a single bit of humanity in the institution of state slavery.

This is what the Haggadah emphasized: We were slaves not only to Pharaoh, but "to Pharaoh in Egypt." Egypt was a corporate state, whose head was Pharaoh. The Pharaoh was not an individual; indeed, we do not know his individual name. Even the personality of the king was erased! In a slave society, individuality submerges into a common pool, the faceless crowd of slaves. This is the meaning of the phrase *Avadim hayinu le-Far'oh be-Mizrayim*. We

not taken our fathers out of Egypt, then we, our children and our children's children would have remained enslaved to Pharaoh in Egypt. Even if all of us were wise, all of us understanding, all of

---

were his faceless slaves, and the relationship was impersonal. And, of course, an impersonal relationship is a cruel relationship. (*Festival of Freedom*)

וַיּוֹצִיאֵנוּ ה׳ אֱ־לֹהֵינוּ The Haggadah uses the possessive case of *Elokeinu*, "our God," in addition to *Hashem*, the Tetragrammaton. It could have said, "*Va-yoẓi'einu Hashem mi-sham*, Hashem took us out of there." To understand what is achieved by adding "*Elokeinu*, our God" to this statement, we must understand the semantics of "*Elokeinu*" and that of the phrase "*Hashem Elokeinu*."

In the verse "*Shema Yisra'el Hashem Elokeinu Hashem eḥad*, Hear O Israel, *Hashem Elokeinu*, God is one" (Deut. 6:4), the phrase *Hashem Elokeinu* expresses the idea that Hashem has been accepted as our God, our Master, our Lawgiver, our King, and our Ruler – He to whom we are committed, to whom we are obedient, and whose laws and commands we are duty-bound to implement.

Contemporary man is an unfree being because he is insecure; he is tied to the moment, never knowing whether disaster will strike the next second. There is only one way for man to free himself from all his restrictions, from all his fears, from all his phobias. Surrender to God frees man from his serfdom to his fellow man. Man rids himself of his fright by faith in God and surrender to Him. It is a great price, of course. One must fear God. This surrender to God is very hard; the biological pressures push, and nature summons action – often an action that has been prohibited by the law, be it in the realm of dietary law, be it in the realm of sexual morality. All man has to do is to exert his ability to give up pleasure for a few seconds, and the next hour he will find freedom at a higher level; he will be more of a free man than he was before.

If we had been taken out of Egypt without *Elokeinu*, without accepting His code, without surrendering to His authority, without reaching a covenant with Him, without obligating ourselves to surrender freedom in order to gain a higher form of freedom – then we would have been in bondage again. Instead of bondage to Pharaoh, it would have been bondage to our own fears, to our own phobias, to nature, to society, to slogans. On Passover, we celebrate our freedom. (*Festival of Freedom*)

כֻּלָּנוּ חֲכָמִים, כֻּלָּנוּ נְבוֹנִים, כֻּלָּנוּ יוֹדְעִים אֶת הַתּוֹרָה The Haggadah introduces here three types of scholars: the *ḥakham*, the scholar who is a creative genius; the *navon*, the scholar who can formulate, explain, and systematize; and the *yode'a*, the scholar who can apply. All of them are supposed to engage in the study of *Yeẓi'at*

הַתּוֹרָה מִצְוָה עָלֵינוּ לְסַפֵּר בִּיצִיאַת מִצְרָיִם. וְכָל הַמַּרְבֶּה לְסַפֵּר בִּיצִיאַת מִצְרַיִם, הֲרֵי זֶה מְשֻׁבָּח:

Miẓrayim. The *ḥakham* can behold things that are invisible to others. The *navon* can develop and systematize a whole philosophy of Jewish fate and destiny. And the *yode'a et ha-Torah* can apply it to present problems, to the events of the day. We study the Jewish people, its past, present, and future, its aspirations and destiny, under all three aspects – and every scholar can contribute a share. *Yeẓi'at Miẓrayim* is not just a story about an event that lies in a dark past. It is the doctrine of the Jewish people; it is the philosophy of our history. It is the Jewish people's outlook on the world; and to that, the Haggadah says, the entire process of intellectual understanding can be applied.

Pesaḥ night is the restaging and the reenacting of the drama of the Exodus, at which time every Jew beheld God's revelation. On that night, they did not just leave Egypt; they were confronted by the public spectacle of *gillu'i Shekhinah*, divine revelation. For one minute or one hour, everyone was wise and clever and intelligent and sensitive – and felt the presence of God. For an hour or two, everyone was initiated into the greatest of all mysteries and was considered a *ḥakham*, *navon*, and *ba'al de'ah*. Permission was granted that night to all of us to address ourselves *as ḥakhamim*, *nevonim*, *yode'im et ha-Torah*, because "In every generation, one must see himself as if he had left Egypt." All the Jews who left Egypt were confronted by God, and so, too, each Jew, at every *Seder* table, is confronted by *gillu'i Shekhinah*. Every Jew claims a share in Torah at the *Seder*; no matter who he is, he has the right to call himself "wise, understanding, and knowledgeable in Torah." "Moses commanded us the Torah, the inheritance of the congregation of Jacob" (Deut. 33:4). (*Kol ha-Rav*)

מִצְוָה עָלֵינוּ לְסַפֵּר בִּיצִיאַת מִצְרַיִם We do not recite a *birkat ha-miẓvah* upon the *miẓvah* of *sipur Yeẓi'at Miẓrayim*. Rosh (*Berakhot* 1:1) quotes the position of Riẓ Geiot and Rav Amram Gaon that if a person has said *ma'ariv* early, that is, before nightfall (and hence did not fulfill his obligation to say *keri'at Shema* at night), he should say the *berakhah* "*al miẓvat keri'at Shema*" upon reciting *keri'at Shema al ha-mittah* later. The logic underlying this position is that when *keri'at Shema* is recited during *shaḥarit* and *ma'ariv*, it is said in the context of other *berakhot*, and therefore requires no *birkat ha-miẓvah*. However, when one recites *keri'at Shema* outside the context of any other *berakhot*, a *birkat ha-miẓvah* must be recited. Similarly, Ba'al ha-Ma'or (*Rosh ha-Shanah* 10b *bedapei ha-Rif*) posits that our practice of reciting a *birkat ha-miẓvah* on *teki'at shofar* followed by thirty shofar blasts prior to *tefillat musaf* is a later decree not referred to in the Talmud. No *birkat ha-miẓvah* was recited in earlier times;

us knowing the Torah, it is a *miẓvah* to tell the story of the exodus from Egypt; and everyone who discusses the exodus from Egypt at length is praiseworthy.

---

instead, the thirty blasts would be sounded only within the *Amidah*, after *Mal-khuyyot*, *Zikhronot*, and *Shofarot*, respectively (and not preceding the *Amidah*, as is our practice now). Apparently, Ba'al ha-Ma'or, too, held that a *birkat ha-miẓvah* is not said for a *miẓvah* that is fulfilled within the framework of other *berakhot*, and that is the reason why no *birkat ha-miẓvah* was recited prior to those *teki'ot* during *musaf* when the earlier practice was still followed. For this reason, we also do not recite a *birkat ha-miẓvah* upon the *miẓvah* of *sipur Yeẓi'at Miẓrayim*, because we fulfill this *miẓvah* in the context of many other *berakhot*, namely the *berakhot* of *Kiddush*, *asher ge'alanu*, *Birkat ha-Mazon*, *birkat ha-Shir*, and those said before the *arba kosot*, *maẓẓah*, and *maror*.

The same principle applies as well to *nesi'at kapayim*, the Priestly Blessing, recited in the context of the *berakhot* of the repetition of the *Amidah*. The Talmud (*Megillah* 27b) relates that before Rabbi Eleazar ben Shammua passed away, his students asked why he had merited a long life. Among other explanations, Rabbi Eleazar explained that he never recited *nesi'at kapayim* without first reciting a *berakhah*. At first glance, this seems quite strange. Would not every *kohen* make sure to recite a *berakhah* before intoning *birkat kohanim*? Rather the Gemara must be telling us that it was he who had instituted the *berakhah*. Fundamentally, there is no requirement to recite a *birkat ha-miẓvah* upon *birkat kohanim*, since *nesi'at kapayim* is performed in the context of the *berakhot* that comprise the *Amidah*. However, the objective of this specific *berakhah* is "*le-barekh et ammo Yisra'el be-ahavah*, to bless His nation, Israel, with love." This is not a *birkat ha-miẓvah per se*, but a request for the Priestly Blessing to be accompanied by love. The love of the *kohen* for Israel is a pre-requisite to the Priestly Blessing and an important enough principle to merit a special *berakhah*. (*Reshimot*)

The slave is deprived of the meaningfulness of speech. He lives in silence – if such a meaningless existence may be called life. He has no message to deliver. In contrast with the slave, the free man bears a message, has a good deal to tell, and is eager to convey his life story to anyone who cares to listen. No wonder the Torah has emphasized the duty of the father – a liberated slave – to tell his children, born in freedom, the story of his liberation. Free man, who is eager to tell his story, is always surrounded by an audience willing to listen to his story. The slave has neither a story nor a curious audience.

(*Redemption, Prayer, Talmud Torah*)

מַעֲשֶׂה בְּרַבִּי אֱלִיעֶזֶר וְרַבִּי יְהוֹשֻׁעַ וְרַבִּי אֶלְעָזָר בֶּן־עֲזַרְיָה וְרַבִּי עֲקִיבָא

וְכָל הַמַּרְבֶּה לְסַפֵּר בִּיצִיאַת מִצְרַיִם הֲרֵי זֶה מְשֻׁבָּח Maimonides notes the difference between the two dimensions of our liberation when he introduces a seeming repetition into his formulation of the obligation to narrate the Exodus: "Even great sages are commanded to tell the story of the Exodus from Egypt; and whoever expands upon the things *she-ir'u ve-she-hayu*, which happened and took place, is to be praised" (*Hilkhot Ḥameẓ u-Maẓẓah* 7:1). *She-ir'u* always denotes passivity: something happened to me; I am the object; I was overpowered. *She-hayu* can also denote active participation, a free decision, purposive action. Apparently, *sipur Yeẓi'at Miẓrayim* encompasses two classes of events, one imposed upon the Jew, and the other precipitated, invited, and caused by him.

In the processes of physical enslavement and redemption, the Jews were completely inactive. The Jew was not ready for *Yeẓi'at Miẓrayim*; he did not expect the redemption to come immediately. This is *she-ir'u*; the events simply happened to them. However, the spiritual redemption is different. It dates back to Abraham. The Jew, of his own free will, has chosen God. Since the Jew is an active participant in his spiritual redemption, it is properly defined as *she-hayu*. And God, in turn, accepted the Jews and chose them: "And now the *Makom* has drawn us close to His service."

(*Festival of Freedom*)

מַעֲשֶׂה...שֶׁהָיוּ מְסֻבִּין בִּבְנֵי בְרַק Moses is described as the "*safra rabah*, the great scribe of Israel" (*Sotah* 13b). Moses was surely a scribe in the technical sense; as Rambam noted in his Introduction to the *Mishneh Torah*, Moses wrote a Torah scroll for each of the twelve tribes and one to be placed in the Holy Ark. The reference here, however, is not to Moses' technical skill or superior handwriting. The reference is to the art of writing God's living word upon a sensitive, passionate heart, the art of projecting God's fiery and flaming letters upon the blank patches and uncharted lanes of human memory, the art of impressing God's image upon the receptive and questing human personality. Moses was called "*Safra rabah de-Yisrael*" because he was a scribe in the same sense in which *Ha-Kadosh Barukh Hu* is referred to in the *Sefer Yeẓirah*, "*Be-sheloshah devarim ha-olam nivra: be-sefer, be-sofer, be-sipur*, the world was created by a Scribe who wrote a book with a story."

According to the *Kuzari* (4:25), when the Torah repeatedly mentions "And God said," it refers to the act of *sipur*, the result of which was the *sefer* of all of creation. It was the word of God that created the world and which is embedded in nature and continues to drive it. If the flowers bloom, the birds fly, man walks,

It happened that Rabbi Eliezer, Rabbi Yehoshua, Rabbi Eleazar ben

and the heavenly bodies remain in motion, it is because this is the will of God. Moses earned the title of the great scribe in Israel because the Torah he taught was inscribed on the parchment of the hearts and souls of the people so that they might act as the scribes that would teach the next generation. Just as the original word of God continues to drive nature, so, too, the Torah that Moses taught in the desert is as alive for us today as it was thousands of years ago.

Megillat Ester refers to itself first as an *iggeret*, a letter (Es. 9:26, 29), and later as a *sefer*, a book (Es. 9:30, 32). There are significant differences between these two forms of writing. A letter is written for a temporary purpose. In contrast, a *sefer* refers to a text that is meant to endure, to survive and communicate to future generations. For example, the prophet Jeremiah commands that the contracts for sale of land be written in a *sefer* and placed in earthen vessels so that they will last a long time (Jer. 32:10–14). A *sefer* documents an event for present and future generations. Similarly, God commanded Moses to document the eternal conflict between God and Amalek in a *sefer* and transmit it to Joshua (Ex. 17:14).

The obligation of *sipur Yeẓi'at Miẓrayim* is the obligation to view one's child as a *sefer* to be written with care and not as an *iggeret*. A Jew must feel that he has participated in the entire collective Jewish experience, and he must inscribe this knowledge into the book that is his child – it is the child who is the *sefer* upon whom the parent writes the history of God's encounter with the Jewish people.

The night of *Pesaḥ* is a symbol for this intergenerational transmission process. We are all familiar with the story of the great rabbis who were assembled in Bene-Berak and were involved in *sipur Yeẓi'at Miẓrayim* all that night until dawn. The "night" symbolizes the long, dark exile that we have endured for two thousand years; the long night of pogroms and blood libels and crusades and inquisitions and Holocaust that we have suffered. Not only were Rabbi Eliezer, Rabbi Akiva, Rabbi Tarfon, and Rabbi Joshua at that table, but the great *Gedolei Yisrael* throughout the ages were present as well. Yet despite all the difficulties, *Gedolei Yisrael* recognized that they had a mission to serve as the scribes of their generation, not in terms of writing books, but as scribes that engrave a love of Torah in the heart of each Jew. *Gedolei Yisrael* carried the burden, and transmitted their Torah as an intergenerational *sefer* and not as a fleeting *iggeret*. They seized on the method God uses, the *sipur be-sefer*, writing on the book of creation, to ensure the continuity of faith in God and the eternity of the Jewish people. The Torah remains alive to us today because of them. If not for their efforts, we would not be able to sit at our *Seder* table and discuss the Exodus on the night of *Pesaḥ*. Jews are called the *Am ha-Sefer*, the people of

וְרַבִּי טַרְפוֹן, שֶׁהָיוּ מְסֻבִּין בִּבְנֵי־בְרַק, וְהָיוּ מְסַפְּרִים בִּיצִיאַת מִצְרַיִם כָּל־אוֹתוֹ הַלַּיְלָה, עַד שֶׁבָּאוּ תַלְמִידֵיהֶם וְאָמְרוּ לָהֶם: רַבּוֹתֵינוּ, הִגִּיעַ זְמַן קְרִיאַת שְׁמַע שֶׁל שַׁחֲרִית:

---

the book, not because they are avid readers, but because each and every Jew is a living book that has been authored by the preceding generations.

(*Kol ha-Rav*)

Maggidim have a beautiful interpretation to this paragraph. They say this refers to the *Pesaḥ* that preceded the outbreak of the insurrection on the part of Bar Kokhba against Rome. "They would talk of *Yeẓi'at Miẓrayim*," but it was not only the story of the past, what happened to Pharaoh and us so many thousand years ago; it was the story of the present and what was going to happen tomorrow. The study of the Exodus was supposed to guide them in their revolt. "They would talk of *Yeẓi'at Miẓrayim* all the night." It was a long night, and the Bar Kokhba revolt was planned at that *Seder* night. They studied *Yeẓi'at Miẓrayim* not only as an event of the past, but also as a clue and a key to the future.

These great rabbis did not belong to the same generation. Rabbi Akiva was much younger than Rabbi Tarfon, and Rabbi Eleazar ben Azariah was younger than Rabbi Akiva. The passage tells us how the Sages of Israel were concerned with just one problem: how to transmit the Torah from generation to generation. They were a community of old and young scholars, but they were all united. They knew that the story of the Exodus is the great story of the Torah. They spoke of the Exodus "the whole night" – not only the night of Passover, but also the great night of the *Galut*, of Jewish exile. It was a very long night during which they had to face Roman detectives, investigators, and executioners.

It was not only these five named Sages who participated in this dialogue. After Rabbi Akiva was executed, after Rabbi Eleazar and Rabbi Joshua died, another generation assumed leadership. They kept on teaching and preaching and propagating Torah, without any interruption, in spite of all opposition and religious persecution and torture.

The tale of the rabbis in Bene-Berak was not just an isolated historical event, but rather a perennial drama that has been enacted since antiquity hundreds, indeed thousands, of times. The people who acted out this drama with tears and blood were not five or ten scholars, but countless individuals in each generation, anonymous fathers, unknown mothers, forgotten teachers, nursemaids, servants, lonely souls, and tragic people. All of them were involved in one task, dedicated to one goal: "They were talking of *Yeẓi'at Miẓrayim* all night."

Azaryah, Rabbi Akiva and Rabbi Tarfon were reclining [at a seder] in Bene-Berak. They were discussing the exodus from Egypt all that night, until their students came and told them: "Our Masters! The time has come for reciting the morning *Shema*!"

This is the central story of our destiny. We have survived; we are now building the Land of Israel. The key to the riddle of how we survived, the solution to this enigma of how we are able to read the Haggadah for thousands of years, lies with the teachers and parents who told the story of the Exodus throughout the whole night, throughout their lifespan. We mention here only one day, one generation, but it continued generation after generation. We are continuing it now, too. While waiting impatiently for daybreak, we shall continue to narrate the story of the Exodus, the tale of all tales, the *sipur* which never becomes obsolete, which is always replete with fervor, always powerful and fascinating.

(*Kol ha-Rav*)

There was a revolutionary message in Rabbi Akiva's urging his people to revolt against the Romans. The concept of a slow historical process that was so popular among the peoples who lived under the influence of Greek philosophy, the endless morphological evolution from matter into form, from a lower to a higher eidetic stage, carries weight and significance so far as time is lived through quantitatively. Then the forces of history move with an extremely slow pace; years, decades, and centuries are nothing but drops in the sea of eternity. A nation, not comprehending the Janus-face of time or the alternatives that time proffers may be subject to the same laws and regulations of the cosmic process in nature. Under the aspect of *minyan ha-shanim*, "quantitative years," any rebellion is *a priori* doomed to a stillbirth. If man leaves his fate to the principle of blind, mechanical causality and circumstantial determination, he can never attain salvation and redemption. *Keẓ* is nonexistent for him as chaos and confusion are precluded in the realm of nature.

The Jews have inherited from Abraham the alternative to *minyan ha-shanim*. The prophecy of the "generations" challenges man, not to live in time, but to mold it, to give to the indifferent *chronos* new aspects and new interpretation. Time is computed according to man's own creativity and self-determination. A qualitative time experience enables a nation to span a distance of hundreds and thousands of years in but a few moments. In the seventy years from the destruction of the Temple until the outbreak of the Bar Kokhba upheaval, the Jewish people may have lived through an endless continuum of time, Rabbi Akiva concluded. "*Ve-hu ha-Keẓ* – and then will be your Redemption!"

(*Sacred and Profane*)

אָמַר רַבִּי אֶלְעָזָר בֶּן־עֲזַרְיָה: הֲרֵי אֲנִי כְּבֶן שִׁבְעִים שָׁנָה, וְלֹא זָכִיתִי שֶׁתֵּאָמֵר יְצִיאַת מִצְרַיִם בַּלֵּילוֹת, עַד שֶׁדְּרָשָׁהּ בֶּן־זוֹמָא. שֶׁנֶּאֱמַר: לְמַעַן תִּזְכֹּר אֶת יוֹם צֵאתְךָ מֵאֶרֶץ מִצְרַיִם כֹּל יְמֵי חַיֶּיךָ (דברים ט"ז, ג'). יְמֵי חַיֶּיךָ הַיָּמִים. כֹּל יְמֵי חַיֶּיךָ, הַלֵּילוֹת. וַחֲכָמִים אוֹמְרִים: יְמֵי חַיֶּיךָ, הָעוֹלָם הַזֶּה. כֹּל יְמֵי חַיֶּיךָ, לְהָבִיא לִימוֹת הַמָּשִׁיחַ:

אָמַר רבי אֶלְעָזָר בֶּן עֲזַרְיָה *Sipur Yeẓi'at Miẓrayim* must be fulfilled through the study of the written Torah in conjunction with its interpretation and exposition in the oral tradition. One who wishes to fulfill this *miẓvah* properly must not only tell, but must also study this section in accordance with the methodology we apply when learning Torah generally. The obligation of *sipur Yeẓi'at Miẓrayim* and telling children about the Exodus is actually an obligation to study Torah and pass on the tradition. This demands understanding the material on the level of *talmud Torah*, within the framework of the Oral Law. Not only must we explain and expound upon the events from the perspective of the written and oral traditions, but there is as well a special obligation to study the laws of *Pesaḥ*. This study itself constitutes a fulfillment of the obligation of *sipur Yeẓi'at Miẓrayim*.

At first glance, this Mishnah, which deals with *zekhirah* and not *sipur*, bears no relevance to the Haggadah. But Rambam's text of the Haggadah reads, "Rabbi Eleazar ben Azariah said to them…." In other words, at the time the rabbis sat in Bene-Berak and engaged in *sipur Yeẓi'at Miẓrayim*, they were discussing the laws pertaining to the Exodus. The obligation of *zekhirat Yeẓi'at Miẓrayim*, though relevant throughout the year and not just on *Pesaḥ*, clearly relates to the wonders and miracles performed for our forefathers in Egypt. Therefore, the laws of *zekhirat Yeẓi'at Miẓrayim* are included among the *halakhot* that one may study in order to fulfill the obligation of *sipur Yeẓi'at Miẓrayim*.

(*Kol ha-Rav*)

Rambam does not enumerate the obligation to remember the Exodus, *zekhirat Yeẓi'at Miẓrayim*, as one of the 613 precepts. He does state (*Hilkhot Keri'at Shema* 1: 2,3) that although the *miẓvah* of *ẓiẓit* does not apply at night, one must recite the verses pertaining to *ẓiẓit* when reciting the *Shema* at night because they mention the Exodus, and it is a *miẓvah* to remember the Exodus every day and every night. Why, then, does he not enumerate this obligation as one of the 613 precepts?

Rav Hayim explained the omission as follows: In *Sefer ha-Miẓvot*, Rambam sets forth the principle that only a permanent precept, a *miẓvah le-dorot*, can

Rabbi Eleazar ben Azaryah said: "I am like a man seventy years old, yet I did not succeed in proving that the exodus from Egypt must be mentioned at night, until Ben Zoma explained it: "It is said, 'That you may remember the day you left Egypt all the days of your life' (Deut. 16, 3); now 'the days of your life' refers to the days, [and the additional word] 'all' indicates the inclusion of the nights!" The sages, however, said: "'The days of your life' refers to the present-day world; and 'all' indicates the inclusion of the days of Mashiaḥ."

---

be enumerated as one of the 613 precepts. According to Ben Zoma (in the Mishnah quoted here in the Haggadah) there is no verse that establishes an obligation to remember the Exodus in post-messianic times, so the precept of remembering the Exodus is of a temporary nature. Rambam, in setting forth an obligation to remember the Exodus at night, follows the opinion of Ben Zoma. Accordingly, Rambam holds that the precept to remember the Exodus is temporary.

Rav Hayim offered another explanation, that the obligation to remember the Exodus is subsumed under the obligation to accept the yoke of Heaven's Kingship, *kabalat ol malkhut shamayim*. The Talmud (*Rosh ha-Shanah* 32a) explains that the words "I am the Lord your God" are synonymous with the idea of Kingship and accepting the yoke of Heaven's Kingship. Likewise, this phrasing is also used in the third paragraph of the *Shema*: "I am the Lord your God, who brought you out of Egypt to be your God, I am the *Hashem* your God" (Num. 15:41). The juxtaposition of God's Kingship and the Egyptian Exodus implies that the remembrance of the Exodus is an inherent part of accepting the yoke of Heaven's Kingship. This concept is also apparent in the Ten Commandments, which state, "I am *Hashem* your God who took you out of the Land of Egypt" (Ex. 20:2). Accordingly, the obligation to remember the Exodus is not an independent obligation; rather, it is a particular manner of fulfilling the more general obligation of accepting the yoke of Heaven's Kingship in reciting the *Shema*. According to Rambam's system of counting the 613 precepts, various requirements that are part of a general *mizvah* are not counted as separate *mizvot*. Rather, they are all subsumed under the general precept. Therefore, the obligation of remembering the Exodus is part of the more general obligation of accepting the yoke of Heaven's Kingship while reciting the *Shema*.

The exact characteristic of the obligation to remember the Exodus in the third paragraph of the *Shema* can be further understood from the talmudic passage:

> Rav Judah bar Zebida said, they [the Sages] wanted to "set forth" the

בָּרוּךְ הַמָּקוֹם, בָּרוּךְ הוּא. בָּרוּךְ שֶׁנָּתַן תּוֹרָה לְעַמּוֹ יִשְׂרָאֵל, בָּרוּךְ הוּא.

> verses about Balak in the recitation of the *Shema*, why did they exclude them? To avoid burdening the congregation. Why [did they consider including the Balak verses]? If it is because they mention the Exodus, why not consider including the verses dealing with usury or the verses dealing with weight calibration, since those verses also mention the Exodus?...the verses of *ẓiẓit* were picked because they have [in addition to the reference to the Exodus] five qualities: the *miẓvah* of *ẓiẓit*, the yoke of the *miẓvot* in general, the prohibition against heretical ideas, the prohibition against contemplating transgressions, and the prohibition against contemplating idolatry (*Berakhot* 12b).

This talmudic passage implies that the Sages determined the content of the third paragraph of the *Shema*, yet Rambam states that the obligation to recite the verses of *ẓiẓit* is a biblical requirement (*Hilkhot Keri'at Shema* 1:3). How then, does Rambam understand this talmudic passage? Rambam holds that the biblical obligation to recite the first two paragraphs of the *Shema* differs from the biblical obligation to recite the third. The first two paragraphs are biblically determined and they can only consist of those particular verses. Similarly, the verses of the Priestly Blessing and the verses recited by the pilgrim offering his first fruits are biblically set forth, and cannot be substituted by other verses. That is not the case, however, with respect to the third paragraph of the *Shema*. Reciting any verse mentioning the Exodus would satisfy the biblical requirement. The talmudic passage therefore discusses how the Sages came to establish a normative text for the third paragraph of the *Shema*, although in fact, they could have chosen any verse that mentions the Exodus.

(*Shi'urim le-Zekher Abba Mori*)

בָּרוּךְ הַמָּקוֹם, בָּרוּךְ הוּא "Rava said that everything that Ezekiel saw, Isaiah saw. What does Ezekiel resemble? A villager who saw the king; while Isaiah resembles a city dweller" (*Ḥagigah* 13b). Rava is explaining why Ezekiel is so elaborate in describing his vision of God's Heavenly Abode, whereas Isaiah's description of God is relatively terse.

The intent of Rava's metaphor of the villager and city dweller is to communicate that though both prophets saw the same vision, Ezekiel's prophecy is more elaborate because he is like a villager who rarely sees the king, and therefore is more effusive in describing his encounter with the king, while Isaiah is like a person who lives in the capital city and sees the king more often and thus is less elaborate in describing the event.

Blessed is the Omnipresent One, blessed be He! Blessed is He who gave the Torah to His people Israel, blessed be He! The Torah

---

The difference between Ezekiel and Isaiah is not in the intensity of their prophecy. Rather, their different visions reflect the different times and circumstances in which they lived. Isaiah lived while the Temple was still standing, and God's presence was palpable. Isaiah, therefore, proclaims "*Kadosh kadosh kadosh melo kol ha-areẓ kevodo*, Holy, Holy, Holy, the whole world is filled with His Majesty" (Isa. 6:3). Ezekiel, however, lived after the time of the Temple's destruction and prophesied while in exile. God is no longer immanent; He has receded to His Heavenly Abode, hidden by many veils of transcendence. Ezekiel, therefore, declares "*Barukh kevod Hashem mi-Mekomo*, blessed is the Majesty of God from His Place" (Ezek. 3:12).

These two prophecies, which represent two perspectives, comprise the *Kedushah* prayer depicting how the angels praise God. The appellation *ha-Makom*, "the Place," refers to God when He retreats and seems distant, at times of travail, trauma, and tragedy. Yet, even when He recedes to His Place, nonetheless, from a distance *ha-Makom* appears to us. When God relates to us from a distance, we refer to Him as *ha-Makom*. Therefore, when we console the mourners, we use the appellation *ha-Makom*, and we say, "*Ha-Makom yenaḥem etkhem*, God, *ha-Makom*, should console you."

As we sit at the *Seder*, even in dark and foreboding periods of Jewish history, we know that *ha-Makom* watches over us.

(*Reshimot*)

בָּרוּךְ שֶׁנָּתַן תּוֹרָה לְעַמּוֹ יִשְׂרָאֵל We start the recital of the section relating to the questions of the four types of children with several words of praise to the Almighty: "Blessed be the *Makom*, blessed be He! Blessed be He who gave the Torah to His people..." The formula is an abbreviation of the blessings on the Torah that we pronounce every morning: "Blessed are You...who gave us His Torah..." These blessings are also concerned with passing on the Torah from generation to generation: "Please, Lord our God, sweeten the words of Your Torah in our mouth.... May we and our offspring, and the offspring of our offspring, and the offspring of all Your people, the House of Israel, be privileged to know Your Name and learn Your Torah for its own sake. Blessed are You, Who teaches Torah to His nation Israel."

We repeat it at the *Seder* because the concern of the *Seder* is *masorah* and *kabalah*. When we are about to proclaim the ideal of *masorah* – "The Torah speaks about four kinds of children" – we offer thanks to the Almighty in

כְּנֶגֶד אַרְבָּעָה בָנִים דִּבְּרָה תוֹרָה: אֶחָד חָכָם, וְאֶחָד רָשָׁע, וְאֶחָד תָּם, וְאֶחָד שֶׁאֵינוֹ יוֹדֵעַ לִשְׁאֹל:

חָכָם מַה הוּא אוֹמֵר? מָה הָעֵדֹת וְהַחֻקִּים וְהַמִּשְׁפָּטִים, אֲשֶׁר צִוָּה יְיָ אֱלֹהֵינוּ אֶתְכֶם? (דברים ו׳, כ׳) וְאַף אַתָּה אֱמָר־לוֹ כְּהִלְכוֹת הַפֶּסַח: אֵין מַפְטִירִין אַחַר הַפֶּסַח אֲפִיקוֹמָן:

---

the same manner as we do every morning. The blessing is related not only to *talmud Torah* but to the *masorah* of Torah as well.

(*Kol ha-Rav*)

כְּנֶגֶד אַרְבָּעָה בָנִים דִּבְּרָה תוֹרָה *Sipur Yeẓi'at Miẓrayim* adjusts itself to the level of the child and also involves instilling love rather than knowledge. Everyone can have a share in accordance with his or her individual ability. When God gave the Torah, He did not give it only for great minds. The Torah is humble enough to be concerned with the *tam*, the dull child, and give him a version of Judaism that he can understand and which will give him joy and happiness. The Torah is also concerned with "*she-eino yode'a li-she'ol*, the child who does not know how to ask," the indifferent, assimilated child, who does not care enough to ask questions. Even the *rasha*, the wicked child, is included. If he had been in Egypt, he would not have deserved redemption; but apparently there is still hope of bringing him back, for he is still at the *Seder* – if he were not at the *Seder*, the Torah would not have spoken about him. The Torah prepared a place for all in the Haggadah.

(*Kol ha-Rav*)

וְאַף אַתָּה אֱמָר לוֹ כְּהִלְכוֹת הַפֶּסַח The *Seder* is celebrated by a community within which one shares not only his material goods, but also his own selfhood, his spiritual treasures, his knowledge, experiences, aspirations and hopes. The *Seder* community is a teaching community. The form which the *halakhah* has prescribed for the narration of the events of the Exodus is more a study than a tale, more a discourse about *miẓvot* than a narrative. Had *Ḥazal* simply wanted the story to be told, the events to be recounted in detail, they would have introduced as mandatory the recital of the sections of Exodus dealing with the saga of slavery and freedom.

Every Jewish home on the *Seder* night becomes a teaching community, a didactic fellowship, a school where a class of disciples is instructed in Judaism. The teacher tells the wondrous story of slaves who in one night turned into princes, into a kingdom of priests. But, basically, he does not relate a story.

addresses itself to four sons: One is wise, one is wicked, one is simple and one does not know how to ask.

The wise one, what does he say? "What are the testimonies, the statutes and the laws which the Lord, our God, has commanded you?" (Deut. 6, 20) You, in turn, shall instruct him in the laws of Passover, [up to] "one is not to eat any dessert after the Passover-lamb."

Rather, he teaches them how to act as free people and how to utilize their freedom. He informs them of laws entailed by the acquisition of freedom. Halakhically, *sipur Yeẓi'at Miẓrayim* requires the study of the laws of *Pesaḥ*, not only the telling of the story. With regard to the wise child, the *halakhah* commands us to "apprise him of the laws of *Pesaḥ*." Passover night is the night of *masorah*, of handing down, transmitting the knowledge, the ancient tradition, our world outlook, commitments, aspirations, and visions to all kinds of children – bright and dull, obedient and rebellious, engaged and indifferent. The meal thus is turned into a "symposium," into a rendezvous with Torah, with the logos. The meal becomes the vehicle of *ḥesed* in its highest form: teaching and enlightening.

(*Festival of Freedom*)

וְאַף אַתָּה אֱמָר לוֹ כְּהִלְכוֹת הַפֶּסַח אֵין מַפְטִירִין אַחַר הַפֶּסַח אֲפִיקוֹמָן The Torah's answer to the wise child's question (Deut. 6:20) is "You shall say to your child: We were slaves to Pharaoh in Egypt, and the Lord took us out of Egypt with a mighty hand; and the Lord placed signs and wonders, great and terrible, upon Egypt, upon Pharaoh and upon all his house, before our eyes. And He took us out of there, that He might bring us in, to give us the land which He swore to our forefathers" (Deut. 6:21–23). Why, then, does the Haggadah answer instead, "You shall tell him the laws of *Pesaḥ*: One must not eat any dessert after the *Pesaḥ* sacrifice"?

The reason is to be found in the Bible's next verse: "And the Lord commanded us to do all these statutes, *kol ha-ḥukkim ha-elleh*, to fear the Lord our God, for our good always, that He might keep us alive, as it is this day" (Deut. 6:24). A part of the Bible's response relates to "*ha-ḥukkim ha-elleh*," and therefore one has to explain what these are. In fact, the Vilna Gaon's version of the answer to the wise son is, "You too should tell him the laws of *Pesaḥ*, until 'One must not eat any dessert after the *Pesaḥ* sacrifice'" – in other words, tell him all the laws until the end of tractate *Pesaḥim*. Studying the laws of *Pesaḥ* is part of *miẓvat sipur Yeẓi'at Miẓrayim*.

(*Kol ha-Rav*)

רָשָׁע מַה הוּא אוֹמֵר? מָה הָעֲבֹדָה הַזֹּאת לָכֶם? (שמות י״ב, כ״ו) לָכֶם וְלֹא לוֹ. וּלְפִי שֶׁהוֹצִיא אֶת־עַצְמוֹ מִן הַכְּלָל, כָּפַר בָּעִקָּר. וְאַף אַתָּה הַקְהֵה אֶת־שִׁנָּיו, וֶאֱמָר־לוֹ: בַּעֲבוּר זֶה, עָשָׂה יְיָ לִי, בְּצֵאתִי מִמִּצְרָיִם (שמות י״ג, ח׳), לִי וְלֹא־לוֹ. אִלּוּ הָיָה שָׁם, לֹא הָיָה נִגְאָל:

תָּם מַה הוּא אוֹמֵר? מַה זֹּאת? וְאָמַרְתָּ אֵלָיו: בְּחֹזֶק יָד הוֹצִיאָנוּ יְיָ מִמִּצְרַיִם מִבֵּית עֲבָדִים: (שמות י״ג, י״ד)

וְשֶׁאֵינוֹ יוֹדֵעַ לִשְׁאוֹל, אַתְּ פְּתַח לוֹ. שֶׁנֶּאֱמַר: וְהִגַּדְתָּ לְבִנְךָ, בַּיּוֹם הַהוּא לֵאמֹר: בַּעֲבוּר זֶה עָשָׂה יְיָ לִי, בְּצֵאתִי מִמִּצְרָיִם: (שמות י״ג, ח׳)

רָשָׁע מַה הוּא אוֹמֵר The *rasha*, the evil child, challenges us, saying that *Yeẓi'at Miẓrayim* no longer has any significance. However, this is not so, as the great story of our tradition can encounter any opposition or challenge. One may emerge victorious even with the radical atheist if one uses the proper terms and the proper categories. The Torah that God gave us is all-inclusive, all-embracing, all-pervading. It has the answers to all problems, even though we cannot always decode its language. The Torah is not afraid. We do not have to retreat into isolation or solitude because the street is "contaminated." To retreat means to lose. "*Teḥillat nefilah nisah*, the beginning of defeat is flight," the Talmud says (*Sotah* 44b). The enemy will conquer when the army begins to withdraw, to retreat, to flee. On the contrary, we face the *rasha*. The Torah did not say to throw the *rasha* out of the house. Rather, engage him in debate and show him that he is wrong: "blunt his teeth." *Talmud Torah* requires bringing the one who got lost, the child who was alienated, back into the fold. He or she is a *rasha* now, but there is potential in the *rasha*.

(*Kol ha-Rav*)

אִילוּ הָיָה שָׁם, לֹא הָיָה נִגְאָל Rambam states (*Hilkhot Teshuvah* 3:12), "One who separates himself from the ways of the community, even though he commits no sins, but isolates himself from the community of Israel, and does not perform *miẓvot* together with them and separates himself from their pain, such a person has no share in the world-to-come."

Thus the *rasha*, by separating himself from the community, is *per se* an apostate.

(*Reshimot*)

The wicked one, what does he say? "What is this service to you?!" (Ex. 12, 26) He says "to you," but not to him! By thus excluding himself from the community he has denied that which is fundamental. You should therefore blunt his teeth and say to him: "It is because of this that the Lord did for me when I left Egypt" (Ex. 13, 8); "for me" – but not for him! If he had been there, he would not have been redeemed!

The simple child, what does he say? "What is this?" Thus you shall say to him: "With a strong hand the Lord took us out of Egypt, from the house of slaves." (Ex. 13, 14)

As for the one who does not know how to ask, you must initiate him, as it is said: "You shall tell your child on that day, 'It is because of this that the Lord did for me when I left Egypt.'" (Ex. 13, 8)

וְהִגַּדְתָּ לְבִנְךָ "*Ve-higgadta le-vinkha*, and you shall tell your child," is *haggadat edut*, a formal act of testimony by an eyewitness who testifies before *beit din* about an event he personally witnessed. Hence we use the term *haggadah*. The *halakhah* requires that in each generation a person is obligated to view himself as if he himself left Egypt. It is the overpowering experience of the Exodus that compels one to act in a way that testifies to his great fortune and joy, and to demonstrate, without restraint, his happiness and enthusiasm. He becomes a witness to the Exodus; the events did not occur to another, but to himself. The entire Haggadah becomes eyewitness testimony.

(*Shi'urim le-Zekher Abba Mori*)

The Haggadah consists of two separate components – narrative and *hallel*, praise, and the word *haggadah* is in fact used in the Torah with these same two connotations. The Torah states "*ve-higgadta le-vinkha*, and you shall tell your son" (Ex. 13:8), which means that one must relate and narrate events. The Torah also uses the word *haggadah* in the sense of offering praise, as in the verse "*higgadti ha-yom la-Hashem Elokekha*" (Deut. 26:3). In that verse, the word *higgadti* is translated by Rashbam and the *Targum Yerushalmi* in the sense of giving praise to God. Thus, the themes of both narrative and *hallel* are included in the word *haggadah*.

(*Reshimot*)

יָכוֹל מֵרֹאשׁ חֹדֶשׁ, תַּלְמוּד לוֹמַר: בַּיּוֹם הַהוּא. (שמות י״ג, ח׳) אִי בַּיּוֹם הַהוּא, יָכוֹל מִבְּעוֹד יוֹם, תַּלְמוּד לוֹמַר: בַּעֲבוּר זֶה. (שמות י״ג, ח׳) בַּעֲבוּר זֶה לֹא אָמַרְתִּי, אֶלָּא בְּשָׁעָה שֶׁיֵּשׁ מַצָּה וּמָרוֹר מֻנָּחִים לְפָנֶיךָ:

מִתְּחִלָּה עוֹבְדֵי עֲבוֹדָה זָרָה הָיוּ אֲבוֹתֵינוּ, וְעַכְשָׁו קֵרְבָנוּ הַמָּקוֹם לַעֲבוֹדָתוֹ.

יָכוֹל מֵרֹאשׁ חֹדֶשׁ Why should we consider the possibility of applying the obligation of *sipur* from *Rosh Ḥodesh*? Never did our Sages ask with regard to the obligation of *lulav*, "Perhaps from *Rosh Ḥodesh*? The verse states, 'on the first day.'" However, the answer becomes abundantly clear when we realize that Rambam (*Sefer ha-Mizṿot*, positive commandment 157, quoting the Mekhilta de-Rashbi to Ex. 13:3) derives the obligation of *sipur Yeẓi'at Miẓrayim* from the word *zakhor* – "Remember this day [that you left Egypt]" (Ex. 13:3) and the parallel "Remember the Sabbath day, to keep it holy" (Ex. 20:8)." The *zakhor* obligation of the Sabbath begins, in effect, on the first day of the week. All week long, a person anticipates the Sabbath, yearns for it, and thinks only of it. This is reflected, as Ramban (Ex. 20:8) points out, by the *halakhah* that assigns the weekdays no names of their own, and instead names them in reference to the Sabbath, e.g., "*yom sheni ba-Shabbat*, the second day of the week," and so forth. Perhaps, then, here too we should begin on *Rosh Ḥodesh* counting toward the fifteenth. The *baraita* therefore found it necessary to establish that this *miẓvah* begins only when one has *maẓẓah* and *maror* placed before him.

(*Kol ha-Rav*)

בְּשָׁעָה שֶׁיֵּשׁ מַצָּה וּמָרוֹר מֻנָּחִים לְפָנֶיךָ The association between *sipur Yeẓi'at Miẓrayim* and the obligation to eat *maẓẓah* and *maror* indicates that the commandment of *sipur Yeẓi'at Miẓrayim* is inherently connected to the *miẓvah* of eating *maẓẓah*. This is supported by Rambam's language in his listing of the *miẓvot* at the beginning of *Hilkhot Ḥameẓ u-Maẓẓah*. He writes that it is a *miẓvah* to eat *maẓẓah* "*be-leilei ha-Pesaḥ*, on the night of Passover." Rambam then lists the *miẓvah* of *sipur Yeẓi'at Miẓrayim* "*be-oto ha-laylah*, on that very night," meaning the same night that one must eat *maẓẓah*. The use of "*be-oto ha-laylah*" as opposed to "*be-leilei ha-Pesaḥ*" implies that the *miẓvah* of *sipur Yeẓi'at Miẓrayim* must be fulfilled in conjunction with the *miẓvah* of eating the *maẓẓah*. Thus, the *miẓvah* of *sipur Yeẓi'at Miẓrayim* does not have its own independent time; rather, it is contingent on the *miẓvah* of eating *maẓẓah* and *maror*.

(*Reshimot*)

מִתְּחִלָּה עוֹבְדֵי עֲבוֹדָה זָרָה הָיוּ אֲבוֹתֵינוּ The Mishnah (*Pesaḥim* 116a) sets forth an obligation to begin the *sipur Yeẓi'at Miẓrayim* by recounting our degradation

One may think that [the discussion of the exodus] must be from Rosh Ḥodesh, the first of the month. The Torah therefore says, "On that day." (Ex. 13, 8) "On that day," however, could mean while it is yet daytime; the Torah therefore says, "It is because of this." (Ex. 13, 8) The expression "because of this" can only be used when *mazzah* and *maror* are placed before you.

In the beginning our ancestors worshipped idols; but now the

---

and then proceeding with our praise. Shmuel says that "degradation" refers to *Avadim hayinu*, the mentioning of our servitude to Pharaoh. Rav says it refers to *Mi-teḥillah ovedei avodah zarah*, the fact that our ancestors were idol worshippers.

The dispute between Rav and Shmuel might be understood as follows. There are two aspects of slavery, the physical and the spiritual. In approaching the shameful aspects of slavery, Rav emphasizes the spiritual degradation of the enslaved Jews. Shmuel, however, emphasizes the physical degradation of the Jews that resulted from bondage. Thus, Rav and Shmuel are each focusing on one of the two dimensions of slavery.

This dispute between Rav and Shmuel is consistent with another dispute between them. The Talmud (*Gittin* 38–39) discusses the issue of a Jew who is "*mafkir*" his slave – a master who relinquishes his ownership of a slave. According to Rav, although the master no longer owns the slave, he must still provide the slave with a *get shiḥrur*, a formal "document of freedom." The opinion of Shmuel, however, is that a master who relinquishes ownership of a slave is not obligated to write and give a "document of freedom," since the slave becomes free by virtue of the master's relinquishing ownership.

This dispute can be understood as follows. There are two elements with respect to the status of a Canaanite slave. First, a slave is the property and monetary asset of the master – *kinyan mamon*. Another dimension of the slavery is the diminished personal status of the slave (e.g., he cannot marry and is not fully obligated in *mizvot*; this is known as *kinyan issur*).

Rav considers the diminished personal status, the *kinyan issur*, as the primary dimension of slavery. Therefore, even if the *kinyan mamon* aspect, the fact that he is the property of his master, has been removed, the slave still needs a *get shiḥrur* because the ties to his master still manifest themselves by his diminished personal status. However, Shmuel holds that the primary aspect of slavery is that he is owned by his master, *kinyan mamon*; the personal status of the slave, *kinyan issur*, is contingent on that. Therefore, if the *kinyan mamon*, the monetary ownership, is eliminated, the slave automatically goes completely free and his personal status is elevated to that of a free man.

שֶׁנֶּאֱמַר: וַיֹּאמֶר יְהוֹשֻׁעַ אֶל־כָּל־הָעָם. כֹּה אָמַר יְיָ אֱלֹהֵי יִשְׂרָאֵל, בְּעֵבֶר הַנָּהָר יָשְׁבוּ אֲבוֹתֵיכֶם מֵעוֹלָם, תֶּרַח אֲבִי אַבְרָהָם וַאֲבִי נָחוֹר, וַיַּעַבְדוּ אֱלֹהִים אֲחֵרִים: וָאֶקַּח אֶת־אֲבִיכֶם אֶת־אַבְרָהָם מֵעֵבֶר הַנָּהָר, וָאוֹלֵךְ אוֹתוֹ בְּכָל־אֶרֶץ כְּנָעַן. וָאַרְבֶּה אֶת־זַרְעוֹ, וָאֶתֶּן לוֹ אֶת־יִצְחָק: וָאֶתֵּן לְיִצְחָק אֶת־יַעֲקֹב וְאֶת־עֵשָׂו. וָאֶתֵּן לְעֵשָׂו אֶת־הַר שֵׂעִיר, לָרֶשֶׁת אוֹתוֹ. וְיַעֲקֹב וּבָנָיו יָרְדוּ מִצְרָיִם: (יהושע כ"ד, ב-ד)

Thus, Rav emphasizes the spiritual dimension of slavery, *Mi-teḥillah ovedei avodah zarah*, representing the diminished personal status, whereas Shmuel emphasizes the physical dimension of the enslavement in Egypt, *Avadim hayinu*, representing the monetary ownership. (*Reshimot*)

מִתְּחִלָּה עוֹבְדֵי עֲבוֹדָה זָרָה הָיוּ אֲבוֹתֵינוּ וְעַכְשָׁיו קֵרְבָנוּ הַמָּקוֹם לַעֲבֹדָתוֹ In the ancient world, other nations usually explained their origins as the product of a love affair between a god and a human; these nations or peoples viewed themselves as descendants of gods, princes, and kings. This is not the story of Judaism. On the night of *Pesaḥ*, the night of the election of Israel as a covenantal nation, we say that our election is not because we have distinguished ourselves. "At first, our ancestors were idolaters," we declare, and we would have remained idolaters and pagans had not God "brought us close to His service."

We are of humble origin. Our ancestors were simple idol worshippers. The fact that we are the people who brought to the world monotheism, a new morality, and a new set of spiritual values, is not due to our efforts or to our greatness. God came to us and invited us to join Him; the initiative belonged to Him. Our greatness came because of a special act of grace on the part of the Almighty. He could have elected any of the seventy nations but, as an act of *ḥesed*, He chose us. We did not display the characteristics that would have qualified us for the honor of being selected as God's people, the *am nivḥar*, a covenantal community. We are undeserving and unworthy. Our Torah is very much concerned with gratitude. Therefore, on *Pesaḥ* night, even before we begin to tell the story of the Exodus, we express our indebtedness to the Almighty. We are indebted not only for the miracles, which happened later, but also for the very fact that He called us into His service.

(*Festival of Freedom*)

קֵרְבָנוּ הַמָּקוֹם לַעֲבֹדָתוֹ It was the *Makom* who brought us close to His service and not the *Kadosh Barukh Hu*, because the *Kadosh Barukh Hu* would not have touched Terah and raised idol worshippers to the level of a kingdom of priests

Omnipresent One has brought us close to His service, as it is said: "Joshua said to all the people: Thus said the Lord, the God of Israel, 'Your ancestors used to live on the other side of the river – Terah, the father of Abraham and the father of Nahor, and they served other gods. I took your father Abraham from beyond the river, and I led him throughout the whole land of Canaan. I increased his seed and gave him Isaac, and to Isaac I gave Jacob and Esau. To Esau I gave Mount Seir to possess it, and Jacob and his children went down to Egypt.'" (Josh. 24, 2–4)

---

and a holy nation. But the *Makom* embraces everyone, regardless of their moral standing in life, regardless of their attributes, regardless of whether they are good or wicked. The *Makom* does not desert anyone. God is ubiquitous and omnipresent, enveloping everything and everyone. No one is outside of Him, just as no one can be outside of space, which is all-penetrating, all-inclusive, all-embracing, and all-pervading. Nothing is so big that it cannot be encompassed by space, and nothing so small that space has no place for it. Of course, the very moment we are brought close, God's appellation changes from *ha-Makom* to *ha-Kadosh Barukh Hu*. The very next paragraph says, "*Ha-Kadosh Barukh Hu* calculated the *keẓ*." (*Kol ha-Rav*)

When Rav declared that the Haggadah's response to the child's question should begin with "In the beginning our forefathers were idolaters, and now the *Makom* has drawn us close to His service," he meant that one can fulfill his obligation of *sipur Yeẓi'at Miẓrayim* with the words "God drew us close to His service." There is undoubtedly a commandment to discourse in detail and at length. But Rav said that the supreme motif must consist of talking about Israel's election, and the story of this election must be conducted through a discourse of the laws of *Pesaḥ*. In fact, *sipur Yeẓi'at Miẓrayim* must begin with the statement of the commandments of *Pesaḥ*, with the laws and statutes, and only then should we tell the story of the Exodus. The telling of the story is an explanation for the laws. That is why the laws governing *sipur Yeẓi'at Miẓrayim* itself were introduced into the Haggadah. Usually, the learned person can go beyond this, as the Haggadah says, "Whoever elaborates on the story of the Exodus is to be praised"; but a minimum was established and standardized in the Haggadah. (*Festival of Freedom*)

וָאֶתֵּן לְעֵשָׂו אֶת הַר שֵׂעִיר לָרֶשֶׁת אֹתוֹ וְיַעֲקֹב וּבָנָיו יָרְדוּ מִצְרָיִם Mount Seir is suddenly mentioned here because the Haggadah wants to contrast Jacob and Esau, twin

בָּרוּךְ שׁוֹמֵר הַבְטָחָתוֹ לְיִשְׂרָאֵל, בָּרוּךְ הוּא. שֶׁהַקָּדוֹשׁ בָּרוּךְ הוּא חִשַּׁב אֶת־הַקֵּץ, לַעֲשׂוֹת כְּמָה שֶׁאָמַר לְאַבְרָהָם אָבִינוּ בִּבְרִית בֵּין הַבְּתָרִים, שֶׁנֶּאֱמַר: וַיֹּאמֶר לְאַבְרָם, יָדֹעַ תֵּדַע כִּי־גֵר יִהְיֶה זַרְעֲךָ בְּאֶרֶץ לֹא לָהֶם

---

brothers with the same parents. Their destinies should have been identical – but they were not. "Esau took his wives, his sons, his daughters, every soul of his household, his livestock, and all the possessions he had acquired in the land of Canaan, and he went to another land" (Gen. 36:6). He did not stay forty years in a desert; he did not eat manna; he had no problems with the Golden Calf or with the spies. There was no resistance; God's promise turned into a reality within a short time. But God did not fulfill His promise to our forefathers immediately.

(*Kol ha-Rav*)

The destinies of Jacob and Esau are inversely proportional. The Talmud (*Megillah* 6a) states: "Caesarea and Jerusalem: If someone tells you both have been destroyed, do not believe him. If someone says both are settled, do not believe him. But if he tells you that Caesarea has been destroyed and Jerusalem settled, or that Jerusalem has been destroyed and Caesarea settled, believe him, as it states, 'I will fill the destroyed one.' If one is settled, the other is destroyed; if one is destroyed, the other is settled. Rav Nahaman son of Isaac derived this principle from the verse in Genesis 25:23, which states, 'One kingdom will be stronger than the other kingdom.' Therefore, in keeping with this relationship, the verse tells us that as Esau inherited Mount Seir, Jacob immediately went into exile to Egypt."

(*Reshimot*)

שֶׁהַקָּדוֹשׁ בָּרוּךְ הוּא חִשַּׁב אֶת הַקֵּץ Rabbi Akiva cited an enigmatic statement regarding the process of redemption: "The father endows his son with his beauty, strength, means, wisdom, years, and the number of generations to come. And this is the *kez*, the redemption; as it is written (Gen. 15:13), 'And they shall enslave them and afflict them for four hundred years'; and it is written (Gen. 15:16), 'In the fourth generation they shall return here'" (*Eduyyot* 2:9).

We may conjecture that Rabbi Akiva delivered this message in the chaotic, strife-torn days of his time. Israel tottered precariously on the brink of the tentative explosion of Bar Kokhba's revolt, which Rabbi Akiva had prophesied and urged so zealously. Rabbi Akiva delivered a grand view of the twofold approach to time. It is undoubtedly true, if time is measured quantitatively,

Blessed is He who keeps His promise to Israel, blessed be He! For the Holy One, blessed be He, calculated the end [of the bondage], in order to do as He had said to our father Abraham at the "Covenant between the Portions," as it is said: "He said to Abraham, 'You shall know that your seed will be strangers in a land that is not theirs, and they will enslave them and make them suffer, for

---

by *minyan ha-shanim*, that only seventy years separate the Bar Kokhba revolt from the destruction of the Temple, and that is too short a period to bring about a national renaissance and prepare a nation for political autonomy. But if time is measured qualitatively by *mispar ha-dorot*, by what the "generations" accomplish in time, by the creativity of a nation, then in seventy years a nation may condense an eternity and become worthy of liberty. If "the father endows the son," then the future is already born.

As a divine proof, he quoted two contradictory decrees as to the duration of the Egyptian bondage. Should the Jew develop the qualitative consciousness of time, his transitional period would expire in four generations. With a qualitative consciousness of time, the Jew could create a prophet, a Moses, in four generations. But if he measured time quantitatively, by the sands of time sweeping endlessly over the pyramids of the Pharaohs, then even four hundred years would be too little. The ideal of *keẓ*, of "the end of the road," can never be realized if it is sought after in quantitative terms; then the process is snail-paced and the stages demarcated by infinite coulisses of time. *Keẓ*, redemption, is not something static and distant towards which man gravitates, for as such it would be only an ever-regressing mirage in the deserts of time. Rather, it is an ideal or norm which man himself quickens into life. Only by qualitative criteria of norms and creativity can man shorten the distance and span time with great leaps. Modern technology has conquered space. It is the ideal of *keẓ* to conquer time.

(*Sacred and Profane*)

יָדֹעַ תֵּדַע כִּי גֵר יִהְיֶה זַרְעֲךָ God tells Abraham, "*Yado'a teda*," You will be intensely dedicated to the land, *ki*, because "your seed shall be a stranger in a land that is not theirs," because you will not get the land immediately and will have to wait a long time for it. They will be slaves and ill-treated for four hundred years. Throughout the dark night of *galut*, you will have only one dream, one vision, one aspiration, one hope: to get back to the Land of Israel! "Next year in Jerusalem!" And after you return to the land, I assure you that you will be deeply in love with the land. It will be an eternal love, not just a passing affair.

וַעֲבָדוּם, וְעִנּוּ אֹתָם אַרְבַּע מֵאוֹת שָׁנָה: וְגַם אֶת־הַגּוֹי אֲשֶׁר יַעֲבֹדוּ דָּן
אָנֹכִי, וְאַחֲרֵי כֵן יֵצְאוּ בִּרְכֻשׁ גָּדוֹל: (בראשית ט"ו, י"ג-י"ד)

Ereẓ Yisrael was not given immediately to Jacob the way Mount Seir was turned over to Esau. The Torah tells us how Esau moved from Canaan to Mount Seir the way one moves from one apartment to another. "And Esau took his wives, and his sons, and his daughters, and all the persons of his house, and his cattle, and all his beasts, and all his substance, which he had acquired in the land of Canaan; and went into another country away from his brother Jacob" (Gen. 36:6). But in order for Jacob and his children to get the Land of Israel, they first had to go down to Egypt.

(*Abraham's Journey*)

וְגַם אֶת הַגּוֹי אֲשֶׁר יַעֲבֹדוּ דָּן אָנֹכִי "And so, too, the nation that will enslave them I will judge" (Gen. 15:14). God promised Abraham at the time of the *berit bein ha-betarim*, the Covenant of the Pieces, that He would judge the Egyptians. God is the universal judge who always sits in judgment and resolves every situation in accordance with the dictates of justice. Why, then, did God need to promise Abraham that He would judge the Egyptians? Rav Hayim of Brisk explained that if God's intent was that He Himself would judge the Egyptians, the words "*adin Anokhi*" would have been more precise. "*Dan Anokhi*," however, implies that God will not merely judge the Egyptians. A judge must be an impartial, dispassionate arbiter of the case. With respect to judging Israel's oppressors, God will not judge dispassionately. Rather, God will passionately advocate and seek judgment against Israel's oppressors. God will be a litigant. This is so because God and Israel are intrinsically connected. The Mishnah (*Sanhedrin* 6:5) states, "When man suffers, what expression does the Divine use? 'My head is too heavy for me, My arm is too heavy for me,'" thus God suffers along with man. When Israel is oppressed, God is oppressed. When Israel is oppressed, God becomes a litigant because He too is oppressed. God's reputation, as it were, is God's destiny. Thus, God's promise to Abraham was an assurance that God would not merely sit and judge the Egyptians, but "*dan Anokhi*," God will advocate and litigate Israel's cause because Israel's cause is also God's cause.

With respect to the judgment against Israel's oppressors, the Midrash (*Gen. Rabbah* 82:9) highlights two seemingly inconsistent verses. One verse states "God stands to fight" (Isa. 3:13), while the other verse states "I will sit to judge the nations" (Joel 3:12). The Midrash explains that initially God will sit and

four hundred years. But I shall also judge the nation whom they shall serve, and afterwards they shall leave with great wealth.'" (Gen. 15, 13–14)

---

deliberate with care and patience, but then God will become a litigant, and He will stand and fight for Israel. Rav Hayim explains that the appropriate protocol calls for the judge to sit, whereas the litigants are to stand (*Shevu'ot* 30b). Accordingly, the Midrash is explaining that God will assume two roles when He judges Israel's oppressors. At the outset, God will function as a judge, sitting and carefully deliberating, as a judge is required to do. However, His passionate desire to advocate for Israel will prevail. God will then stand, assuming the role of a fervent litigant. That is the meaning of God's promise to Abraham, "*dan Anokhi*."

(*Kol ha-Rav*)

וְאַחֲרֵי כֵן יֵצְאוּ A slave upheaval haunted all tyrants of antiquity, as well as those of modern times. Rebellion by slaves meant total destruction. History records many bloody and ruthless insurrections of slaves against their masters. The stories about the cruelty of the rebels are blood-chilling. They were eager to settle a long account of cruelty. Horrific massacres were typical. The brutish drive for vengeance, for gratification of the satanic in man, was irresistible.

Did anything of that kind happen on the night of the Exodus? Were Egyptian babies taken out of the embrace of their mothers and thrown into the Nile, as the babies of the slaves had been murdered just a short while before? Did the Hebrew beat up his taskmaster who just several days ago had tortured him mercilessly? Nothing of the sort. Not one person was hurt, not one house destroyed.

The liberated slaves had the courage to withdraw, to defy the natural call of their blood. What did the Jews do at the hour of freedom? Instead of swarming the streets of Goshen, they were locked up in their houses, eating the paschal lamb and reciting the *Hallel*. It is unique in the history of revolutions. "None of you shall go out of the door of his house until the morning" (Ex. 12:22).

Would we have blamed the Jews if they had engaged in a few acts of vandalism and even murder on the night of the fifteenth of Nisan, killing a few taskmasters who had thrown their babies in the Nile? Still, the Jews, at the command of God, said no. They defied themselves and refused to gratify a basic need of the human being, the need for revenge. But by defeating themselves, they also won the greatest of all victories: they became free.

(*Festival of Freedom*)

מכסים את המצות ומגביהים את הכוס ואומרים:

וְהִיא שֶׁעָמְדָה לַאֲבוֹתֵינוּ וְלָנוּ. שֶׁלֹּא אֶחָד בִּלְבָד, עָמַד עָלֵינוּ לְכַלּוֹתֵנוּ, אֶלָּא שֶׁבְּכָל דּוֹר וָדוֹר, עוֹמְדִים עָלֵינוּ לְכַלּוֹתֵנוּ. וְהַקָּדוֹשׁ בָּרוּךְ הוּא מַצִּילֵנוּ מִיָּדָם:

מניחים את הכוס ומגלים את המצות.

צֵא וּלְמַד, מַה בִּקֵּשׁ לָבָן הָאֲרַמִּי לַעֲשׂוֹת לְיַעֲקֹב אָבִינוּ. שֶׁפַּרְעֹה לֹא גָזַר אֶלָּא עַל הַזְּכָרִים, וְלָבָן בִּקֵּשׁ לַעֲקֹר אֶת־הַכֹּל. שֶׁנֶּאֱמַר: אֲרַמִּי אֹבֵד אָבִי,

---

וְהִיא שֶׁעָמְדָה As an introduction to *Arammi oved avi*, we raise our cup and say, "*Ve-hi she-amedah la-avoteinu*, This [promise] has sustained our ancestors and us." *Yeẓi'at Miẓrayim* is a steady occurrence, an everyday event. There is always a Pharaoh, or somebody worse, who is possessed by psychopathic, cruel, bloodthirsty hate. Only the steady vigilance of the Almighty has saved us from complete annihilation.

We celebrate the festival of *Yeẓi'at Miẓrayim* not only because we remember it, nor just because we re-experience it, but rather because it is a permanent drama. Every generation lives through the actual experience of *Yeẓi'at Miẓrayim*. Hence, before we start reciting, commenting on, and explaining the *parashah* of *Arammi oved avi*, we inform the listener that our method is one of total interpretation, of translating the past into the present, of identifying memory with reality. The *parashah* tells us that we are a lonely people, that we are all a band of wandering Arameans facing hostility, that our very existence is a miracle. The story of the Exodus is the story of our destiny!

Yeẓi'at Miẓrayim is relevant and worthy of remembering. We experience it in retrospection and feel worthy of giving thanks; we also recognize that it is the story of this generation, for whose salvation we pray. We lift up the cup when we say *Ve-hi she-amedah*. In biblical Hebrew, the word *kos*, cup, symbolizes destiny: "You anointed my head with oil; my cup overflows" (Ps. 23:5); "I will raise the cup of salvations" (Ps. 116:13). Raising the cup symbolizes that the Haggadah is the book of Jewish destiny.

(*Festival of Freedom*)

שֶׁפַּרְעֹה לֹא גָזַר אֶלָּא עַל הַזְּכָרִים וְלָבָן בִּקֵּשׁ לַעֲקוֹר אֶת הַכֹּל Our Sages introduced Laban in the Haggadah as the enemy of our people. Laban himself admitted this later. He said: "It lies within the power of my hand, *la-asot immakhem ra*, to do evil to you" (Gen. 31:29). It is noteworthy that the word *immakhem* is in the plural

The wine cup is raised and the mazzot are covered.

This is what has stood by our ancestors and us! For not just one alone has risen against us to destroy us, but in every generation they rise against us to destroy us; and the Holy One, blessed be He, saves us from their hand!

The wine cup is put down and the mazzot are uncovered.

Go forth and learn what Laban the Aramean wanted to do to our father Jacob. Pharaoh had decreed only against the males, but Laban wanted to uproot everyone – as it is said: "The Aramean wished

---

form. Since he was addressing Jacob, he should have used the singular form, but he was really speaking of his two daughters and his grandchildren. Laban was ready to kill his own daughters because they had adopted a God he did not understand; he felt so alienated from his own children that he was kindled with an insane hatred against them. Nothing short of divine intervention would have stopped Laban from implementing his plan. In comparison, Pharaoh was sane. Pharaoh ordered the Hebrew sons cast into the Nile – but not his own son. He was quite concerned about his sons; when his eldest died, he came running to Moses and told him to take the Israelites and leave immediately. Pharaoh was immoral, an exploiter, a slave driver, but he was normal. He made money from his slave society. He wanted to keep the Jews downtrodden, but he did not try to wipe them out, nor did he wish to harm his own family.

(*Kol ha-Rav*)

אֲרַמִּי אֹבֵד אָבִי This is the same text the pilgrim used to recite (with an additional one and one-half verses) on the occasion of *hava'at bikurim*, bringing the first fruits to the Temple. Apparently, the recital of this *parashah* by the pilgrim constituted, as far as the substance of the *mizvah* is concerned, an act of *sipur Yezi'at Mizrayim*. We are thus obligated to tell the story of the Exodus on two occasions: first, when we offer the *bikurim*, and second, on the fifteenth night of Nisan. The Torah did not specify the text we are supposed to use on the first night of Passover. It just stated in general terms, "*Ve-higgadta le-vinkha*, You shall tell your child" (Ex. 13:8). However, it did point out the text to be read in the Temple at the time of *hava'at bikurim*: "You shall speak and say before the Lord your God, 'A wandering Aramean…' (Deut. 26:5)." There is good reason to assume that the narration on the first night of Passover should avail itself of the same text. In both cases, we were commanded "*le-saper bi-Yezi'at Mizrayim*, to tell the story of the Exodus."

וַיֵּרֶד מִצְרַיְמָה, וַיָּגָר שָׁם בִּמְתֵי מְעָט. וַיְהִי שָׁם לְגוֹי גָּדוֹל עָצוּם וָרָב:

(דברים כ"ו, ה')

Even though *haggadah* (as in "*ve-higgadta le-vinkha*") and *mikra bikurim* constitute two separate, independent *mizvot*, their common root is to be found in the norm of *hakarat ha-tov*, expressing gratitude and thanksgiving. However, even though *mikra bikurim* and *haggadah* are both rooted in *hakarat ha-tov*, the manner in which gratitude is expressed differs. *Mikra* consists of *shevaḥ*, praise; *haggadah* consists of *shirah*, song.

In *mikra bikurim*, the precept of gratitude is fulfilled indirectly, by telling the story of *Yeẓi'at Miẓrayim*. There are no special words of glorification, no explicit words of praise. The narrative description of what happened suffices; all addenda are superfluous. The duty of *hakarat ha-tov* is discharged by describing the events, similar to the reading of the *Megillah* on *Purim*. When explaining why we do not recite the *Hallel* on Purim, the Talmud (*Megillah* 14a) declares: "*Keriyaitah zu halleila*, reading the story [of Esther] is itself the highest praise." In other words, the thanksgiving is implicit in the narration itself. All one is required to do is tell the truth.

On the night of the *Seder*, we praise God in an explicit manner. Although we describe the events and narrate the entire story, we are not satisfied with implicit praise. We sing a hymn; we recite *Hallel*; we say *shirah ḥadashah*, a new song. On *Pesaḥ* night, we are not only grateful but overflowing with gratitude and love. It is a night of ecstasy, when man is God-intoxicated; it is the night of "*Ani le-Dodi ve-Dodi li*, I am my Beloved's and my Beloved is mine" (Song 6:3). We must sing; we must recite *shirah* over a cup overflowing with wine! "We shall say before Him a new song; *haleluyah*."

(*Kol ha-Rav*)

There are fundamental differences between remembering and telling. First, *zekhirah*, remembering, means briefly recalling the Exodus from Egypt when we recite the section of *ẓiẓit* in *keri'at Shema*. On concluding with the final verse, "I am the Lord your God who took you out of the land of Egypt" (Num. 15:41), we have fulfilled this commandment. On the other hand, *sipur*, telling, requires relating the story at length, including the hardships of slavery and the signs and miracles that God performed in Egypt to redeem us. Second, *zekhirah* is done in private, for oneself, whereas *sipur* entails a commandment to tell someone else, as the verse states: "You shall tell your child…" (Ex. 13:8). Third, *zekhirat Yeẓi'at Miẓrayim* does not constitute a *miẓvah* in itself, but rather derives from the *miẓvah* of *keri'at Shema* and the acceptance of the yoke of Heaven. *Sipur*

to destroy my father; and he went down to Egypt and sojourned there, few in number; and he became there a nation – great and mighty and numerous." (Deut. 26, 5)

Yeẓi'at Miẓrayim, on the other hand, is an autonomous *miẓvah*, one of the 613 biblical commandments. I heard all the above distinctions from my father and teacher, *zt"l*, in the name of my grandfather, *zt"l*. It seems to me that we can add a further distinction: *Sipur* entails a commandment to offer praise and thanksgiving, as we say in the Haggadah: "Therefore we are obligated to thank, praise, extol…." No such obligation accompanies *zekhirah*.

An additional distinction is that *sipur* is accomplished through study, *talmud Torah*, while *zekhirah* entails merely mentioning the fact of the Exodus. We know that *sipur Yeẓi'at Miẓrayim* revolves around the biblical section of "*Arammi oved avi*" (Deut. 26:5–8). The Mishnah (*Pesaḥim* 10:4, 116a) indeed states explicitly, "One expounds [the verses] from *Arammi oved avi* until he concludes the entire passage." Rambam formulates this *halakhah* similarly (*Hilkhot Ḥameẓ u-Maẓẓah* 7:4): "One expounds from *Arammi oved avi* until he finishes the entire passage." It would appear that in Rambam's view, one cannot achieve the desired "elaboration" on the Haggadah simply by telling the story. In order to complete the *miẓvah*, we require the act of studying and expounding with the Oral Torah, not merely reading, the verses of *Arammi oved avi*. Elaborating by reading the narratives in the Book of Exodus does not fulfill the *miẓvah* of elaborating upon *sipur Yeẓi'at Miẓrayim*. Expounding upon the section of *Arammi oved avi* is indispensable.

(*Kol ha-Rav*)

The Mishnah (*Pesaḥim* 10:4) requires that "he expound from *Arammi oved avi* until he concludes the entire passage." But, in fact, we do not recite the whole passage from beginning to end. We omit the last verse and a half: "He brought us to this place, and gave us this land, a land flowing with milk and honey. And now, behold, I have brought the first fruits of the land, which You, O Lord, have given me" (Deut. 26:9–10). Why was the verse discussing the entry into the Land of Israel not included in our version of Haggadah?

There are several approaches to a resolution of this problem. First, if the Haggadah had included this reference to the Land of Israel, it would convey the impression that there are five languages of, or references to, *Ge'ullah* and not four. *Ḥazal* apparently felt that "*ve-heve'ti*" (Ex. 6:8) should not be mentioned on the *Seder* night. This was so because, unlike the other references to *Ge'ullah*, which were stated by the Almighty to Moses as new ideas that had not been expressed to the patriarchs, "*ve-heve'ti*, and I shall bring you into the land" was already promised to Abraham, Isaac, and Jacob in their respective *Berit Avot*.

וַיֵּרֶד מִצְרַיְמָה, אָנוּס עַל פִּי הַדִּבּוּר. וַיָּגָר שָׁם, מְלַמֵּד שֶׁלֹּא יָרַד יַעֲקֹב אָבִינוּ לְהִשְׁתַּקֵּעַ בְּמִצְרַיִם, אֶלָּא לָגוּר שָׁם, שֶׁנֶּאֱמַר: וַיֹּאמְרוּ אֶל־פַּרְעֹה, לָגוּר בָּאָרֶץ בָּאנוּ, כִּי אֵין מִרְעֶה לַצֹּאן אֲשֶׁר לַעֲבָדֶיךָ, כִּי כָבֵד הָרָעָב בְּאֶרֶץ כְּנָעַן. וְעַתָּה, יֵשְׁבוּ־נָא עֲבָדֶיךָ בְּאֶרֶץ גֹּשֶׁן: (בראשית מ"ז, ד')

Second, although the Jewish people did enter into the Land of Israel subsequent to the Exodus from Egypt, this was not the primary goal of *Yeẓi'at Miẓrayim*. The Land of Israel was their destination but not their destiny. The direct goal of the Exodus was the revelation at Sinai, the transformation of a subjugated people into "a nation of priests and a holy nation" (Ex. 19:6). It was not just to grant them political and economic freedom, but also to create a sacred people. Moses, at the episode of the burning bush, asked the Almighty: "Who am I that I should go unto Pharaoh, and that I should bring forth the Children of Israel out of Egypt?" (Ex. 3:11) And the Almighty gives an answer that seems at first unresponsive to Moses' question: "Certainly I will be with you, and this shall be unto you the sign that I have sent you: When you have brought forth the people out of Egypt they shall serve God upon this mountain" (Ex. 3:12). In effect, the Almighty was stating, "Know, Moses, that the purpose of the redemption from Egypt is not political and social freedom. For that task I would not have chosen you. I did not select you to be a diplomat or a king or a political leader. Rather, the purpose of the Exodus is to create a holy nation, to forge the Jewish people into a Torah nation. For this purpose, I need a *rebbe*, a teacher and mentor, who will lead and guide this people. And for this role, you, Moses, are the best candidate." *Pesaḥ* leads into *Shavu'ot*, and the dominant theme of these holidays is the Exodus leading to the giving of the Torah. These two festivals do not focus on the Land of Israel as a central theme.

Third, I have no doubt that on *Pesaḥ* night, when the Temple stood on Mount Moriah, we used to recite with great love and gratitude the verse "He brought us." We felt duty-bound to thank God not only for the Exodus, but for the entry into the Promised Land and the construction of the Temple as well. The Mishnah describes how *Pesaḥ* was observed when the Temple stood, not during the period of *galut*, exile. However, times changed. The Temple was destroyed; the Land of Israel was conquered by the enemy; and the Jewish people were driven from the land. *Ḥazal* apparently doubted the propriety of thanksgiving on the night of *Pesaḥ* for the land and sanctuary that were snatched away from us.

(*Kol ha-Rav*)

אָנוּס עַל פִּי הַדִּבּוּר The expression "*anus al pi ha-dibur*," which emphasizes coercion, is a strange one, and appears only in the Haggadah. One would have expected the passage to read, "'*Va-yered Miẓraymah al pi ha-dibur*," with no mention

"He went down to Egypt" – forced by Divine decree. "He sojourned there" – this teaches that our father Jacob did not go down to Egypt to settle, but only to live there temporarily. Thus it is said, "They said to Pharaoh, We have come to sojourn in the land, for there is no pasture for your servants' flocks because the hunger is severe in the land of Canaan; and now, please, let your servants dwell in the land of Goshen." (Gen. 47, 4)

---

of coercion. Therefore, I wish to suggest that this phrase means not that God commanded him, but that the Almighty arranged circumstances in such a way that it was impossible for Jacob to continue living in Canaan, for in order to recover his beloved son Joseph years later, Jacob would have to reluctantly descend to Egypt. Jacob did not want to leave Canaan, but God had to bring about the fulfillment of His promise to Abraham, "Your seed will be strangers in a land not theirs." Jacob was forced by the situation brought about by God: that is the meaning of *anus al pi ha-dibur.*

Jacob and his children did not forfeit their ownership claims over the land the very instant they left Canaan, because Jacob's departure from Canaan was "compelled by word of God." He did not do it voluntarily. After all, the grant of the land was dependent upon Abraham's arrival and sojourn in Canaan. On his way to Haran, Jacob was assured by the Almighty that the land would be his after his return: "I shall give it to you and your progeny" (Gen. 28:13). Yet such a promise is not to be found in the prophecy revealed to Jacob on his way to Egypt. The Almighty merely told Jacob, "I will go down with you to Egypt, and I will also surely bring you up again" (Gen. 46:4), without promising him the land.

The reason for *anus al pi ha-dibur* is the *halakhah* that an act done under coercion neither cancels rights nor generates obligations. In spite of the fact that Jacob and his children absented themselves from the Promised Land, their claims to the land were not undermined.

Interestingly, Rambam omitted this passage from his Haggadah. The Mishnah (*Pesaḥim* 115a) states that there is an obligation on *Pesaḥ* night to study and elucidate the passage of *Arammi oved avi*. Apparently, Rambam believed that the obligation cited by the Mishnah refers only to matters that can be elucidated directly from the *parashah*. Since there is no allusion in the verse of *Va-yered Miẓraymah* ("Jacob descended to Egypt") to the idea that Jacob was coerced by God to descend to Egypt, Rambam felt it should not be included in the Haggadah.

(*Reshimot*)

לָגוּר בָּאָרֶץ בָּאנוּ, כִּי אֵין מִרְעֶה לַצֹּאן אֲשֶׁר לַעֲבָדֶיךָ The Jews came to Egypt as shepherds. The land was promised to Abraham, Isaac, and Jacob in the form of a covenant

בִּמְתֵי מְעָט, כְּמָה שֶׁנֶּאֱמַר: בְּשִׁבְעִים נֶפֶשׁ, יָרְדוּ אֲבֹתֶיךָ מִצְרָיְמָה. וְעַתָּה, שָׂמְךָ יְיָ אֱלֹהֶיךָ, כְּכוֹכְבֵי הַשָּׁמַיִם לָרֹב. (דברים י׳, כ״ב)

---

concluded between the Almighty and the patriarchs. However, there was a stipulation in the agreement: the implementation of the latter was contingent upon the sojourn of Abraham's children in a strange land as bondsmen and servants. Prior to the fulfillment of this stipulation, the gift was held in abeyance; the finalization and the full consummation of the covenant took place after the Israelites met the challenge of "Your seed shall be strangers" (Gen. 15:13). Hence, their rights to the Promised Land were limited. The most they had was a *kinyan perot*, the right to use the land and enjoy the produce. Later, after the Exodus, they acquired *kinyan ha-guf*, full ownership. Hence, before the Exodus they had no right to develop an agricultural economy, to dig, to build, to destroy, to change the structure of the land. All they possessed was the right to enjoy the fruit, and that is exactly what the pastoral community did. It did not exploit the land like the agricultural society. It took whatever the land offered. As they left Egypt, the Torah began to prepare them with *mizvot* for the new challenge they were facing: the change from shepherds into farmers, the transformation of the simple pastoral society into a relatively complex agricultural society.

The Torah gave the Jew an ethic of an agricultural economy as well as an ethic of a pastoral economy. It tries to teach both farmer and shepherd how to engage in their respective trades with honesty, kindness, and dignity – not to grab and not to reach out for something beyond one's grasp. The Torah did not discriminate between these two human activities. Each one must comply with its respective ethic. *Arammi oved avi va-yered Mizraymah.* Jacob went to Egypt because he was a nomad with restricted rights to the land. Only the descent to Egypt expanded his rights.

The agricultural and pastoral societies differ not only economically but psychologically as well. The agriculturist knows how to defend his homestead; he is capable of fighting should someone try to steal his land or produce. The farmer loves his homestead and is loyal to it. He does not surrender territory. The shepherd or nomad does not know how to protect his property, since he is not committed to a specific locus. If someone encroaches upon his territory, he will move on to another spot. On the other hand, the shepherd is kind and hospitable, while the farmer is ruthless, insensitive, and at times cruel. His motto is: My homestead is my fortress.

The Torah wants the Jew to be as kind and gentle as the legendary shepherd. On the other hand, the Torah is concerned with defense. The Jew is engaged in a permanent struggle, and in order to emerge victorious from his historical

"Few in number" – as it is said: "Your ancestors went down to Egypt with seventy persons, and now, the Lord, your God, has made you as numerous as the stars of heaven." (Deut. 10, 22)

---

engagement he must be tough and brave. To be kind and gentle when firmness and resoluteness are necessary is a sin. At times, though, overzealousness and a lack of consideration are disjunctive emotions. Hence, the Torah wanted the Jew to be both shepherd and farmer.

(*Festival of Freedom*)

In my opinion, the quotation of what Jacob's sons said to Pharaoh is important for two reasons. First, they explained to Pharaoh that they had not moved from Canaan to Egypt because Egypt was a progressive country, technologically as well as agriculturally, whereas Canaan was a backward land with a primitive economy. They did not say that their moving was due to the superiority of Egypt to Canaan. They explained their choice in terms of a transient event – the famine. Second, they wanted to impress Pharaoh with their love and affection for their cattle. In other words, they told Pharaoh: We are nomads, shepherds, cattlemen. We will not change our pastoral way of life, even though the Egyptians do not respect our profession. The purpose of this introduction was to inform Pharaoh that they would not assimilate into the Egyptian people. They suggested to Pharaoh that they settle in Goshen, in a ghetto. They did not intend to change their habits and way of life.

(*Kol ha-Rav*)

בִּמְתֵי מְעָט...כְּכוֹכְבֵי הַשָּׁמַיִם לָרֹב Man is a weak as well as a strong being. He is master of his environment, as well as prisoner of the same environment. He is wise as well as foolish. He possesses fortitude, and at the same time is a frightened being. His main preoccupation is the fear of death. The word *met* is used to refer to man as a mortal being: "*ir metim*" (Deut. 2:34, 3:6) means "the town and its mortals." *Met* portrays man as a weak, helpless, transient being "who is here today and tomorrow in the grave" (*Berakhot* 28b, 33a), who is the weakest link in the biological chain, short-lived, perplexed, horrified by the vision of death and fleeing extinction. In a similar fashion, the word *nefesh*, quoted here by the Haggadah, is used by the Torah to point to man's deficits, his limitations – physical as well as spiritual – and his insecurity: "*Nefesh ki teḥeta bi-shegagah*, When a soul shall sin in error" (Lev. 4:2). "*Bi-metei me'at*" thus denotes a few mortals, poor erring immigrants.

Our anthropology is a dialectical one. Man is a big lie, a non-being; he is also

וַיְהִי שָׁם לְגוֹי, מְלַמֵּד שֶׁהָיוּ יִשְׂרָאֵל מְצֻיָּנִים שָׁם:

גָּדוֹל עָצוּם, כְּמָה שֶּׁנֶּאֱמַר: וּבְנֵי יִשְׂרָאֵל, פָּרוּ וַיִּשְׁרְצוּ, וַיִּרְבּוּ וַיַּעַצְמוּ בִּמְאֹד מְאֹד, וַתִּמָּלֵא הָאָרֶץ אֹתָם: (שמות א׳, ז׳)

---

a mighty being who can rise to the stars. Man is both weak and powerful; he errs, but he also illuminates and shines. The *metim* who were concerned with the fleshpots rose to dizzying heights a few months later when they responded to God's inquiry, "*Kol asher diber Hashem na'aseh ve-nishma*, All that God has spoken we shall do and heed" (Ex. 24:7).

Thus, the parallel verse, which the Haggadah introduces, expresses just the opposite of the term *metim*: "Now the Lord your God has made you as the stars of heaven for multitude" (Deut. 10:22). Man is not just a transient being who is today here and tomorrow in the grave, but also a star radiating light and twinkling to us from endless distances.

(*Kol ha-Rav*)

וַיְהִי שָׁם לְגוֹי The Jews became a people in Egypt. The Zohar (Ex. 189a) emphasizes "*sham*" – only there in Egypt could the Jews become a great people; had they not been in Egypt, they would not have been transformed into a *goy gadol*. The Jewish people become great in crisis. *Keneset Yisrael* had to spend many years in slavery in order to attain nationhood and greatness. It had to see and experience evil, tyranny, ruthlessness – for one cannot hate Satan unless one knows him well and has dealt with him. To hear stories about Satan is not enough; direct experience and involvement are indispensable. Joseph was sold to Potiphar, the chief executioner, in order to acquaint him with human cruelty.

Had Jacob remained in Canaan, his children and future generations would not have developed extra sensitivity vis-à-vis fairness and honesty. We would not have hated cruelty and ruthlessness with passion and zeal. Had we not been in Egypt, had we not felt the pain caused by the whip, we would not have understood the divine law of not oppressing the stranger or the law of loving one's neighbor. Had we not spent years of horror, we could not have grown and developed into a great nation. In pain and despair, we have attained greatness and nationhood. "Like the rose among thorns, so is my beloved among the maidens" (Song 2:2).

(*Festival of Freedom*)

The Jews became there a nation, a *goy*, because they were distinct; they stood out as a separate entity in Egypt. The Vilna Gaon pointed out that the term *goy* is derived from *geviyah*, a physiognomy, a countenance, a form. *Goy* is rooted

"He became there a nation" – teaches that Israel was distinctive there.

"Great, mighty" – as it is said: "The children of Israel were fruitful and increased abundantly, and multiplied and became very, very mighty, and the land became filled with them." (Ex. 1, 7)

---

in the idea of individuality, the exclusiveness of the face. When one stands out in a crowd, when a people is different, it is appropriate to speak of a *goy*, an individuality, be it a single person or a group of people.

That is exactly what the Haggadah says: "'And there he became a great *goy*,' which indicates that the Jews were distinguished there." The Israelites stood out as a distinct group, and this distinctness made them a *goy*, a nation. In light of the above, we understand also the saying "Because of four things the Jews merited redemption from Egypt: they did not change their names, they did not change their language, they harbored no informers, and there was not one among them who was licentious" (*Lev. Rabbah* 32:5; *Song Rabbah* 4:12). They were distinct; they constituted an individualistic community.

(*Festival of Freedom*)

גָּדוֹל Many Haggadot derive that the Jews were distinguished from the phrase *goy gadol*, not the word *goy* alone. The combination of *goy* and *gadol* has the meaning of *meẓuyyanim*, distinct, unique. A *goy gadol*, a great nation, distinguishes itself in two areas. First, it distinguishes itself in the area of righteousness – "And what *goy gadol* is there that has statutes and ordinances so righteous as this law?" (Deut. 4:8) If a nation is emotionally capable of approving injustice, it cannot lay claim to greatness, no matter how powerful it is militarily and economically, or however ingenious it is in matters of science and technology. Real greatness consists in the innate quality of fairness and righteousness, in the spontaneous indignation whenever one is confronted with hypocrisy and selfishness.

Second, a *goy gadol* distinguishes itself in the area of prayer. A great nation is a prayerful nation, a nation that knows the secret of prayer. This is also true of an individual: a great person knows the secret of prayer. Abraham, Isaac, and Jacob were great because they were acquainted with prayer. "'I shall make you a *goy gadol*' (Gen. 12:2) – therefore, we say [in the *Amidah* prayer], 'the God of Abraham'" (*Pesaḥim* 117b). A great nation consists of many praying individuals who feel each other's pain, and who suffer and pray in community.

God told Moses, "Come now, therefore, and I will send you to Pharaoh, that you may bring *ammi*, My people, the children of Israel, out of Egypt" (Ex. 3:10). The Vilna Gaon pointed out that the term *am* derives from the preposition *im*, denoting a people whose individual members are bound to lead one another by a

וָרָב, כְּמָה שֶׁנֶּאֱמַר: רְבָבָה כְּצֶמַח הַשָּׂדֶה נְתַתִּיךְ, וַתִּרְבִּי, וַתִּגְדְּלִי, וַתָּבֹאִי בַּעֲדִי עֲדָיִים: שָׁדַיִם נָכֹנוּ, וּשְׂעָרֵךְ צִמֵּחַ, וְאַתְּ עֵרֹם וְעֶרְיָה: (יחזקאל ט"ז, ז') וָאֶעֱבֹר עָלַיִךְ וָאֶרְאֵךְ מִתְבּוֹסֶסֶת בְּדָמָיִךְ, וָאֹמַר לָךְ בְּדָמַיִךְ חֲיִי, וָאֹמַר לָךְ בְּדָמַיִךְ חֲיִי: (יחזקאל ט"ז, ו')

---

strong sense of solidarity and sympathy. The Egyptian exile gave birth to two entities: a *goy gadol* and an *am kadosh*. While *goy* refers to a spiritual-psychological singularity, a singular way of life, a distinct philosophy and morality, *am* signifies the aspect of love and compassion that all share: experientially, they have one destiny. The Exodus is the wellspring of that great experience of *goy* and *am*.

(*Kol ha-Rav*)

עצום...וַיִּרְבּוּ וַיַּעַצְמוּ *Aẓum* refers to numbers; there were many Jews in Egypt. They were fruitful and they increased abundantly and multiplied. However, an abundant population does not always coincide with power. In fact, history tells us that the powerful nations are not necessarily the largest numerically. On the contrary, smaller nations have often ruled larger ones. Rome in antiquity ruled over a population many times greater than itself. The same was true of England and her empire. There is sometimes a tendency on the part of the greater nation to become inert, while the lesser is driven by fear and envy to great accomplishments and steady progress. It is quite simple to wake up the small child. It is harder to wake up the sleeping giant. In Egypt, the *va-yirbu* and the *va-yaʿaẓmu* coincided. The more they increased, the stronger they became spiritually, the greater were their accomplishments. Numerical size and sheer strength complemented each other.

(*Kol ha-Rav*)

וְאַתְּ עֵרֹם וְעֶרְיָה The most amazing thing about the Exodus, far greater than the signs and wonders, is the transformation of a nation of slaves who lived in a boundless state, who "preferred a dissolute life," who did not understand the meaning of laws and strictures, of obeying laws when no taskmaster threatens you. As slaves, they understood only one thing: you must obey the taskmaster, because if you do not, he will beat you with his baton. Why should one obey a commandment like *maẓẓah*, like the eating of the paschal lamb, like "You shall not break a bone of it" (Ex. 12:46) or "You may not leave over any of it until the morning" (Ex. 12:10) if no taskmaster stands over you? Why not break the bones of the paschal sacrifice? If the bone is tasty, we'll snap it and suck out its marrow."

"You have increased and waxed great…yet you are naked and bare" (Ezek. 16:7) – the sages apply this verse to the slaves destined to leave Egypt, saying that

"Numerous" – as it is said: "I caused you to thrive like the plants of the field, and you increased and grew and became very beautiful, your bosom fashioned and your hair grown long, but you were naked and bare. (Ezek. 16, 7) I passed over you and saw you wallowing in your blood, and I said to you 'By your blood you shall live,' and I said to you 'By your blood you shall live!'" (Ezek. 16, 6)

---

they were "naked of commandments" (*Ex. Rabbah* 1:35; Mekhilta, *Bo*, 5). Their life was a naked one, a beastly one, controlled by lusts and desires. And then there occurred the greatest of all miracles: "And all the people of Israel did as God commanded Moses and Aaron, so they did" (Ex. 12:28)! The slaves suddenly felt the duty of commandments, the power of a life devoted to higher ideas and goals. They understood what it means to possess spiritual ideals, and what it means to enter into a covenant with the Almighty. This transformation is a hidden miracle of great import. The Jews were able to distinguish between sacred and profane.

(*Festival of Freedom*)

וָרָב...וָאֹמַר לָךְ בְּדָמַיִךְ חֲיִי Ezekiel tells us the story of a girl who thought of herself as a child without responsibilities, who was told by a passerby that she was an adult, possessing a great potential to form a community and to give her friendship and loyalty to the thou. *Rav*, which usually means "numerous," is translated by the Haggadah as "grown up," emotionally developed, mature.

The portrait is magnificent, breathtaking. The Jews in Egypt thought very little of themselves; they did not believe that they were worthy of freedom, that they were qualified to conclude a covenant of love and devotion with the Almighty. When Moses came with the message of freedom, they were not certain that a band of day laborers was capable of both loving and being loved by God. Of course, they were primitive and ignorant – yet in their ignorance they discovered greatness. "In your blood live!" The potential was there.

Moses himself was skeptical about their readiness for freedom, but God saw a different picture. "*Ra'oh ra'iti*" (Ex. 3:7) – I see two images: one of a wild, uncouth adolescent, and another of a mature, capable woman. Indeed, the people were mature and ready to enjoy the fruits of liberty. Instead of taking revenge on their former masters in their hour of freedom, the Jews stayed in their houses, eating the paschal lamb and reciting the *Hallel*. It was unique in the history of revolutions. *Va-rav* – they were ripe and ready to meet the historical challenges before them. They were ready for self-government and the establishment of a free society.

(*Kol ha-Rav*)

וָאֹמַר לָךְ בְּדָמַיִךְ חֲיִי The individual participates in the fate and the destiny of the chosen people-nation. Therefore, a Gentile who comes to attach himself to

וַיָּרֵעוּ אֹתָנוּ הַמִּצְרִים וַיְעַנּוּנוּ, וַיִּתְּנוּ עָלֵינוּ עֲבֹדָה קָשָׁה: (דברים כ"ו, ו')

וַיָּרֵעוּ אֹתָנוּ הַמִּצְרִים, כְּמָה שֶׁנֶּאֱמַר: הָבָה נִתְחַכְּמָה לוֹ. פֶּן־יִרְבֶּה, וְהָיָה כִּי־תִקְרֶאנָה מִלְחָמָה, וְנוֹסַף גַּם הוּא עַל־שֹׂנְאֵינוּ, וְנִלְחַם־בָּנוּ וְעָלָה מִן־הָאָרֶץ: (שמות א', י')

---

the Jewish community must accept upon himself the yoke of both covenants. He must enter into the magic circle of Jewish fate and, in a spirit of holiness, dedicate himself to Jewish destiny. Conversion consists in a person's joining himself to both the people formed by the covenant in Egypt and the holy nation formed by the covenant at Sinai.

The act of circumcision, *milah*, was the charge given to Abraham the Hebrew, *Avraham ha-Ivri*, the father of Jewish fate; it was performed by the Israelites in Egypt prior to their sacrificing and eating the paschal lamb, the symbol of redemption from Egypt. For this reason it signifies the people's special fate, its isolation and its involuntary singularity. The act of immersion (*tevilah*), in contrast to that of circumcision, denotes the integration of a person in a great destiny and his entry into the covenant at Sinai. The Jews were charged with the commandment of immersion prior to the revelation of the Law at Sinai. In the conversion formula to be found in the book of Ruth, both these aspects are set forth, and their gist is succinctly expressed in its last two phrases (Ruth 1:16): "Your people shall be my people, and your God, my God."

(*Fate and Destiny*)

The Gemara (*Keritot 9a*) identifies the verse "and I [God] saw you wallowing in your bloods" (Ezek. 16:6) as integral to the conversion of *Benei Yisrael* before they left Egypt. Rashi there explains "your bloods" as referring to the bloods of circumcision and *korban Pesaḥ*. This indicates that the *korban Pesaḥ* of Egypt represented not only a sacrifice in its own right but also, like circumcision, an aspect of Israel's conversion, serving as the *korban gerut* required of every convert.

Rashi comments (Ex. 12:48) that the verse "if a convert lives among you and performs the [*korban*] *Pesaḥ*" might be understood as suggesting that in addition to the *korban* required of every convert, a convert must also bring a *korban Pesaḥ* immediately following his conversion even if it is not Passover time. Such a possible interpretation flows from the nature of *korban Pesaḥ* as part of the conversion process. To dispel the conclusion that the convert must do so in this case, the verse continues with the instruction that converts and non-converts follow "one law."

The *korban Pesaḥ* reaffirms the conversion that brought us into God's

"The Egyptians treated us badly and they made us suffer, and they put hard work upon us." (Deut. 26, 6)

"The Egyptians treated us badly" – as it is said: "Come, let us act cunningly with them lest they multiply and, if there should be a war against us, they will join our enemies, fight against us and leave the land." (Ex. 1, 10)

---

covenant. It represents, after the circumcision, the culmination of *gerut*, the conversion process. It is interesting to note that the *korban Pesaḥ* and circumcision are the only positive commandments subject to the punishment of *karet*. Further, a person who is not circumcised may not eat the *korban Pesaḥ*, for the *korban Pesaḥ* and circumcision are fundamental aspects of Jewish identity.

(*Reshimot*)

וַיָּרֵעוּ אֹתָנוּ הַמִּצְרִים In recounting the suffering in Egypt, we say "*Va-yare'u otanu ha-Mizrim*" (Deut. 26:6). This is generally translated as "the Egyptians did evil to us." However, the grammatical form is imperfect; if that were the meaning, the more likely formulation would have been "*Va-yare'u lanu ha-Mizrim*."

Actually, the verse is describing the fact that the Egyptians not only committed evil themselves, but also "made us out to be evil." They accused the Jews of being disloyal fifth columnists, of plotting a rebellion. The proof-text is that the Jews would rebel and leave the land. The Egyptians offended doubly; they caused the Jews to suffer, and also robbed them of their good name.

(*Reshimot*)

There is a significant difference between "*va-yare'u otanu*" and "*va-yare'u lanu ha-Mizrim*." *Le-hara*, in the dative case, denotes "to hurt"; *le-hara*, in the accusative case, means to afflict someone terribly. But if "*va-yare'u otanu*" refers to the Egyptians' cunning preparation of a blueprint of persecution to be implemented later, how does this constitute *ra*, "harm" or ill-treatment? The Egyptians did harm to our ancestors merely by planning evil. Not only hurting a person, but also thinking of the possibility of inflicting pain is immoral. Any joy derived from a malicious and hostile thought is sinful. The last commandment in the Decalogue is "*Lo taḥmod*, You shall not covet." Conspiracy to hurt is like actual hurting. The Haggadah identifies "*va-yare'u*" with "*Havah nitḥakemah*, Come, let us deal wisely with them." The term *va-yare'u* has a very specific meaning, and teaches us that the desire to do evil is the beginning of doing evil.

(*Kol ha-Rav*)

וַיְעַנּוּנוּ. כְּמָה שֶׁנֶּאֱמַר: וַיָּשִׂימוּ עָלָיו שָׂרֵי מִסִּים, לְמַעַן עַנֹּתוֹ בְּסִבְלֹתָם: וַיִּבֶן עָרֵי מִסְכְּנוֹת לְפַרְעֹה, אֶת־פִּתֹם וְאֶת־רַעַמְסֵס: (שמות א׳, י״א)

וַיִּתְּנוּ עָלֵינוּ עֲבֹדָה קָשָׁה, כְּמָה שֶׁנֶּאֱמַר: וַיַּעֲבִדוּ מִצְרַיִם אֶת־בְּנֵי יִשְׂרָאֵל בְּפָרֶךְ: (שמות א׳, י״ג)

וַנִּצְעַק אֶל־יְיָ אֱלֹהֵי אֲבֹתֵינוּ, וַיִּשְׁמַע יְיָ אֶת־קֹלֵנוּ, וַיַּרְא אֶת־עָנְיֵנוּ, וְאֶת־עֲמָלֵנוּ, וְאֶת לַחֲצֵנוּ: (דברים כ״ו, ז׳)

וַנִּצְעַק אֶל־יְיָ אֱלֹהֵי אֲבֹתֵינוּ, כְּמָה שֶׁנֶּאֱמַר: וַיְהִי בַיָּמִים הָרַבִּים הָהֵם, וַיָּמָת מֶלֶךְ מִצְרַיִם, וַיֵּאָנְחוּ בְנֵי־יִשְׂרָאֵל מִן־הָעֲבֹדָה וַיִּזְעָקוּ. וַתַּעַל שַׁוְעָתָם אֶל־הָאֱלֹהִים מִן־הָעֲבֹדָה: (שמות ב׳, כ״ג)

וַיִּשְׁמַע יְיָ אֶת־קֹלֵנוּ, כְּמָה שֶׁנֶּאֱמַר: וַיִּשְׁמַע אֱלֹהִים אֶת־נַאֲקָתָם, וַיִּזְכֹּר אֱלֹהִים אֶת־בְּרִיתוֹ, אֶת־אַבְרָהָם, אֶת־יִצְחָק, וְאֶת יַעֲקֹב: (שמות ב׳, כ״ד)

וַתַּעַל שַׁוְעָתָם אֶל הָאֱ־לֹהִים Basically, the Jews did not pray. They did not yet know the secret of prayer. According to the *Midrash* (*Mekhilta*, *be-Shallaḥ*, *massekhet de-va-Yehi*, 2), prayer was discovered at the Red Sea. In Egypt, prayer was alien to them. They instinctively groaned, but their sighs were not intentional – they were merely reacting to torture and suffering. They cried. That is not exclusively a human action; even a dumb animal will react to pain with a loud shriek. It is an instinctual reaction to discomfort.

God accepted their shouts as a prayer. In reality, though, it was just a spontaneous sigh, a sudden cry in the night. Until the death of Pharaoh, they were unaware of their horrible condition. They were anaesthetized against pain. They were silent, mute. When the Egyptian beat the Jew, the latter did not even complain. He thought that the situation of "an Egyptian smiting a Hebrew" (Ex. 2:11) represented the normal course of events.

Only with Pharaoh's death did the absurdity and the ugliness of the slavery dawn upon them. They began to complain. Silent slaves turned into a vocal, suffering group. They were no longer a band of mute bondsmen who did not even understand the horrible wrong inflicted on them. They began to protest, to feel pain.

However, they still did not know the act of prayer. They complained without directing it to the Almighty. And yet, "their cry came up unto God." Their shriek, their purposeless cry, rose up to God, who accepted it as if it were

"They made us suffer" – as it is said: "They set taskmasters over [the people of Israel] to make them suffer with their burdens, and they built storage cities for Pharaoh, Pitom and Ramses." (Ex. 1, 11)

"They put hard work upon us" – as it is said: "The Egyptians made the children of Israel work with rigor." (Ex. 1, 13)

We cried out to the Lord, the God of our ancestors, and the Lord heard our voice and saw our suffering, our labor and our oppression. (Deut. 26, 7)

"We cried out to the Lord, the God of our ancestors" – as it is said: "During that long period, the king of Egypt died; and the children of Israel groaned because of the servitude, and they cried out. And their cry for help from their servitude rose up to God." (Ex. 2, 23)

"The Lord heard our voice" – as it said: "God heard their groaning, and God remembered His covenant with Abraham, Isaac and Jacob." (Ex. 2, 24)

---

conscious prayer. The reason for this was God's covenant with the patriarchs, as the next verse makes clear.

(*Kol ha-Rav*)

וַיִּשְׁמַע אֱ־לֹהִים אֶת נַאֲקָתָם The twelfth article of faith requires of every Jew to believe not only in redemption, but in the Messiah's role in the process of redemption. The Almighty will avail Himself of a human being as an instrument and implementer of His inscrutable will. Redemption entails agency. God is the principal, the human being the agent. When God heard the cries of the Israelites in Egypt, when He saw their affliction, felt their pain, and decreed that the time of redemption had arrived, He summoned Moses to accept the agency, to be His representative. How impressive is the transition from the verse "And God heard their groaning…And God looked upon the children of Israel and God apprehended" (Ex. 2:24–25) to "Now Moses kept the flock of Jethro" (Ex. 3:1). Everything was ready. The process of redemption was about to commence. What held up the dramatic events associated with redemption? What delayed the realization of the great promise to Abraham, Isaac, and Jacob? The absence of Moses. The next verse begins with an exclamation: Yet Moses was still a shepherd! Everything, everybody, angels and humans, the Almighty Himself, had to wait for Moses to accept the great assignment to be the Divine agent.

(*Family Redeemed*)

וַיַּרְא אֶת־עָנְיֵנוּ. זוֹ פְּרִישׁוּת דֶּרֶךְ אֶרֶץ. כְּמָה שֶׁנֶּאֱמַר: וַיַּרְא אֱלֹהִים אֶת־בְּנֵי יִשְׂרָאֵל, וַיֵּדַע אֱלֹהִים: (שמות ב׳, כ״ה)

וְאֶת־עֲמָלֵנוּ. אֵלּוּ הַבָּנִים. כְּמָה שֶׁנֶּאֱמַר: כָּל־הַבֵּן הַיִּלּוֹד הַיְאֹרָה תַּשְׁלִיכֻהוּ, וְכָל־הַבַּת תְּחַיּוּן: (שמות א׳, כ״ב)

וַיַּרְא אֶת עָנְיֵנוּ There are certain travails and events in a person's life that cause him to scream and cry out to God for relief. We find reference to this type of prayer in the preceding passage when it says, "God heard our voices." However, there are other calamities that a person suffers in silence, in which he does not call out to God. Such was the case here, where Israel's travails included the most private of domains. However, God, who sees everything, is cognizant of these afflictions and it is with respect to these calamities that the author of the Haggadah cites the verse "And God took cognizance of them." God hears the cries and suffering contained within a person's heart and provides salvation for all of his troubles.

In fact, the *Amidah*'s blessing "*Re'eh ve-anyenu*, See our afflictions" was established for exactly this purpose. God bears witness to all of our sufferings and redeems us from our troubles, even if we suffer in silence. The closing of the *berakhah* "*Go'el Yisra'el*, Who Redeems Israel" constitutes a request that "He should redeem us from the troubles that constantly beset us." Rashi (*Megillah* 17b) points out that this does not refer to the future messianic redemption, since this theme is covered later in the *Amidah* in the *berakhot* of *Boneh Yerushalayim* and *Maẓmi'aḥ keren yeshu'ah*.

On a communal fast-day, we insert into the blessing of *Go'el Yisra'el* the words "The One who answered our forefather, Abraham, at Mount Moriah, He will answer you and listen to your cries today" (Mishnah, *Ta'anit* 2:4). Yet we do not find that Abraham prayed to God at the *Akedah*. The Midrash (*Gen. Rabbah* 56:11) tells us that the very moment that Abraham reached out with his knife to slaughter his son, tears streamed from his eyes and fell into Isaac's eyes. While his heart was filled with happiness because of the fulfillment of God's request, Abraham was also experiencing the powerful emotions of a merciful father on the verge of losing a beloved son. God, who sees our afflictions, saw Abraham's tears and answered them even though Abraham did not beseech God to save Isaac. God answers even prayers that are never expressed by our lips and are solely contained within our hearts.

(*Reshimot*)

וַיַּרְא...וַיֵּדַע The Torah states (Ex. 2:24) that God hearkened to their cry and remembered His covenant. Yet in the very next verse, the Torah repeats that "God saw...and God knew," or took notice. The latter is not a redundancy, because

"He saw our suffering" – this refers to the separation of husband and wife, as it is said: "God saw the children of Israel and God took note." (Ex. 2, 25)

"Our labor" – this refers to the "sons," as it is said: "Every boy that is born, you shall throw into the river and every girl you shall keep alive." (Ex. 1, 22)

---

the hidden wrong done to the slave is by far more terrible and destructive than that wrong of which he is aware.

The real tragedy of the slave consists in the fact that he himself does not understand how shameful and horrible the experience of slavery is. The Jewish slaves in Egypt complained only about the work, the physical labor they were forced to do. However, they did not cry about the disintegration of the family community caused by Pharaoh's edict. They did not indict Pharaoh for denying them the basic rights that God granted to every human being, that a man and woman may join in a marriage. God "heard our voice," but He saw further – "our affliction," namely, the separation of husband and wife. *Yezi'at Mizrayim* would not have been a total act of redemption if God had been guided only by their prayers.

Indeed, I always say that we would be a most unfortunate people if God were guided exclusively by our prayers. Sometimes we pray for things that are a menace to us, and sometimes we do not pray for things that are of the greatest importance. We say, "*Shema kolenu*, hear our prayers," but with one stipulation: "*kabel be-raḥamim u-ve-razon*" – You choose which prayers to fulfill and which to reject, because we do not rely on ourselves.

It is true that "they cried, and their cry came up unto God by reason of the bondage" (Ex. 2:23). Yet the redemption was precipitated by other wrongs the Egyptians did to the Jews, even though the Jews did not complain. "God saw the children of Israel and God knew" (Ex. 2:25). Only God saw the real damage done to the Jews; only He knew.

(*Kol ha-Rav*)

וַיֵּדַע אֱ־לֹהִים *Va-yeda Elokim* means that He experienced their travail, their pain, their suffering, their humiliation. It is complete sympathy, compassion, and involvement. Similarly, "*Ki yadati* their sorrows" (Ex. 3:7) means "I felt their pain." "Adam *yada* Eve his wife" (Gen. 4:1) means that he loved her and they were intimate.

(*Abraham's Journey*)

וְאֶת עֲמָלֵנוּ *Amal* has the connotation of incessant labor, work that is endless. Koheleth uses *amal* in such a framework: "What advantage is there to man in all that he labors (*amalo she-ya'amol*) under the sun?" (Eccl. 1:3).

וְאֶת לַחֲצֵנוּ. זֶה הַדְּחַק. כְּמָה שֶׁנֶּאֱמַר: וְגַם־רָאִיתִי אֶת־הַלַּחַץ, אֲשֶׁר מִצְרַיִם לֹחֲצִים אֹתָם: (שמות ג', ט')

וַיּוֹצִאֵנוּ יְיָ מִמִּצְרַיִם, בְּיָד חֲזָקָה, וּבִזְרֹעַ נְטוּיָה, וּבְמֹרָא גָּדֹל וּבְאֹתוֹת וּבְמֹפְתִים: (דברים כ"ו, ח')

The objective to whose achievement man dedicates his whole life is his children! He engages in constant worrying, unending concern, complete surrender to his involvement with the destiny of the child. That is exactly what the Haggadah meant to say: "*et amalenu – et mi she-anu omelim bishevilo*," our children, to whom our commitment is unlimited.

Yet, with the passage of time, the outrage of the murder of the male children was forgotten. The events referred to in the quoted verse happened when Moses was an infant, some eighty years before the Exodus. Eventually, the edict to murder the sons was abolished, and "a new king arose" with his own laws. He forgot about the law issued by his predecessor, and did not want to continue the same policy when Moses came back as an old man. Sons were not murdered anymore. Even the parents themselves – those whose children had been taken away – no longer remembered. They complained "*min ha-avodah*" – against the intolerable hard labor pressing upon them. But the fact that eighty years before there had been an inhuman law in Pharaoh's statute book decreeing that every male infant was to be killed was completely forgotten. They had turned a new page in history, forgotten what had happened, and did not mention it in their prayers.

In their prayers, the Jews did not point out the cruelty of the Egyptians. They complained only about the physical labor, but not about children who had been killed decades ago. But God did not forget. God insisted that the Egyptians, whether under the same Pharaoh or under his successor, would have to pay for the lives extinguished years before. "*Ve-et amalenu – ellu ha-banim*": this refers to the sons whom we have forgotten, whose tragic martyred deaths were not mentioned in our prayers.

(*Kol ha-Rav*)

וְאֶת לַחֲצֵנוּ *Lahazenu* means the pressure exerted by their enemies upon them to terminate their covenantal identity. The redemption from Egypt was precipitated by three crimes that the Egyptians had perpetrated against the Jews: *oni*, *amal*, and *lahaz* – affliction, toil, and oppression. These terms refer to (1) the attempt to destroy the marital community and condemn man and woman to a lonely life, contrary to the divine dictum that "It is not good for man to be alone"; (2) the murder of the infants; and (3) the exertion of great pressure on the Jews. Notwithstanding the Jews' crying and praying, the liberation would

"Our oppression" – this refers to the pressure, as it is said: "I have seen the oppression with which the Egyptians oppress them." (Ex. 3, 9)

"The Lord took us out of Egypt with a strong hand and an outstretched arm, and with a great manifestation, and with signs and wonders." (Deut. 26, 8)

---

have not taken place by reason of *oni* alone, for the time of redemption had not arrived. The Almighty had said to Abraham, "They shall serve them, and they shall afflict them for four hundred years" (Gen. 15:13), and the Jews had not spent this many years in exile and slavery. But the Almighty had to act quickly, because a delay would have resulted in the complete disintegration of *Keneset Yisrael*. They were so tightly integrated into the Egyptian people, culture, and economy that waiting would have destroyed all hopes and promises. God skipped several hundred years in order to save the people.

Every human being has a capacity to suffer without losing his dignity. This ability gives man his humanity and distinctiveness. The same applies to nations. Some have a very high persecution threshold and can bear distress and evil of every kind in stride. They sustain their identity in spite of the fact that to be identified with the community means suffering and agony, sacrificial action. Others have a low persecution threshold. They cannot be subjected to agony and pain for a long time; they simply yield to pressure and disintegrate quickly. The Jews in Egypt had reached the boundary beyond which loomed total assimilation and national betrayal. There were only two alternatives: immediate liberation or complete breakdown of the covenantal community.

(*Kol ha-Rav*)

בְּיָד חֲזָקָה וּבִזְרֹעַ נְטוּיָה Jewish morality is based upon the principle of "*Ve-halakhta bi-derakhav*, You shall walk in His ways" (Deut. 28:9), or *imitatio Dei*. We read that God took us out of Egypt "*be-yad ḥazakah u-vi-zero'a netuyah*, with a strong hand and an outstretched arm." This teaches us a normative lesson: If God uses a strong hand and an outstretched arm, we are also supposed to use them from time to time. In times of crisis or distress, man receives the call to stand up and defend a certain position. *Yad ḥazakah* means effective action, and *zero'a netuyah*, the Haggadah later tells us, means "a drawn sword in his hand, outstretched over Jerusalem" (1 Chron. 21:16). This indicates vigilance, watchfulness, alertness, and preparedness.

Judaism has taught us time and again that our responsibility is not limited to our own actions; we are also charged with historical responsibility. Man is called upon to shape history, to be historically involved, to direct history's

וַיּוֹצִאֵנוּ יְיָ מִמִּצְרַיִם. לֹא עַל־יְדֵי מַלְאָךְ, וְלֹא עַל־יְדֵי שָׂרָף, וְלֹא עַל־יְדֵי

unfolding toward worthwhile objectives. An individual is called upon, from time to time, to participate in the emergence and development of the *Keneset Yisrael.* In order to participate in the historical drama, we must possess two capabilities: first, to be vigilant, always ready for action; second, when action is called for, to act effectively.

Sometimes, if one is sensitive to events and knows that he has to act immediately, he cannot give reasons for this feeling. We can easily rationalize secondary, marginal decisions. But what will we answer if someone asks us why we love a certain person, why we are committed to certain ideals, why we sacrifice for certain values? We cannot always explain the central decisions that decide the destiny of a human being, a people, or a community.

The verse says, "Return, return, O Shulamite, return, that we may look upon you" (Song 7:1). The Midrash (*Tanḥuma*, Num. 11) interprets this as the Gentiles inviting the community of Israel to join them: "Return, return, O Shulamite," come back to us. Why do the Jews display such dedication, why such commitment, why so many sacrifices, why so much torture and misery and agony? The Shulamite replies: "What will you see in the Shulamite, *ki-meḥolat ha-maḥanayim*, as it were a dance between two camps?" (Song 7:1). In effect, she is saying, "What can I tell you? I am involved in a dance between two camps; I cannot free myself from the dance." I must be a Jew because I cannot be a non-Jew. Being a Jew is part of our I-awareness, part of our own existence. Can we explain our own existence, who we are, why we want to live, why we are afraid of death, our relationship to our children, our relationship to our parents? Being a Jew is a basic experience, a central experience that cannot be rationalized or explained and expounded to an audience. We are caught in an eternal dance from which we cannot free ourselves, and we will continue dancing until the day on which "God will be One, and His name One" (Zech. 14:9).

(*Kol ha-Rav*)

In *Parashat Va-etḥannan* the Torah tells us, "Then you shall say unto your son: 'We were Pharaoh's slaves in Egypt; and God brought us out of Egypt with a mighty hand'" (Deut. 6:20–21), but fails to make any mention of God's outstretched arm. In contrast, in regard to both *Pesaḥ* night and the recitation of *Arammi oved avi* when the *bikurim* are brought to the *kohen* in the *Beit ha-Mikdash*, we are commanded to mention both God's mighty hand and His outstretched arm.

God's outstretched arm symbolizes the idea that God's arm is forever out-

"The Lord took us out of Egypt" – not using an angel, not using a

---

stretched over the nation of Israel to shield them from their enemies. Even after God has saved the Jewish people from one calamity, His arm remains outstretched to protect them from future troubles. The passage in *Va-etḥannan* is focused only on recounting the story of the Exodus, not on past or future salvations. Consequently, the Torah mentions the mighty hand of God that redeemed us, but omits any reference to God's outstretched arm. In contrast, at a time of thanking God, it is appropriate to recognize that His kindness toward us never ends. Even unto this very day, His sword remains drawn in His hand, outstretched over Jerusalem to protect us.

On *Pesaḥ* night, in addition to the obligation of recounting the story of the Exodus, it is incumbent upon each individual to thank God. As the Talmud relates, it is incumbent upon the slave who is freed by his master to offer him thanks and praise. Consequently, as part of the obligation of thanksgiving, the Haggadah cites God's outstretched arm.

(*Reshimot*)

וּבְמֹרָא גָּדֹל This verse enumerates God's spectacular miracles at the time of the Exodus. The revelation of the Divine Presence, however, does not seem to be in the same category as the other miracles referred to in the verse. The "strong hand" and "outstretched arm" were miracles that specifically pertained to the Exodus. They were one-time occurrences designed to convince Pharaoh to allow the Jews to leave. The revelation of the Divine Presence, however, seems to have a much broader scope that does not seem to pertain specifically to the Exodus. Why, therefore, does the verse list the revelation of the Divine Presence along with the miracles of the "strong hand" and "outstretched arm"?

The miraculous events of the Exodus had a dual purpose. One was to free the Jewish nation from their enslavement in Egypt. Another, equally important aspect, was to reveal to all, including Pharaoh, that there is a Divine Presence in the world. These two purposes of the miracles of the Exodus are very much intertwined and help us understand certain aspects of the Exodus narrative.

For example, Moses initially asked Pharaoh for permission to let the Jews go into the desert for three days and worship God (Ex. 5). Moses' discussion with Pharaoh was not a labor dispute; rather it was a pretext to teach Pharaoh about God's Presence. Had Pharaoh acquiesced to the request and acknowledged that God is present in the world and should be worshipped, that very realization would have led Pharaoh to eventually free the Jewish nation. Had Pharaoh allowed the Jews to worship God, both goals of the Exodus would have been attained. Pharaoh would have learned about God's Presence and

שָׁלִיחַ, אֶלָּא הַקָּדוֹשׁ בָּרוּךְ הוּא בִּכְבוֹדוֹ וּבְעַצְמוֹ. שֶׁנֶּאֱמַר: וְעָבַרְתִּי בְאֶרֶץ מִצְרַיִם בַּלַּיְלָה הַזֶּה, וְהִכֵּיתִי כָל־בְּכוֹר בְּאֶרֶץ מִצְרַיִם, מֵאָדָם וְעַד בְּהֵמָה, וּבְכָל־אֱלֹהֵי מִצְרַיִם אֶעֱשֶׂה שְׁפָטִים אֲנִי יְיָ: (שמות י״ב, י״ב)

וְעָבַרְתִּי בְאֶרֶץ־מִצְרַיִם בַּלַּיְלָה הַזֶּה, אֲנִי וְלֹא מַלְאָךְ. וְהִכֵּיתִי כָל בְּכוֹר

---

would have ultimately freed the Jews, thus permanently permitting them to worship God (see Ex. 5:2, where Pharaoh says, "I do not know God, I will not let Israel go").

Throughout the narrative of the Exodus we encounter Pharaoh's struggle with recognizing God. Therefore, the *mora gadol*, the revelation of the Divine Presence, is indeed an integral part of the Exodus, and that is why the revelation of the Divine Presence is included with the other miraculous manifestations of the Exodus.

(*Reshimot*)

לֹא עַל יְדֵי מַלְאָךְ God did not send a *mal'akh* because the Jews were not yet deserving of redemption; the conditions had not been met. From the viewpoint of justice and truth, the redemption should have been postponed for many years. Only God Himself, with His *middat ha-ḥesed*, His quality of loving-kindness, knew that a Jew, no matter how low he falls, has a crisis capacity; in times of distress, he becomes a great and wondrous human being. He begins to act heroically. He can fall to horrible depths, yet he also is capable, under pressure, of reaching the stars. Only God could precipitate the *ge'ullah*. *Emet*, truth, did not warrant this kind of redemption.

In order to bring about a redemption that the people did not deserve, God had to intervene in the natural cosmic order and let the miraculous divine order overrule the causal. God does not like doing this. He wants man to find Him within the cosmic order, to experience Him in the beautiful *gillu'i shekhinah*, divine revelation, in the world itself. That is why God said, "*Va-ered le-haẓẓilo*, I have come down to save him" (Ex. 3:8) – regretfully, I have to descend. In order to save My people, I have to suspend the causal universal experience and let a supernatural order replace it.

Our Sages say that the splitting of the sea was difficult for the Almighty (*Pesaḥim* 118a, *Sotah* 2a, *Sanhedrin* 22a). When He has to use a mighty hand and an outstretched arm, this is, so to speak, a "descent" for the Creator of the world. The Midrash (*Ex. Rabbah* 15:5) compares God's miraculous descent to save the Jews to a priest defiling himself in order to save his *terumah* (sanctified food) that fell into a cemetery. He says to himself, "What shall I do? I cannot

seraph and not using a messenger. The Holy One, blessed be He, did it in His glory by Himself!

Thus it is said: "In that night I will pass through the land of Egypt, and I will smite every first-born in the land of Egypt, from man to beast, and I will carry out judgments against all the gods of Egypt, I the Lord." (Ex. 12, 12)

"I will pass through the land of Egypt" – I and not an angel; "I will smite every first-born in the land of Egypt" – I and not a *seraph*; "I

---

defile myself and I cannot forfeit my *terumah*! It is better that I defile myself one time and then purify myself so that I do not lose my *terumah*." Thus were our forefathers the *terumah* of the Holy One, Blessed be He.

(*Kol ha-Rav*)

וְלֹא עַל יְדֵי שָׁלִיחַ How can the Haggadah say "not through a messenger" when the Almighty Himself said to Moses, "Therefore, I shall send you to Pharaoh" (Ex. 3:10)? The answer is that Moses was a *shali'aḥ* who served only as a companion for the Almighty. When God chose Moses, the latter was very reluctant to accept the mission. He considered himself unqualified to be the leader of the people and to confront Pharaoh; he was too modest, too humble. God answered him: "*Ki ehyeh immakh* – I shall accompany you" (Ex. 3:12). God promised Moses that He would never desert him; He would participate in the implementation of the mission, and together they would enter Pharaoh's chambers. Therefore, when God instructed Moses to appear before Pharaoh, He used the imperative *bo* instead of *lekh*. When Moses addresses Pharaoh, God will be present; when he raises the staff, God will be with him. In effect, God says, "*Bo immadi el Far'oh*, Come along with Me to Pharaoh." Such a *shali'aḥ* does not deserve credit, so his name is not mentioned. Every miracle executed by Moses was performed by the Almighty.

(*Festival of Freedom*)

וְהִכֵּיתִי כָל בְּכוֹר The oldest child is, of course, the strongest among the children of the household. The oldest son is capable of exercising authority over his younger siblings. Quite often, the older children can simply torture younger ones. In the parental home, the seven-year-old can order around the five-year-old, and the twelve-year-old can order around an eight-year-old sibling. In the patriarchal society of antiquity, the father was the supreme law simply because he was the strongest and could use force. It was a slave society, and

בְּאֶרֶץ־מִצְרַיִם, אֲנִי וְלֹא שָׂרָף, וּבְכָל־אֱלֹהֵי מִצְרַיִם אֶעֱשֶׂה שְׁפָטִים, אֲנִי וְלֹא הַשָּׁלִיחַ. אֲנִי יְיָ, אֲנִי הוּא וְלֹא אַחֵר:

בְּיָד חֲזָקָה. זוֹ הַדֶּבֶר, כְּמָה שֶׁנֶּאֱמַר: הִנֵּה יַד־יְיָ הוֹיָה, בְּמִקְנְךָ אֲשֶׁר בַּשָּׂדֶה, בַּסּוּסִים בַּחֲמֹרִים בַּגְּמַלִּים, בַּבָּקָר וּבַצֹּאן, דֶּבֶר כָּבֵד מְאֹד: (שמות ט׳, ג׳)

וּבִזְרֹעַ נְטוּיָה. זוֹ הַחֶרֶב. כְּמָה שֶׁנֶּאֱמַר: וְחַרְבּוֹ שְׁלוּפָה בְּיָדוֹ, נְטוּיָה עַל־יְרוּשָׁלָיִם: (דברי הימים א׳ כ״א, ט״ז)

וּבְמֹרָא גָּדֹל. זוֹ גִּלּוּי שְׁכִינָה, כְּמָה שֶׁנֶּאֱמַר: אוֹ הֲנִסָּה אֱלֹהִים, לָבוֹא לָקַחַת לוֹ גוֹי מִקֶּרֶב גּוֹי, בְּמַסֹּת בְּאֹתֹת וּבְמוֹפְתִים וּבְמִלְחָמָה, וּבְיָד חֲזָקָה וּבִזְרוֹעַ נְטוּיָה, וּבְמוֹרָאִים גְּדֹלִים. כְּכֹל אֲשֶׁר־עָשָׂה לָכֶם יְיָ אֱלֹהֵיכֶם בְּמִצְרַיִם, לְעֵינֶיךָ: (דברים ד׳, ל״ד)

---

cruel tyranny reigned from the old man at the top straight down to the bottom of the societal pyramid. The Hebrews were slaves in Egypt, but they were slaves not only to Pharaoh. Defenseless and weak, they were subjected to the brutality and cruelty of every official and every person who wielded power in Egypt, every person who was stronger than they were. *Bekhor* represents not only the oldest, but the strongest, the one who exercises power.

On the night of Passover, the Almighty smote the firstborn – which means those who were born first and exercised brutal authority and compelled people to comply with their will. Each one was a master of slaves. God also punished their gods, because if a nation is punished, the philosophy of the people must also be destroyed. If somebody is punished but his philosophy is not refuted, he will repeat the same mistake.

"The Lord executed judgments upon their gods" (Num. 33:4). This means that on the night of *Pesaḥ*, God punished the whole ideology of slavery, of oppressing through force and violence, of ruling people through fear.

(*Festival of Freedom*)

אֲנִי הוּא וְלֹא אַחֵר The protagonist of the night of redemption in Egypt is not Moses, but solely the Holy One; hence Moses' name cannot be found in the Haggadah. The Midrash to the verse "By night I sought him whom my very soul loves; I sought him but found him not" (Song 3:1) can be interpreted as referring to *Pesaḥ* night, when we search for Moses' name in the Haggadah and cannot find it. However, Rambam mentions Moses in the context of the response to the wise child: "If the child is mature and wise, the father informs him what occurred in Egypt and the miracles that were performed by our teacher Moses"

will carry out judgments against all the gods of Egypt" – I and not a messenger; "I the Lord" – it is I, and none other!

"With a strong hand" – this refers to the *dever* (pestilence) as it is said: "Behold, the hand of the Lord will be upon your livestock in the field, upon the horses, the donkeys, the camels, the herds and the flocks, a very severe pestilence." (Ex. 9, 3)

"With an outstretched arm" – this refers to the sword, as it is said: "His sword was drawn, in His hand, stretched out over Jerusalem." (I Chron. 21, 16)

"With great awe" – this refers to the revelation of the *Shekhinah* (Divine Presence), as it is said: "Has any God ever tried to take for himself a nation from the midst of another nation, with trials, signs and wonders, with war and with a strong hand and an outstretched arm, and with great revelations, like all that the Lord your God, did for you in Egypt before your eyes!" (Deut. 4, 34)

(*Hilkhot Ḥameẓ u-Maẓẓah* 7:2). When speaking to the wise child, we mention Moses, the giver of the Torah. We call him *Mosheh Rabenu*, our teacher, not *Mosheh Go'alenu*, our redeemer. Man cannot usurp God's attributes of power; only God can redeem. But man has a right – even a duty – to imitate God, who is the great teacher.

(*Shi'urim le-Zekher Abba Mori*)

זוֹ הַדֶּבֶר *Dever* was the first plague to shatter the very economic and military foundations of the Egyptian empire. The previous plagues made life uncomfortable; they did not, however, inflict irreparable harm upon Egypt's economy and military posture. Pharaoh considered the Jews his property and did not let them go. The Almighty taught Pharaoh that even the property he possessed did not belong to him. How, then, could Pharaoh lay claim to human beings who merely sojourned in the land of Egypt? Thus, "a mighty hand" means the hand that strips man of property, of his illusions that he owns everything. The outstretched arm holds a sword ready to strike. It represents a lack of security – the human exposure to disaster and the suddenness with which catastrophe strikes. A slave surely lacks the right of property and the right of security. God demonstrated that no one, not even Pharaoh, is endowed with these rights in an absolute sense.

(*Shi'urim le-Zekher Abba Mori*)

וּבְאֹתוֹת. זֶה הַמַּטֶּה, כְּמָה שֶׁנֶּאֱמַר: וְאֶת הַמַּטֶּה הַזֶּה תִּקַּח בְּיָדֶךָ. אֲשֶׁר תַּעֲשֶׂה־בּוֹ אֶת־הָאֹתֹת: (שמות ד', י"ז)

וּבְמֹפְתִים. זֶה הַדָּם, כְּמָה שֶׁנֶּאֱמַר: וְנָתַתִּי מוֹפְתִים, בַּשָּׁמַיִם וּבָאָרֶץ: (יואל ג', ג')

בכל מילה מהמילים "דם ואש ותימרות עשן" נוהגים להטיף טיפת יין מן הכוס.

דָּם, וָאֵשׁ, וְתִימְרוֹת עָשָׁן:

דָּבָר אַחֵר: בְּיָד חֲזָקָה שְׁתַּיִם. וּבִזְרֹעַ נְטוּיָה שְׁתַּיִם. וּבְמוֹרָא גָּדוֹל שְׁתַּיִם. וּבְאֹתוֹת שְׁתַּיִם. וּבְמֹפְתִים שְׁתַּיִם:

אֵלּוּ עֶשֶׂר מַכּוֹת שֶׁהֵבִיא הַקָּדוֹשׁ בָּרוּךְ הוּא עַל־הַמִּצְרִים בְּמִצְרַיִם, וְאֵלּוּ הֵן:

בכל מכה ומכה וכן בסימנים דצ"ך עד"ש באח"ב נוהגים להטיף טיפת יין מן הכוס.

דָּם, צְפַרְדֵּעַ, כִּנִּים, עָרוֹב, דֶּבֶר, שְׁחִין, בָּרָד, אַרְבֶּה, חֹשֶׁךְ, מַכַּת בְּכוֹרוֹת:

רַבִּי יְהוּדָה הָיָה נוֹתֵן בָּהֶם סִמָּנִים:

דְּצַ"ךְ, עֲדַ"שׁ, בְּאַחַ"ב:

רַבִּי יוֹסֵי הַגְּלִילִי אוֹמֵר: מִנַּיִן אַתָּה אוֹמֵר, שֶׁלָּקוּ הַמִּצְרִים בְּמִצְרַיִם עֶשֶׂר מַכּוֹת, וְעַל הַיָּם לָקוּ חֲמִשִּׁים מַכּוֹת? בְּמִצְרַיִם מַה הוּא אוֹמֵר: וַיֹּאמְרוּ הַחַרְטֻמִּם אֶל־פַּרְעֹה, אֶצְבַּע אֱלֹהִים הִוא. (שמות ח', ט"ו) וְעַל הַיָּם מַה הוּא אוֹמֵר? וַיַּרְא יִשְׂרָאֵל אֶת־הַיָּד הַגְּדֹלָה, אֲשֶׁר עָשָׂה יְיָ בְּמִצְרַיִם,

---

וְעַל הַיָּם לָקוּ חֲמִשִּׁים מַכּוֹת Although our Haggadah refers to the miracle of the splitting of the sea, these passages are omitted from the text of Rambam's Haggadah. Rambam writes, "There is a biblical positive commandment to speak about the miracles and wonders that were done for our fathers in Egypt on the fifteenth of Nisan" (*Hilkhot Ḥamez u-Mazzah* 7:1). The latter part of this statement is ambiguous. Is Rambam specifying the precise date on which we are to speak about the miracles (i.e., on *Pesaḥ* night, the fifteenth of Nisan), or is he saying that we should discuss only the miracles that took place specifically on, or as a

"With signs" – this refers to the staff, as it is said: "Take into your hand this staff with which you shall perform the signs." (Ex. 4, 17)

"And with wonders" – this refers to the blood, as it is said: "I shall show wonders in heaven and on earth." (Joel 3, 3)

Some wine is spilled from the cup during the recitation of the words "blood, and fire, and pillars of smoke."

Blood, and fire, and pillars of smoke.

Another explanation: "Strong hand" indicates two [plagues]; "Outstretched arm," another two; "Great awe," another two; "Signs," another two; and "Wonders," another two.

These are the Ten Plagues which the Holy One, blessed be He, brought upon the Egyptians, namely as follows:

Some wine is spilled from the cup during the recitation of each of the ten plagues.

Blood. Frogs. Lice. Wild Beasts. Pestilence. Boils. Hail. Locusts. Darkness. Smiting the First-born.

Rabbi Yehudah referred to them by acronyms:

DeẒaKh (blood, frogs, lice); **ADaSh** (beasts, pestilence, boils); **BeAḤaV** (hail, locusts, darkness, first-born).

Rabbi Yossi the Gallilean said: How do you know that the Egyptians were stricken by ten plagues in Egypt, and then were struck by fifty plagues at the sea? In Egypt it says of them, "The magicians said to Pharaoh 'This is the finger of God.' (Ex. 8, 15) At the sea it says,

---

prelude to, the fifteenth of Nisan? If the latter is true, then we can understand why these passages were omitted, since the miracle of the splitting of the sea took place after the fifteenth of Nisan. Similarly, if the latter interpretation of this passage from Rambam is correct, this may be the reason that *Az yashir*, Moses' song at the splitting of the sea, is not recited at the *Seder* even though it would seem to be so well suited for inclusion in the Haggadah.

Another reason that *Az yashir* is not included in the Haggadah may be that it was not composed by King David, and all formal praise to God is required to have been composed by King David, who was "*ne'im zemirot Yisrael*, the

וַיִּירְאוּ הָעָם אֶת־יְיָ. וַיַּאֲמִינוּ בַּייָ, וּבְמֹשֶׁה עַבְדּוֹ: (שמות י״ד, ל״א) כַּמָּה לָקוּ בְּאֶצְבַּע? עֶשֶׂר מַכּוֹת. אֱמוֹר מֵעַתָּה: בְּמִצְרַיִם לָקוּ עֶשֶׂר מַכּוֹת, וְעַל־הַיָּם לָקוּ חֲמִשִּׁים מַכּוֹת:

רַבִּי אֱלִיעֶזֶר אוֹמֵר: מִנַּיִן שֶׁכָּל־מַכָּה וּמַכָּה, שֶׁהֵבִיא הַקָּדוֹשׁ בָּרוּךְ הוּא עַל הַמִּצְרִים בְּמִצְרַיִם, הָיְתָה שֶׁל אַרְבַּע מַכּוֹת? שֶׁנֶּאֱמַר: יְשַׁלַּח־בָּם חֲרוֹן אַפּוֹ, עֶבְרָה וָזַעַם וְצָרָה, מִשְׁלַחַת מַלְאֲכֵי רָעִים: (תהלים ע״ח, מ״ט) עֶבְרָה אַחַת. וָזַעַם שְׁתַּיִם. וְצָרָה שָׁלֹשׁ. מִשְׁלַחַת מַלְאֲכֵי רָעִים אַרְבַּע. אֱמֹר מֵעַתָּה: בְּמִצְרַיִם לָקוּ אַרְבָּעִים מַכּוֹת, וְעַל הַיָּם לָקוּ מָאתַיִם מַכּוֹת:

רַבִּי עֲקִיבָא אוֹמֵר: מִנַּיִן שֶׁכָּל־מַכָּה וּמַכָּה, שֶׁהֵבִיא הַקָּדוֹשׁ בָּרוּךְ הוּא עַל הַמִּצְרִים בְּמִצְרַיִם, הָיְתָה שֶׁל חָמֵשׁ מַכּוֹת? שֶׁנֶּאֱמַר: יְשַׁלַּח־בָּם חֲרוֹן אַפּוֹ, עֶבְרָה וָזַעַם וְצָרָה, מִשְׁלַחַת מַלְאֲכֵי רָעִים: (תהלים ע״ח, מ״ט) חֲרוֹן אַפּוֹ אַחַת. עֶבְרָה שְׁתַּיִם. וָזַעַם שָׁלֹשׁ. וְצָרָה אַרְבַּע. מִשְׁלַחַת מַלְאֲכֵי רָעִים חָמֵשׁ. אֱמֹר מֵעַתָּה: בְּמִצְרַיִם לָקוּ חֲמִשִּׁים מַכּוֹת, וְעַל הַיָּם לָקוּ חֲמִשִּׁים וּמָאתַיִם מַכּוֹת.

---

sweet singer of Israel." As Rashi notes, the *shirot ve-tishbeḥot*, the praises sung in the Temple, are required to have been composed by King David (II Sam. 23:1, Rashi s.v. *u-ne'im zemirot Yisrael*). Similarly, Rambam states, based on King David's status as the *ne'im zemirot Yisrael*, that the verses for *Malkhuyyot*, *Zikhronot*, and *Shofarot* in the *Rosh ha-Shanah Amidah* which are from *Ketuvim*, the biblical writings, are to come exclusively from Psalms (*Hilkhot Shofar* 3:8). This concept is further reflected in *Barukh she-amar*, the opening *berakhah* of *Pesukei de-Zimrah*, the section of praise contained in the daily *Shaharit* prayer, which states "*u-ve-shirei David avdekha nehallelkha*, and with the songs of David Your servant we shall praise you." The requirement that the praises contained in *Pesukei de-Zimrah* be composed by King David explains why Rambam does not include *Az yashir* in the daily *tefillot* as part of *Pesukei de-Zimrah*, but places it after *Yishtabaḥ*.

(*Reshimot*)

וַיַּאֲמִינוּ בַּה' וּבְמֹשֶׁה On *Pesaḥ*, God met not an individual Jew, but the community in its entirety. No individual was singled out; no person, however great and spiritually mighty, stood out; no leader, no matter how inspiring and

"Israel saw the great hand that the Lord laid against Egypt; and the people feared the Lord, and they believed in the Lord and in His servant Moses." (Ex. 14, 31) Now, how often were they smitten by 'the finger'? Ten plagues! Thus you must conclude that in Egypt they were smitten by ten plagues, at the sea they were smitten by fifty plagues!

Rabbi Eliezer said: How do we know that each individual plague which the Holy One, blessed be He, brought upon the Egyptians in Egypt consisted of four plagues? For it is said: "He sent against them His fierce anger, fury, and wrath, and trouble, a discharge of messengers of evil": (Ps. 78, 49) 'Fury,' is one; 'Wrath,' makes two; 'Trouble,' makes three; 'Discharge of messengers of evil,' makes four. Thus you must now say that in Egypt they were struck by forty plagues, and at the sea they were stricken by two hundred plagues.

Rabbi Akiva said: How do we know that each individual plague which the Holy One, blessed be He, brought upon the Egyptians in Egypt consisted of five plagues? For it is said: "He sent against them his fierce anger, fury, and wrath, and trouble, a discharge of messengers of evil": (Ps. 78, 49) "His fierce anger," is one; "fury," makes two; "wrath," makes three; "trouble," makes four; "discharge of messengers of evil," makes five. Thus you must now say that in Egypt they were struck by fifty plagues, and at the sea they were stricken by two hundred and fifty plagues.

---

impressive, was treated differently than the rest of the community. Therefore, it is fitting that the name of Moses does not appear in the Haggadah (except once, tangentially, in a proof-text – and in Maimonides' Haggadah, not at all). On that mysterious night of revelation, God, enveloped in glory and majesty, appeared to the whole community. Everyone, genius and simpleton, king and servant, rich and poor, aristocrat and plebeian, saw God and confronted Him. Even the revelation on Mount Sinai on *Shavu'ot*, in which the redemption culminated, was of a communal character. The entire people stood at the foot of the mount.

(*Festival of Freedom*)

כַּמָּה מַעֲלוֹת טוֹבוֹת לַמָּקוֹם עָלֵינוּ:

אִלּוּ הוֹצִיאָנוּ מִמִּצְרַיִם, וְלֹא עָשָׂה בָהֶם שְׁפָטִים, דַּיֵּנוּ:

אִלּוּ עָשָׂה בָהֶם שְׁפָטִים, וְלֹא עָשָׂה בֵאלֹהֵיהֶם, דַּיֵּנוּ:

אִלּוּ עָשָׂה בֵאלֹהֵיהֶם, וְלֹא הָרַג אֶת־בְּכוֹרֵיהֶם, דַּיֵּנוּ:

אִלּוּ הָרַג אֶת־בְּכוֹרֵיהֶם, וְלֹא נָתַן לָנוּ אֶת־מָמוֹנָם, דַּיֵּנוּ:

אִלּוּ נָתַן לָנוּ אֶת־מָמוֹנָם, וְלֹא קָרַע לָנוּ אֶת־הַיָּם, דַּיֵּנוּ:

אִלּוּ קָרַע לָנוּ אֶת־הַיָּם, וְלֹא הֶעֱבִירָנוּ בְתוֹכוֹ בֶּחָרָבָה, דַּיֵּנוּ:

אִלּוּ הֶעֱבִירָנוּ בְתוֹכוֹ בֶּחָרָבָה, וְלֹא שִׁקַּע צָרֵינוּ בְּתוֹכוֹ, דַּיֵּנוּ:

אִלּוּ שִׁקַּע צָרֵינוּ בְּתוֹכוֹ, וְלֹא סִפֵּק צָרְכֵּנוּ בַּמִּדְבָּר אַרְבָּעִים שָׁנָה, דַּיֵּנוּ:

אִלּוּ סִפֵּק צָרְכֵּנוּ בַּמִּדְבָּר אַרְבָּעִים שָׁנָה, וְלֹא הֶאֱכִילָנוּ אֶת־הַמָּן, דַּיֵּנוּ:

אִלּוּ הֶאֱכִילָנוּ אֶת־הַמָּן, וְלֹא נָתַן לָנוּ אֶת־הַשַּׁבָּת, דַּיֵּנוּ:

אִלּוּ נָתַן לָנוּ אֶת־הַשַּׁבָּת, וְלֹא קֵרְבָנוּ לִפְנֵי הַר סִינַי, דַּיֵּנוּ:

אִלּוּ נָתַן לָנוּ אֶת הַשַּׁבָּת Shabbat and *kibud horim*, honoring one's parents, are tied together in the *Aseret ha-Dibrot* and in the verse in *Kedoshim* that is a repetition of *Aseret ha-Dibrot*. "You shall fear every man his mother and his father, and keep My Sabbaths" (Lev. 19:3). There is another equation. "You shall keep My Sabbaths and revere My Sanctuary" (Lev. 19:30). Sabbath observance is equated with the reverence we have to feel when we enter the Temple.

Infinity limits and contracts itself in order to reside in finitude, in the world, in a small place we call the Holy of Holies. At times, the Holy One, instead of asking for a physical sanctuary built of materials like wood, gold, silver, copper, chooses a human being in which to dwell. He resides in a father or in a mother, in the recesses of their personality. The parent is a dwelling place for God, and that is why the Torah requires unqualified respect for parents.

The same is true of Shabbat. On *yom tov*, each Jew is commanded to come close to the *Shekhinah*; this is the *mizvah* of *aliyah la-regel*. He stepped out of his home, somewhere in the Galil, and walked to Jerusalem in search of the *Shekhinah*. But *yom tov* is not the abode of the *Shekhinah*. The Torah did not

How many levels of favors has the Omnipresent One bestowed upon us:

If He had only brought us out from Egypt, and had not carried out judgments against them, *Dayenu*, it would have sufficed us!

If He had only carried out judgments against them, and not against their idols, *Dayenu*, it would have sufficed us!

If He had only destroyed their idols, and had not smitten their first-born, *Dayenu*, it would have sufficed us!

If He had only smitten their first-born, and had not given us their wealth, *Dayenu*, it would have sufficed us!

If He had only given us their wealth, and had not split the sea for us, *Dayenu*, it would have sufficed us!

If He had only split the sea for us, and had not taken us through it on dry land, *Dayenu*, it would have sufficed us!

If He had only taken us through the sea on dry land, and had not drowned our oppressors in it, *Dayenu*, it would have sufficed us!

If He had only drowned our oppressors in it, and had not supplied our needs in the desert for forty years, *Dayenu*, it would have sufficed us!

If He had only supplied our needs in the desert for forty years, and had not fed us the manna, *Dayenu*, it would have sufficed us!

If He had only fed us the manna, and had not given us the Shabbat, *Dayenu*, it would have sufficed us!

If He had only given us the Shabbat, and had not brought us before Mount Sinai, *Dayenu*, it would have sufficed us!

---

tell a Jew to make a pilgrimage to Jerusalem on Shabbat. There is no need. On Shabbat the *Shekhinah* knocks on the door. All we have to do is to let Her in. The same *Shekhinah* that accompanies the elderly mother or father accompanies a Jew on Shabbat. We revere the *Beit ha-Mikdash* because that is where God found a place to reside. The same is true of Shabbat and parents.

(*Kol ha-Rav*)

אִלּוּ קֵרְבָנוּ לִפְנֵי הַר סִינַי, וְלֹא נָתַן לָנוּ אֶת־הַתּוֹרָה, דַּיֵּנוּ:

אִלּוּ נָתַן לָנוּ אֶת־הַתּוֹרָה, וְלֹא הִכְנִיסָנוּ לְאֶרֶץ יִשְׂרָאֵל, דַּיֵּנוּ:

אִלּוּ הִכְנִיסָנוּ לְאֶרֶץ יִשְׂרָאֵל, וְלֹא בָנָה לָנוּ אֶת־בֵּית הַבְּחִירָה, דַּיֵּנוּ:

עַל אַחַת כַּמָּה וְכַמָּה טוֹבָה כְפוּלָה וּמְכֻפֶּלֶת לַמָּקוֹם עָלֵינוּ: שֶׁהוֹצִיאָנוּ מִמִּצְרַיִם, וְעָשָׂה בָהֶם שְׁפָטִים, וְעָשָׂה בֵאלֹהֵיהֶם, וְהָרַג אֶת־בְּכוֹרֵיהֶם, וְנָתַן לָנוּ אֶת־מָמוֹנָם, וְקָרַע לָנוּ אֶת־הַיָּם, וְהֶעֱבִירָנוּ בְתוֹכוֹ בֶּחָרָבָה, וְשִׁקַּע צָרֵינוּ בְּתוֹכוֹ, וְסִפֵּק צָרְכֵּנוּ בַּמִּדְבָּר אַרְבָּעִים שָׁנָה, וְהֶאֱכִילָנוּ אֶת־הַמָּן, וְנָתַן לָנוּ אֶת־הַשַּׁבָּת, וְקֵרְבָנוּ לִפְנֵי הַר סִינַי, וְנָתַן לָנוּ אֶת־הַתּוֹרָה, וְהִכְנִיסָנוּ לְאֶרֶץ יִשְׂרָאֵל, וּבָנָה לָנוּ אֶת־בֵּית הַבְּחִירָה, לְכַפֵּר עַל־כָּל־עֲוֹנוֹתֵינוּ.

אִלּוּ הִכְנִיסָנוּ לְאֶרֶץ יִשְׂרָאֵל וְלֹא בָנָה לָנוּ אֶת בֵּית הַבְּחִירָה The reference to the *Beit ha-Beḥirah* in the phrase "If He had brought us into the Land of Israel but had not built for us the *Beit ha-Beḥirah*, the chosen dwelling place, it would have been sufficient for us" is more understandable and takes on added significance in light of Rambam's treatment of the *miẓvah* of building the *Beit ha-Mikdash*. The Talmud states (*Sanhedrin* 20b) that the Jewish people received three commandments upon their entry to the Land of Israel: to appoint a king, to destroy the descendants of Amalek, and to build the *Beit ha-Beḥirah*, God's chosen dwelling place. Rambam codifies this Gemara in *Hilkhot Melakhim* (1:1), stating that the Jewish people are commanded to build the *Beit ha-Beḥirah* when they enter the Land of Israel (as well as to appoint a king and destroy Amalek), based on the verse "You shall seek His presence and come there" (Deut. 12:5). In *Hilkhot Beit ha-Beḥirah* (1:1), Rambam also records the obligation to build a "*bayit la-Hashem*, a house for the Lord," based on the verse "And you shall make for Me a sanctuary, and I will dwell among you" (Ex. 25:8). The *Leḥem Mishneh* in his commentary on Rambam asks why Rambam found it necessary to cite two separate biblical sources for the *miẓvah* of building the *Beit ha-Mikdash*.

The answer to the *Leḥem Mishneh*'s question is that Rambam, in fact, views the building of the *Beit ha-Mikdash* as two separate *miẓvot*. One *miẓvah* – the building of a *Beit ha-Mikdash* – is based on the verse "And you shall make for Me a sanctuary" and is not contingent upon entering the Land of Israel. Thus, the construction of the *mishkan* in the desert is a fulfillment of this *miẓvah*. There is, however, a second *miẓvah* – the building of the *Beit ha-Beḥirah*, God's

If He had only brought us before Mount Sinai, and had not given us the Torah, *Dayenu*, it would have sufficed us!

If He had only given us the Torah, and had not brought us into the land of Israel, *Dayenu*, it would have sufficed us!

If He had only brought us into the land of Israel, and had not built for us the Temple, the Chosen House, *Dayenu*, it would have sufficed us!

Thus how much more so should we be grateful to the Omnipresent One for the doubled and redoubled goodness that He has bestowed upon us; for He brought us out of Egypt, and carried out judgments against them, and against their idols, and smote their first-born, and gave us their wealth, and split the sea for us, and took us through it on dry land, and drowned our oppressors in it, and supplied our needs in the desert for forty years, and fed us the manna, and gave us the Shabbat, and brought us before Mount Sinai, and gave us the Torah, and brought us into the land of Israel and built for us the Chosen House to atone for all our sins.

---

chosen house, in Jerusalem – based on the verse "And you shall seek His presence." Rambam states that once the *Beit ha-Beḥirah* was ultimately constructed in its destined place in Jerusalem, it never moved to another location. Establishment of the *Beit ha-Beḥirah* in Jerusalem excludes the performance of the *avodah* in any other location.

Thus, the Jewish people may have entered the Land of Israel after having fulfilled the *mizvah* of building a *Beit Mikdash* and experiencing the spiritual presence of the *mishkan* in the desert and the various *Batei ha-Mikdash* in places other than Jerusalem, such as Shiloh and Nob and Gibeon. But we are additionally thankful for God having bestowed upon us the *Beit ha-Beḥirah*, His ultimate dwelling place, in its destined location in Jerusalem.

(*Kovez̤ Ḥiddushei Torah*)

וְנָתַן לָנוּ אֶת הַשַּׁבָּת The topical *halakhah* is interested in the cognitive substance, not axiological validity, in formal constructs like those of physicists or mathematicians, and their logical interrelatedness within the system. At the level of topical *halakhah*, Shabbat is just a twenty-four hour stretch or period during which one must abstain from work and discontinue his daily routine; that's

רַבָּן גַּמְלִיאֵל הָיָה אוֹמֵר: כָּל שֶׁלֹּא אָמַר שְׁלֹשָׁה דְבָרִים אֵלּוּ בַּפֶּסַח, לֹא יָצָא יְדֵי חוֹבָתוֹ, וְאֵלּוּ הֵן:

all. There is nothing else involved in the topical approach to the Sabbath idea. However, when we shift our attention from halakhic thinking to halakhic feeling, from halakhic topics to axiological themata, we suddenly find ourselves in a new dimension, namely that of *kedushah*, holiness. Suddenly the Sabbath is transmuted or transformed from an abstract norm, from a formal concept, into a "reality," a living essence, a living entity; from a discipline in accordance with which one acts compulsorily into a great experience which one acts out spontaneously. Of course, we have many passages in the Bible dealing with the Sabbath, but the basic biblical text containing the Sabbath idea within the topical frame of formal-systematic reference is the passage in the Decalogue dealing with the normative aspect of the Sabbath: "Remember the Sabbath day to keep it holy, *le-kaddesho.* Six days shall you labor and do all your work but the seventh day is a Sabbath unto the Lord your God; in it you shall not do any manner of work, you, nor your son…." (Ex. 20:8–10).

The verb *le-kaddesho*, "to keep it holy," if analyzed in the light of positive topical *halakhah*, means only abstention from the daily routine or separation from work. In the topical context, the term *le-kaddesho* does not refer to or imply a charismatic quality inherent in the seventh day. It is just set aside as a day in the week on which one must abstain from work; that is all. This is a formal approach to the Sabbath idea.

In contrast to the topical *halakhah*, the text which forms the main motto of the thematic *halakhah* with regard to Shabbat would be, I believe, the mysterious passage in Genesis which concludes the story of creation: "And God blessed the seventh day and hallowed it, *va-yikaddesh oto*" (Gen. 2:3). A twenty-four-hour period was sanctified and hallowed. It has suddenly become a metaphysical entity upon which the Almighty had bestowed a unique endowment, a very strange endowment, namely, that of blessedness and sanctity.

(*Out of the Whirlwind*)

כָּל שֶׁלֹּא אָמַר שְׁלֹשָׁה דְבָרִים אֵלּוּ בַּפֶּסַח, לֹא יָצָא יְדֵי חוֹבָתוֹ *Sipur Yeẓi'at Miẓrayim* is accomplished through two media: the spoken word – the Haggadah, and actions such as the eating of *Pesaḥ*, *maẓẓah*, and *maror*, and the drinking of the *arba kosot*, the four cups of wine. *Sipur Yeẓi'at Miẓrayim* is a blend of storytelling, Torah teaching, and eating symbolic food items. It is a fusion of the spoken word and the physiological functions of eating and drinking, the intermingling of physical pleasure with Torah debate, the combining of the word of God with an activity motivated by biological pressure and characteristic not only of man but of animals.

Eating the paschal sacrifice, *maẓẓah*, and *maror* constitutes a double *miẓvah*.

Rabban Gamliel used to say: Whoever does not discuss the following three things on Passover has not fulfilled his duty, namely:

The *mizvat akhilah*, physically consuming these items, is, *per se*, a religious performance, a *ma'aseh kiyum mizvah*. But eating the *Pesaḥ*, *mazzah*, and *maror* is also the instrument or medium of *sipur Yezi'at Mizrayim*, telling the story of the Exodus. We narrate the story not only through speech but through eating as well. In order to fulfill the *mizvah* of *sipur* in the most perfect manner, one must interpret and explicate the symbolic meaning of *Pesaḥ*, *mazzah u-maror*.

(*Kol ha-Rav*)

The simple interpretation of Rabban Gamliel's ruling is that one who does not discuss these matters on the night of *Pesaḥ* is deficient in his fulfillment of the *mizvah* of reciting the Haggadah. This seems to be the opinion of Rambam (*Hilkhot Ḥamez u-Mazzah* 7:5), who summarizes the *Maggid* section of the Haggadah, then quotes Rabban Gamliel's dictum and concludes, "These recitations comprise the Haggadah." We understand from Rambam that discussing *Pesaḥ*, *mazzah*, and *maror* constitutes *sipur Yezi'at Mizrayim*. Tif'eret Yisrael states explicitly that one who does not discuss the three topics required by Rabban Gamliel is lacking in his fulfillment of *haggadah*.

However, Ramban in *Milḥamot* (*Berakhot* 2b in the Alfasi) adds another dimension to Rabban Gamliel's ruling. Ramban explains that there are instances where the Torah prescribes the optimal manner in which a *mizvah* should be performed and yet allows for a minimal fulfillment as well. For example, *Keri'at Shema* should be recited in the morning only after it is sufficiently light for one to distinguish between the colors blue and white. However, a person who recited *Keri'at Shema* after dawn, but before it was possible to distinguish between blue and white, has fulfilled the basic obligation and need not repeat the *Shema*.

Similarly, the intent of Rabban Gamliel's statement is that anyone who does not discuss *Pesaḥ*, *mazzah*, and *maror* has not *fully* satisfied his obligation to eat the *Pesaḥ*, *mazzah*, and *maror*. If, however, one has eaten the *Pesaḥ*, *mazzah*, and *maror* but not discussed them, he has fulfilled the basic obligation.

As noted above with regard to Rambam's quoting Rabban Gamliel's dictum, the discussion of the *mizvot* of *Pesaḥ*, *mazzah*, and *maror* constitutes *sipur Yezi'at Mizrayim*. Thus, from Ramban's analysis we see that *sipur Yezi'at Mizrayim* is not only an independent *mizvah*, it is also an integral component of the specific *mizvot* of the *Seder*. This idea is consistent with Ramban's statement in his *Hassagot* on the *Sefer ha-Mizvot* (*Mizvot she-Shakhaḥ Otan ha-Rav mi-Mizvot Aseh, Mizvah 15*) that *sipur Yezi'at Mizrayim* is counted as an independent *mizvah* even though it is a component of the *mizvah* of *korban Pesaḥ*.

(*Reshimot*)

פֶּסַח, מַצָּה, וּמָרוֹר:

פֶּסַח, מַצָּה, וּמָרוֹר The Talmud (*Pesaḥim* 28b and 120a) states: "*Kol arel lo yo'khal bo* (Ex. 12:48) – *Bo eino okhel aval okhel be-mazzah u-maror*, an uncircumcised male may not eat from it [the *korban Pesaḥ*] but eats *mazzah* and *maror*." The Talmud also applies this *derashah* to a *mumar*, an apostate, stating that a *mumar* "eats *mazzah* and *maror*." *Tosafot* (*Pesaḥim* 28b, s.v. *Kol*) reason that the basis of the prohibition against the *mumar*'s eating the *korban Pesaḥ* is that the *korban Pesaḥ* has the status of *kodshim*, consecrated items. Accordingly, *Tosafot* wonder why it was necessary for the Talmud to tell us that a *mumar* eats *mazzah* and *maror*, items that are not *kodshim*. *Tosafot* answer that there is, indeed, no reason to think that a *mumar* would be prohibited from eating *mazzah* and *maror*. The *derashah*, however, is not teaching that a *mumar* is permitted to eat *mazzah* and *maror*, but is teaching that a *mumar* is obligated to eat *mazzah* and *maror* even though he is not obligated with respect to *korban Pesaḥ*. Clearly, *Tosafot* assume that the prohibition against a *mumar* eating *korban Pesaḥ* stems from the *kedushat korban*, the sacrificial holiness that inheres within the *korban Pesaḥ*. This understanding of *Tosafot*'s reasoning is consistent with *Tosafot* in *Yevamot* 62a (s.v. *ha-Torah*). The Talmud there elaborates on Moses' rationale for breaking the *luḥot*, the Tablets of the Law, when he saw that the Israelites had sinned by worshipping the Golden Calf. Moses reasoned that if a *mumar* is prohibited from eating *korban Pesaḥ*, the Jewish nation, which had now come within the category of *mumarim*, should certainly be prohibited from receiving the entirety of Torah. *Tosafot* comment that Moses' reasoning needs clarification – "*de-sha'ani Pesaḥ mishum de-kodshim*, the prohibition against the *mumar*'s eating *korban Pesaḥ* is distinguishable because the *korban Pesaḥ* is *kodshim*," while in the case of the breaking of the *luḥot*, Moses could have taught the people the entire Torah in order to enable their repentance. *Tosafot*'s comment demonstrates that *Tosafot* assume that the prohibition against a *mumar* eating *korban Pesaḥ* stems from the *korban Pesaḥ*'s status as *kodshim*.

Rambam, however, understands the prohibition against the *mumar*'s eating *korban Pesaḥ* differently. Rambam (*Hilkhot Korban Pesaḥ* 9:8) states that although an *arel* may not eat from the *korban Pesaḥ*, he eats *mazzah* and *maror*. In the view of Rambam, the Talmud's *derashah* of *okhel hu be-mazzah u-maror* is describing a permissive act rather than an obligation. Rambam understands that the prohibition against the *mumar's* eating the *korban Pesaḥ* does not stem from the fact that the *korban Pesaḥ* is *kodshim*. Indeed, one could not even entertain the possibility (i.e., have a *havvah ammina*) that the prohibition against the *mumar*'s eating the *korban Pesaḥ* is based on the *korban Pesaḥ*'s status of *kodshim*, for if that were the basis, then the prohibition would have

Pesaḥ (the Passover-sacrifice), **Mazzah** (the unleavened bread), and **Maror** (the bitter herbs).

no relation to a prohibition against a *mumar's* eating *mazzah* and *maror*. While there is, in fact, a special prohibition forbidding an *arel* and a *mumar* from partaking of *kodshim*, the *korban Pesaḥ* has an additional dimension. Beyond the *mizvah* of eating the *Pesaḥ*, *mazzah*, and *maror* there inheres within each a fulfillment of the *mizvah* of *sipur Yezi'at Mizrayim*. Rashi (Deut. 16:3) supports this concept by stating "*Lema'an tizkor – al yedei akhilat Pesaḥ ve-ha-mazzah*, we remember *Yezi'at Mizrayim* by consuming the *korban Pesaḥ* and *mazzah*." What seem to be only *mizvot* dealing with the eating of food are also an inherent aspect of *sipur Yezi'at Mizrayim*. Therefore, Rambam learns that the exclusion of a *mumar* from eating the *korban Pesaḥ* is because such a person is precluded from the commandment of *sipur Yezi'at Mizrayim*. Accordingly, we might have thought that just as a *mumar* is prohibited from fulfilling the obligation of *sipur Yezi'at Mizrayim* insofar as it pertains to eating the *korban Pesaḥ*, the *mumar* should likewise be prohibited from partaking of the *mazzah* and *maror*. The Talmud, therefore, needs to tell us that although all three items are aspects of *sipur Yezi'at Mizrayim*, and a *mumar* is not permitted to eat the *korban Pesaḥ*, the *mumar* may nonetheless eat *mazzah* and *maror*.

This understanding of the prohibition against a *mumar's* eating from the *korban Pesaḥ* is explicit in the *Sefer ha-Ḥinnukh* (*Mizvah* 13), which states, "an apostate should not eat from the *korban Pesaḥ* that we use as a remembrance… to entering the covenant of Torah and faith."

(*Reshimot*)

The order in Rabban Gamliel's saying is a bit puzzling. He speaks of *Pesaḥ*, *mazzah*, and *maror*, but he should have started with the *maror*, the bitter herbs, which symbolizes the *genut*, the degrading life of slavery and oppression with which we begin our narration, and only then mentioned *Pesaḥ*, the climactic event, which took place on the night of the fifteenth of Nisan, when God passed over (*pasaḥ*) the houses of the Jews and struck the Egyptians (Ex. 12:27). He should have taken up *mazzah* last, because *mazzah* represents the last event, the redemption that took place in the morning when the Jews left Egypt (Ex. 12:39).

Maimonides (*Hilkhot Ḥamez u-Mazzah* 7:5 and 8:4) also initially quotes "*Pesaḥ, mazzah u-maror*," as in our Haggadah. But when he begins to discuss the *mizvot* there, his order changes to *Pesaḥ*, *maror*, and *mazzah*. Then, in his Haggadah, he reverts to the sequence of our Haggadah, *Pesaḥ, mazzah u-maror*. In either case, the sequence does not follow the chronology of events – *maror*, *Pesaḥ*, and finally *mazzah* – because the Haggadah is a book of studies in

כשאומר פסח שהיו אבותינו אוכלים לא יגביה את התבשיל שהוא זכר לפסח.

פֶּסַח שֶׁהָיוּ אֲבוֹתֵינוּ אוֹכְלִים, בִּזְמַן שֶׁבֵּית הַמִּקְדָּשׁ הָיָה קַיָּם, עַל שׁוּם מָה? עַל שׁוּם שֶׁפָּסַח הַקָּדוֹשׁ בָּרוּךְ הוּא, עַל בָּתֵּי אֲבוֹתֵינוּ בְּמִצְרַיִם, שֶׁנֶּאֱמַר: וַאֲמַרְתֶּם זֶבַח פֶּסַח הוּא לַיְיָ, אֲשֶׁר פָּסַח עַל בָּתֵּי בְנֵי יִשְׂרָאֵל בְּמִצְרַיִם בְּנָגְפּוֹ אֶת־מִצְרַיִם, וְאֶת־בָּתֵּינוּ הִצִּיל, וַיִּקֹּד הָעָם וַיִּשְׁתַּחֲווּ:

(שמות י"ב, כ"ז)

Yeẓi'at Miẓrayim and not a book of stories. Haggadah means *talmud Torah*. The *miẓvot* of *Pesaḥ, maẓẓah u-maror* should be explained and interpreted within the framework of *sipur Yeẓi'at Miẓrayim* – not in accordance with the unfolding of the events, but within the frame of reference of *halakhah*, of the conceptual sequence of *miẓvot*.

The focal *miẓvah* nowadays is *maẓẓah*, for "*maẓẓah* in contemporary times is a biblical command, and *maror* is a rabbinic command" (*Pesaḥim* 120a). The verse states, "With *maẓẓot* and *merorim* you shall eat [the *korban Pesaḥ*]" (Num. 9:11), indicating that *maror* needs to be eaten only when there is a *korban Pesaḥ*. This conclusion would not apply to the *maẓẓah*, for there is another verse requiring its eating: "At the night you shall eat *maẓẓot*" (Ex. 12:18) – without reference to the *korban Pesaḥ*.

Thus, while on the biblical level *maror* is dependent on the *Pesaḥ* sacrifice, *maẓẓah* has two original aspects – one connected to the *Pesaḥ* and one independent of it. During Temple times, one who ate *maẓẓah* fulfilled two commandments, while eating *maror* fulfilled only one Torah obligation. Halakhically, *Pesaḥ* is the central *miẓvah*, because *maẓẓah* and *maror* both depend on it. Fifty percent of *maẓẓah*'s importance depends on it, but *maror* depends on *Pesaḥ* totally, for when *Pesaḥ* is eliminated, there is no *maror mi-de-oraita*.

Therefore, in chapters 7 and 8, when Mamonidies discusses the *Seder* in Temple times, he starts with *Pesaḥ*, which determines the character of *maẓẓah* and *maror*, then continues with that which is more dependent upon *Pesaḥ* – namely, *maror* – and concludes with *maẓẓah*. Yet in 8:9 he informs us that *al ha-sova* applies to both *Pesaḥ* and *maẓẓah*, for "eating them is the *miẓvah*," meaning that eating these items is the central *miẓvah* – *Pesaḥ* during Temple times, and *maẓẓah* today. In Temple times, *Pesaḥ* overrides *maẓẓah* with regard to *al ha-sova*; nowadays, *maẓẓah* takes the place of *Pesaḥ* as the central *miẓvah*. Hence, in Maimonides' Haggadah, which is that "which Israel was accustomed to use in the time of the exile," the order is different. *Pesaḥ* is explained first because it is *zekher la-Mikdash*, a memorial to the Temple. Then we explain *maẓẓah*, for it is the main *miẓvah*, and finally *maror*. Similarly, Rabban Gamliel,

The zero'a is not raised when saying the following:

Pesaḥ, the Passover-lamb that our ancestors ate during the time of the *Beit ha-Mikdash*, was for what reason? It was because the Omnipresent passed over our ancestors' houses in Egypt, as it is said: "You shall say, It is a Passover-offering to the Lord, because He passed over the houses of the children of Israel in Egypt when He struck the Egyptians with a plague, and He saved our houses. And the people bowed and prostrated themselves." (Ex. 12, 27)

(Mishnah *Pesaḥim* 10:5), is discussing the *Seder* in post-Temple times and he therefore uses the order *Pesaḥ*, *maẓẓah*, *maror.*

(*Festival of Freedom*)

פֶּסַח The birth of the *ḥesed* community – of a nation within which people unite, give things away, care for each other, share what they possess – is symbolized by the paschal sacrifice. God did not need the paschal lamb; He had no interest in the sacrifice. He simply wanted the people – slaves who had just come out of the house of bondage – to emerge from their isolation and insane self-centeredness into the *ḥesed* community, where the little that man has is too much for himself, where whatever he possesses transcends his ability to enjoy.

A new fellowship was formed around the paschal lamb; a new community sprang into existence. Being together, living with each other, sharing something many possess in common was made possible by the ceremonial of the paschal lamb. The *halakhah* coined the term *ḥavurah* with reference to the group gathering together for this ceremonial (e.g., Mishnah, *Pesaḥim* 8:7). Eating together is a great medium of communication between individuals. Therefore, everything is shared.

The slave suddenly realized that the little he has saved up for himself, a single lamb, is too much for him. The slave spontaneously does something which he would never have believed that he was capable of doing, namely, he knocks on the door of his neighbor whom he had never noticed, inviting him to share the lamb with him and to eat together.

(*Festival of Freedom*)

עַל שׁוּם מָה There are two versions of this text. One version asks the question "*al shum mah*," and the other version is "*al shem mah*." What is the significance of these two versions?

The words *al shum mah* imply that the author of the Haggadah is asking God's reason for commanding us to eat *maẓẓah*. Thus, in asking *al shum mah*,

מגביה את המצה הפרוסה ומראה למסובים.

מַצָּה זוֹ שֶׁאָנוּ אוֹכְלִים, עַל שׁוּם מָה? עַל שׁוּם שֶׁלֹּא הִסְפִּיק בְּצֵקָם שֶׁל אֲבוֹתֵינוּ לְהַחֲמִיץ, עַד שֶׁנִּגְלָה עֲלֵיהֶם מֶלֶךְ מַלְכֵי הַמְּלָכִים, הַקָּדוֹשׁ בָּרוּךְ הוּא, וּגְאָלָם, שֶׁנֶּאֱמַר: וַיֹּאפוּ אֶת־הַבָּצֵק אֲשֶׁר הוֹצִיאוּ מִמִּצְרַיִם, עֻגֹת מַצּוֹת, כִּי לֹא חָמֵץ, כִּי גֹרְשׁוּ מִמִּצְרַיִם, וְלֹא יָכְלוּ לְהִתְמַהְמֵהַּ, וְגַם צֵדָה לֹא עָשׂוּ לָהֶם. (שמות י"ב, ל"ט)

---

the Haggadah is seeking to explore God's will, to understand why God commands us to eat *mazzah*.

The words *al shem mah* pose a different question: What is the content of the commandment? What is the significance of the commandment to eat *mazzah*? Thus, the question *al shem mah* is not seeking to delve into God's will; God's will is impenetrable. We can only ask what impact should eating *mazzah* have on the person who performs this commandment.

The distinction between *al shum* and *al shem* can be understood in light of the classical medieval Jewish philosophers' discussion regarding the reasons for the commandments.

Rambam, in his *Guide for the Perplexed* (pt. 3, chap. 48) understood that there is a rabbinic dispute with respect to whether we can offer reasons for God's commandments. The Rabbis state, "He who prays saying 'Your mercy extended to a bird's nest' is silenced, because he treats God's commandments as expressions of mercy, whereas they are decrees" (*Berakhot* 33b). Rambam understands that this statement follows the opinion of the Rabbis who hold that one may not offer specific reasons for the commandments, other than the fact that they are God's decrees. Others disagree, and hold that the commandments have specific reasons that can be understood by human beings.

Ramban (Deut. 22:6) elaborates in discussing the precept of *shillu'aḥ ha-ken* (the obligation to drive away the mother before taking her offspring from a nest). Ramban makes a distinction between an explanation of a commandment that involves God's reasons and an explanation that describes the human benefit of a commandment. He uses the commandment of *shillu'aḥ ha-ken* to illustrate this point. The deficiency of the prayer "Your mercy extended to a bird's nest" is the implication that it was God's attribute of mercy that caused God to set forth this commandment. The implication that God decrees a commandment for His benefit, to fulfill His need to be merciful, is an unacceptable limitation of God's perfection. However, it is perfectly appropriate to assert the human benefit in performing a commandment. Thus, it is appropriate to

The broken mazzah is raised and shown.

This M*azzah* is eaten for what reason? It is because the dough of our ancestors did not have time to become leavened before the King of the kings of kings, the Holy One, blessed be He, revealed Himself to them and redeemed them. Thus it is said: "They baked M*azzah*-cakes from the dough that they had brought out of Egypt, because it was not leavened; for they had been driven out of Egypt and could not delay, and they had also not prepared any [other] provisions." (Ex. 12, 39)

---

state that the commandment of *shillu'aḥ ha-ken* was designed to teach human beings to be merciful.

This distinction can explain the difference between *al shum* and *al shem*. *Al shum* is asking why God, from His perspective, commanded us to eat *mazzah*. Vis-à-vis God, the question "why" is not valid. God's will is self-justifying, and requires no explanation. *Al shem*, however, addresses the human perspective in performing a commandment: What do *we* learn? What impact should this commandment have on *us*? Therefore, the more appropriate text should be *al shem*.

Rav Hayim further explained that *ta'amei ha-mizvot* should not be understood as "the reasons for the commandments" but rather as "the flavor of the commandments," as the verse states (Ps. 34:9) "*ta'amu u-re'u ki tov Hashem*, taste and see that God is good."

(*Reshimot*)

וּגְאָלָם Genuine *ge'ullah*, genuine redemption, always comes suddenly, unexpectedly, at a time when people are ready to give up hope. Sometimes historical situations keep deteriorating; people pray and cry, begging for mercy – but there is no answer to their prayer, only silence. At that moment, when the crisis reaches its maximum and threatens the very existence of the community, when people begin to give up, the *ge'ullah* suddenly comes and takes them out of the land of affliction. It comes in the middle of the night and knocks on the door when no one expects it, when everybody is skeptical about it, when everybody laughs off the possibility of redemption.

This is what happened in Egypt. "The children of Israel sighed by reason of the bondage, and they cried, and their cry rose up to God by reason of the bondage" (Ex. 2:23). God did not answer at that moment, and the people had no knowledge that "God looked…and God knew" (Ex. 2:25). When the crisis reached its climax and the Jewish people were on the verge of complete

מגביה את המרור ומראו למסובים.

מָרוֹר זֶה שֶׁאָנוּ אוֹכְלִים, עַל שׁוּם מָה? עַל שׁוּם שֶׁמֵּרְרוּ הַמִּצְרִים אֶת־חַיֵּי אֲבוֹתֵינוּ בְּמִצְרַיִם, שֶׁנֶּאֱמַר: וַיְמָרְרוּ אֶת־חַיֵּיהֶם בַּעֲבֹדָה קָשָׁה, בְּחֹמֶר וּבִלְבֵנִים, וּבְכָל־עֲבֹדָה בַּשָּׂדֶה, אֵת כָּל־עֲבֹדָתָם, אֲשֶׁר עָבְדוּ בָהֶם בְּפָרֶךְ. (שמות א׳, י״ד)

בְּכָל־דּוֹר וָדוֹר חַיָּב אָדָם לִרְאוֹת אֶת־עַצְמוֹ, כְּאִלּוּ הוּא יָצָא מִמִּצְרָיִם, שֶׁנֶּאֱמַר: וְהִגַּדְתָּ לְבִנְךָ בַּיּוֹם הַהוּא לֵאמֹר: בַּעֲבוּר זֶה עָשָׂה יְיָ לִי, בְּצֵאתִי מִמִּצְרָיִם. (שמות י״ג, ח׳) לֹא אֶת־אֲבוֹתֵינוּ בִּלְבָד, גָּאַל הַקָּדוֹשׁ בָּרוּךְ הוּא, אֶלָּא אַף אוֹתָנוּ גָּאַל עִמָּהֶם, שֶׁנֶּאֱמַר: וְאוֹתָנוּ הוֹצִיא מִשָּׁם, לְמַעַן הָבִיא אֹתָנוּ, לָתֶת לָנוּ אֶת־הָאָרֶץ אֲשֶׁר נִשְׁבַּע לַאֲבֹתֵינוּ. (דברים ו׳, כ״ג)

מכסים את המצות ומגביהים את הכוס עד אחר ברכת
בורא פרי הגפן (טור ומחבר סי׳ תע״ג ס״ז):

לְפִיכָךְ אֲנַחְנוּ חַיָּבִים לְהוֹדוֹת, לְהַלֵּל, לְשַׁבֵּחַ, לְפָאֵר, לְרוֹמֵם, לְהַדֵּר, לְבָרֵךְ, לְעַלֵּה וּלְקַלֵּס, לְמִי שֶׁעָשָׂה לַאֲבוֹתֵינוּ וְלָנוּ אֶת־כָּל־הַנִּסִּים הָאֵלּוּ. הוֹצִיאָנוּ

---

assimilation and disappearance, Moses came. At the beginning, he was very far from successful; apparently, the plagues did not convince the Jews that redemption was near. They did not expect divine revelation that night. Indeed, this is the most important feature of *ge'ullat Mizrayim*. The redemption from Egypt consisted not only of the fact that our ancestors went from slavery to freedom, but, more importantly, that this redemption and the revelation of the Almighty were surprises to them. This is the nature of *ge'ullah*.

(*Festival of Freedom*)

חַיָּב אָדָם לִרְאוֹת אֶת עַצְמוֹ כְּאִלּוּ הוּא יָצָא מִמִּצְרַיִם Rambam says that on Passover night, we should each act like a free person and demonstrate our freedom. "In every generation one should show himself – *le-har'ot et aẓmo* – as if he had been liberated from Egypt" (*Hilkhot Ḥameẓ u-Maẓẓah* 7:6). Rambam added the letter *he* to the usual formulation: not *li-re'ot et aẓmo* ("one should see himself"), but rather *le-har'ot et aẓmo* ("one should show himself"). *Li-re'ot* means to experience, to feel, to re-experience the slavery and the Exodus. It should not be an ancient event, lying at the dawn of our history and having no relevance for us. I am to re-experience it. Memory, in Judaism, means not just to remember

The maror is raised and shown.

This *maror* is eaten for what reason? It is because the Egyptians embittered our ancestors' lives in Egypt, as it is said: "They made their lives bitter with hard service, with mortar and with bricks, and with all manner of service in the field; all their service which they made them serve with rigor." (Ex. 1, 14)

In every generation a person is obligated to regard himself as if he had come out of Egypt, as it is said: "You shall tell your child on that day, it is because of this that the Lord did for me when I left Egypt." (Ex. 13, 8) The Holy One, blessed be He, redeemed not only our ancestors from Egypt, but He redeemed also us with them, as it is said: "It was us that He brought out from there, so that He might bring us to give us the land that He swore to our ancestors." (Deut. 6, 23)

The mazzot are covered and the cup of wine raised until after the blessing for the wine.

Thus it is our duty to thank, to laud, to praise, to glorify, to exalt, to adore, to bless, to elevate and to acclaim the One who did all these miracles for our ancestors and for us. He took us from slavery

---

technically, but also to relive the event. *Le-har'ot* adds another dimension: the re-experiencing should be so dynamic and so intense that it breaks through and somehow expresses itself in action. If we are overpowered by an emotion, we cannot suppress it; we cannot control ourselves. We will sing and dance; we will cry and shout; we will shed tears and embrace people. The experience of *Yeẓi'at Miẓrayim* on the night of *Pesaḥ* should be so overpowering, so overwhelming, that we should act it out.

(*Kol ha-Rav*)

לְפִיכָךְ The *Lefikhakh* paragraph speaks of thanking God for miracles done "for our forefathers and us." The paragraph of *Asher ge'alanu*, which follows our singing of the first two chapters of *Hallel*, blesses God "who redeemed us and redeemed our forefathers from Egypt." If one thanks God for a historical event that retains its relevance for us, then one should first mention his forefathers, to whom the event occurred, and then himself. Yet if one has experienced the event himself, he first should thank God for the miracle that happened to

מֵעַבְדוּת לְחֵרוּת, מִיָּגוֹן לְשִׂמְחָה, וּמֵאֵבֶל לְיוֹם טוֹב, וּמֵאֲפֵלָה לְאוֹר גָּדוֹל, וּמִשִּׁעְבּוּד לִגְאֻלָּה. וְנֹאמַר לְפָנָיו שִׁירָה חֲדָשָׁה. הַלְלוּיָהּ:

יש נוהגים להניח כאן את הכוס (ספר המנהגים לר"א קלויזנר)
ומגביהים אותו שוב בברכת אשר גאלנו.

הַלְלוּיָהּ. הַלְלוּ עַבְדֵי יְיָ, הַלְלוּ אֶת־שֵׁם יְיָ: יְהִי שֵׁם יְיָ מְבֹרָךְ, מֵעַתָּה וְעַד עוֹלָם: מִמִּזְרַח שֶׁמֶשׁ עַד מְבוֹאוֹ, מְהֻלָּל שֵׁם יְיָ: רָם עַל־כָּל־גּוֹיִם יְיָ, עַל הַשָּׁמַיִם כְּבוֹדוֹ: מִי כַּייָ אֱלֹהֵינוּ, הַמַּגְבִּיהִי לָשָׁבֶת: הַמַּשְׁפִּילִי לִרְאוֹת,

---

him, and only then thank God for redeeming others as well. The *Lefikhakh* paragraph should read *lanu ve-la-avoteinu*, with ourselves mentioned first, only if we actually are capable of fulfilling and realizing the *halakhah* that "In every generation one must see himself as if he had come out of Egypt." It is not difficult to eat *mazzah* and *maror*. However, *Be-khol dor va-dor* is not a *mizvah* of eating; it is one of an emotion, a state of mind. It is the involvement of a modern person who nevertheless lives within ancient events – a very complicated *mizvah*. We can prove that we have fulfilled the *mizvah* by saying *Hallel* – and so as long as we haven't said *Hallel*, we have not fulfilled *Be-khol dor va-dor*. Before we recite *Hallel*, we have no right to say *lanu ve-la-avoteinu*, so we say *la-avoteinu ve-lanu*. The very instant *Hallel* is recited, we suppose that we did so with ecstasy and joy – as if the event had happened just recently. Therefore, we may now mention ourselves first and let our ancestors follow.

(*Festival of Freedom*)

הַלְלוּיָהּ The Mishnah in *Pesaḥim* (116b) states that we recite *Hallel* over the second cup of wine. From the text of *Hallel* we can infer that the reason for reciting *Hallel* is that this recitation is part-and-parcel of the fulfillment of *sipur Yezi'at Mizrayim* and our obligation to re-enact the Exodus. We lift our cups and declare that because of our miraculous delivery we are obligated to sing and praise God.

However, there is an additional factor that obligates us to recite *Hallel* on the *Seder* night, and that is the *mizvah* of *korban Pesaḥ*. The Talmud (*Pesaḥim* 95a–b) enumerates the differences between the sacrifice brought on the fourteenth of Nisan and the one brought on the fourteenth of Iyar in conjunction with *Pesaḥ Sheni*. One of the differences is that *Hallel* is recited only when we eat the *korban Pesaḥ* brought in Nisan. This is derived from the verse "You shall have a song as on the night when the festival is sanctified" (Isa. 30:29). From this exchange, we can see that the recitation of *Hallel* on the night of

to freedom, from sorrow to joy, and from mourning to festivity, and from deep darkness to great light, and from bondage to redemption. Let us therefore recite before Him a new song, Halleluyah, Praise God!

Some lower the cup for the following two paragraphs and then raise it for the blessing:

Halleluyah – Praise God! Offer praise, you servants of the Lord; praise the Name of the Lord. May the Lord's Name be blessed from now and to all eternity. From the rising of the sun to its setting, the Lord's Name is praised. The Lord is high above all nations, His glory is over the heavens. Who is like the Lord, our God, who dwells

---

the *Seder* is a function of the *miẓvah* of *korban Pesaḥ* as well as a component of the obligation of *sipur Yeẓi'at Miẓrayim*.

Today, when we no longer have a *Beit ha-Mikdash*, and the *korban Pesaḥ* is not brought, it should follow that the obligation of reciting *Hallel* is a function only of the *miẓvah* of *sipur Yeẓi'at Miẓrayim*, which, indeed, is the opinion of Ran and *Kol Bo*. The view of Ramban, however, differs; he holds that even today *Hallel* at the *Seder* is recited on the performance of the *miẓvot* of the *Seder* and not only as an element of *sipur Yeẓi'at Miẓrayim*. Ramban (on *Pesaḥim* 117) writes that although we divide the recitation of *Hallel* with the eating of the *korban Pesaḥ*, this is not to be viewed as an interruption. Quite to the contrary, *Hallel* is recited upon the performance of the *miẓvot* of *korban Pesaḥ* and *maẓẓah*. These *miẓvot* are what give rise to the obligation to recite *Hallel*. Ramban's view, however, requires clarification, as Ramban also cites the *Yerushalmi* to the effect that someone who recites *Hallel* in synagogue has satisfied his obligation. One could ask how the *Hallel* recited in synagogue is connected to the *miẓvah* of eating the *korban Pesaḥ*. Ramban also implies that a person who recites *Hallel* in synagogue on *Pesaḥ* night should repeat it at the *Seder*. If he has essentially fulfilled his obligation to recite *Hallel*, why does Ramban recommend that he recite it again?

The Gemara (*Arakhin* 10b) derives from the verse "You shall have a song as on the night when the festival is sanctified" that one recites *Hallel* only on *yom tov*. It would, therefore, appear that Ramban's intent was not that *Hallel* is recited on the performance of the *miẓvah* of eating the *korban Pesaḥ*, but rather that the *miẓvot* of the night of the *Seder* transform that night into a *yom tov* of redemption, which is the appropriate time for *Hallel*. Therefore, the entire evening, even when one is in *shul*, is the appropriate time for this recitation of *Hallel*.

בַּשָּׁמַיִם וּבָאָרֶץ: מְקִימִי מֵעָפָר דָּל, מֵאַשְׁפֹּת יָרִים אֶבְיוֹן: לְהוֹשִׁיבִי
עִם־נְדִיבִים, עִם נְדִיבֵי עַמּוֹ: מוֹשִׁיבִי עֲקֶרֶת הַבַּיִת, אֵם הַבָּנִים שְׂמֵחָה,
הַלְלוּיָהּ: (תהלים קי"ג)

A proof for this view of Ramban's position is found in the commentary of
Rabbenu Hananel (*Pesaḥim* 98a), who states that if a relative dies on the fourteenth of Nisan after midday, one does not become an *onen* (a mourner prior
to the burial who is exempt from *miẓvot*), because the fourteenth of Nisan
after midday is the time for bringing the *korban Pesaḥ* and recitation of its
accompanying *Hallel*. These *miẓvot* elevate this period of time and confer on
it the status of a *yom tov*, during which *avelut* (mourning) is inapplicable.

(*Reshimot*)

In describing the *miẓvah* of *sipur Yeẓiʾat Mitzrayim* in his *Sefer ha-Miẓvot*
(*Miẓvah* 157), Rambam includes the requirement of praising God for all the
good He has bestowed upon us. From this we see that Rambam is of the view
that the recitation of *Hallel* on the night of the *Seder* is a biblical obligation.
The *Sefer ha-Ḥinnukh* (*Miẓvah* 21) echoes this sentiment. In truth, the text
of the Haggadah itself suggests that the requirement of reciting *Hallel* is an
inherent component of the *miẓvah* of *sipur Yeẓiʾat Miẓrayim*, since we declare,
"*Lefikhakh anaḥnu ḥayyavim le-hodot le-hallel*, therefore we are required to
thank and praise [God]." Indeed, the recitation of *Hallel* at the *Seder* is one of
the features that distinguish the *miẓvah* of *sipur Yeẓiʾat Miẓrayim* at the *Seder*
from the daily *miẓvah* of *zekhirat Yeẓiʾat Miẓrayim*.

Some questions, however, present themselves. *Tosafot* (*Megillah* 21a, s.v. *la-
atuyei*) state that it is permissible to complete the *Hallel* after midnight since its
recitation is only a rabbinic obligation, a view which seems inconsistent with
the text of the Haggadah. Another question arises from Rashi's explanation
(*Pesaḥim* 36, s.v. *she-onin*) that the reason *maẓẓah* is called *leḥem oni* is that
we recite over the *maẓẓah* ("*onin alav*") the complete *Hallel* and the Haggadah.
This passage of Rashi is difficult because we do not recite the entire *Hallel* over
the *maẓẓah* – the *afikoman* is eaten before the *Hallel* is finished.

We can answer these questions by distinguishing between the first half of
Hallel, which is recited as part of the *Maggid* section of the *Seder*, and the second
half of *Hallel*, which is recited after the *Afikoman*. The first half of *Hallel*, which
contains the paragraph "*Be-ẓet Yisraʾel mi-Miẓrayim*, when Israel left Egypt,"
expresses the praise that we owe God for taking us out of Egypt. *Tosafot* would
agree that the recitation of the first half of *Hallel*, which is an integral part
of *Maggid*, is indeed a biblical obligation. It is only the second half of *Hallel*,

on high yet looks down so low upon heaven and earth! He raises the poor from the dust, He lifts the needy from the trash heaps, to seat them with nobles, with the nobles of His people. He restores the barren woman to the house, into a joyful mother of children. *Halleluyah* Praise God. (Ps. 113)

---

which consists of generic praise not directly related to *sipur Yeẓi'at Miẓrayim*, whose recitation is a rabbinic obligation and therefore may occur even after midnight. Permission to recite the second half of *Hallel* after midnight should not, however, be viewed as an indication that one may treat the second half of *Hallel* on the *Seder* night more leniently than the first half; rather it is an indication that the second half of *Hallel* is qualitatively different from the first. While the first half is an element of the fulfillment of the biblical obligation of *sipur Yeẓi'at Miẓrayim* and is therefore subject to the same requirement as *sipur Yeẓi'at Miẓrayim* that it be completed before midnight, the second half is the fulfillment of the rabbinic obligation to praise God for His blessings in all aspects of our lives. The first half of *Hallel* constitutes *hoda'ah*, an expression of thanks to God, while the second half constitutes *shevaḥ*, praise. That the two sections of *Hallel* constitute two *kiyumim*, two separate fulfillments, is further demonstrated by *Tosafot* in *Berakhot* (14a, s.v. *yamim*), where *Tosafot* refer to the practice of reciting two *berakhot* to *Hallel* at the *Seder*, one on the first half of *Hallel* and another on the second half.

This distinction between the first and second halves of *Hallel* would also explain Rashi's intent in stating that we complete the *Hallel* over the *maẓẓah*. In truth, we complete the *Hallel* of *Yeẓi'at Miẓrayim* before we eat the *maẓẓah*. In general, viewing *Hallel* as containing two qualitatively different sections, one concerning *sipur Yeẓi'at Miẓrayim*, and the other pertaining to all of God's blessings, helps to explain the puzzling phenomenon of bifurcating *Hallel* on the *Seder* night and interrupting it with the meal. The deliberate separation of *Hallel* at the *Seder* is to emphasize *sipur Yeẓi'at Miẓrayim* and to incorporate the portion of *Hallel* that concerns *Yeẓi'at Miẓrayim* as a component of the biblical obligation to be recited before midnight while the *maẓẓah* is still present.

Another point is noteworthy. The division of *Hallel* at the *Seder* to which we are accustomed is according to Beit Hillel. Beit Shammai divided the text differently. According to Beit Shammai, only the first paragraph of *Hallel* is recited in the *Maggid* section, while the second paragraph, *Be-ẓet Yisra'el mi-Miẓrayim*, is recited after the *Afikoman* with the rest of *Hallel* in conjunction with the fourth cup of wine. Beit Shammai apparently were of the view that the second half of *Hallel*, like the first, is an expression of *sipur Yeẓi'at Miẓrayim*.

(*Reshimot*)

בְּצֵאת יִשְׂרָאֵל מִמִּצְרָיִם, בֵּית יַעֲקֹב מֵעַם לֹעֵז: הָיְתָה יְהוּדָה לְקָדְשׁוֹ, יִשְׂרָאֵל מַמְשְׁלוֹתָיו: הַיָּם רָאָה וַיָּנֹס, הַיַּרְדֵּן יִסֹּב לְאָחוֹר: הֶהָרִים רָקְדוּ כְאֵילִים, גְּבָעוֹת כִּבְנֵי־צֹאן: מַה־לְּךָ הַיָּם כִּי תָנוּס, הַיַּרְדֵּן תִּסֹּב לְאָחוֹר: הֶהָרִים תִּרְקְדוּ כְאֵילִים, גְּבָעוֹת כִּבְנֵי־צֹאן: מִלִּפְנֵי אָדוֹן חוּלִי אָרֶץ, מִלִּפְנֵי אֱלוֹהַּ יַעֲקֹב: הַהֹפְכִי הַצּוּר אֲגַם־מָיִם, חַלָּמִישׁ לְמַעְיְנוֹ־מָיִם. (תהלים קי"ד)

מכסים את המצות ומגביהים את הכוס.

בָּרוּךְ אַתָּה יְיָ, אֱלֹהֵינוּ מֶלֶךְ הָעוֹלָם, אֲשֶׁר גְּאָלָנוּ וְגָאַל אֶת־אֲבוֹתֵינוּ

בְּצֵאת יִשְׂרָאֵל מִמִּצְרָיִם A slave whose master placed *tefillin* upon him goes free (*Gittin* 40a), because slavery cannot harmonize with the proclamation of God's unity and the acceptance of His commandments expressed in the four passages contained in the *tefillin*. The Sages explain that "One may not return a slave to his master" (Deut. 23:16) refers to a slave from outside Israel who escapes to Israel (*Gittin* 45a). A slave who flees from the profane to the sacred is emancipated.

The difference between freedom through conquest and freedom through sanctity – through escaping to Israel, through immersion with intent to convert, through the putting on of *tefillin* and the reading of the Torah – is very similar to the difference Rambam (*Hilkhot Terumot* 1:5) propounded regarding the first and second sanctifications of the Land of Israel: The first sanctification was canceled when they were exiled. Since the land was obtained by virtue of conquest alone, its sanctification was temporary and not permanent. However, the second sanctification was permanent because those who returned settled the land not through conquest.

A master can reclaim a slave taken through conquest; nothing changes in his personal status, and the slave remains morally and spiritually a slave, vulgar and profane. Conquest is valid only as long as the conqueror is powerful, but when the former master is the stronger, the latter's conquest is annulled. However, when the freedom of a slave stems from a transformation of personality, from the raising of the soul from profanity to sanctity, from the acceptance of the yoke of commandments, from leaving the lands of the nations and moving to the Land of Israel – then his newfound status can never be annulled. "Personal sanctity cannot be annulled of itself" (*Nedarim* 29b). The election of Israel in Egypt did not come about through conquest, through the mighty hand and the outstretched arm, through signs and wonders, but rather through the divine revelation of a still, small voice in the soul of the nation.

The Torah announced the procedure for all the commandments – the

When Israel went out of Egypt, the House of Jacob from a people of a strange language, Judah became His holy one, Israel His dominion. The sea saw and fled, the Jordan turned backward. The mountains skipped like rams, the hills like young sheep. What is with you, O sea, that you flee; Jordan, that you turn backward? Mountains, why do you skip like rams; like young sheep? Tremble, you earth, before the Lord, before the God of Jacob, Who turns the rock into a pool of water, the flint-stone into a spring of water. (Ps. 114)

The maẓẓot are covered and the cup is lifted.

Blessed are You, Lord, our God, King of the universe, who has redeemed us and redeemed our ancestors from Egypt, and enabled

---

paschal lamb, *maẓẓah*, bitter herbs, recounting the story of the Exodus – on the night of the fifteenth, when the Jews were still in Egypt. Rabbi Eleazar ben Azariah claims that all the commandments associated with the *Seder* must be observed specifically before midnight, before the plague of the firstborn took place (*Pesaḥim* 120b). The great sanctity of the night-of-watching is grounded not on the miracles and wonders which God displayed that night, not on the acquisition through conquest accomplished with a mighty hand and an outstretched arm, but rather on acquisition through sanctification, through commandments, through the divine revelation of a still, small voice. The Jews themselves accomplished the greatest miracle: they raised themselves to the level of a holy nation. Only after that miracle took place did the redemption through conquest and the miracles of a mighty hand and an outstretched arm first begin.

Had the Jews not first redeemed themselves by self-sanctification on that night-of-watching in Egypt, the redemption through conquest would not have been complete. "When Israel went out of Egypt, the house of Jacob from a people of strange language, Judah became God's holy one, and Israel became His nation." Only afterwards, "The sea saw and fled; the Jordan was driven back" (Ps. 114:1–3).

(*Festival of Freedom*)

אֲשֶׁר גְּאָלָנוּ The Mishnah (*Pesaḥim* 116b) records two opinions about the structure of the *berakhah* of *Asher ge'alanu*. According to Rabbi Tarfon, the *berakhah* is a short one, mentioning our redemption and that of our forefathers, and ending without a *ḥatimah*, a closing phrase. According to Rabbi Akiva, it is a longer

מִמִּצְרַיִם, וְהִגִּיעָנוּ לַלַּיְלָה הַזֶּה, לֶאֱכָל־בּוֹ מַצָּה וּמָרוֹר. כֵּן, יְיָ אֱלֹהֵינוּ וֵאלֹהֵי אֲבוֹתֵינוּ, יַגִּיעֵנוּ לְמוֹעֲדִים וְלִרְגָלִים אֲחֵרִים, הַבָּאִים לִקְרָאתֵנוּ

---

one that does contain a *hatimah*, one that expresses our desire to celebrate future festivals, especially in a rebuilt Jerusalem with a restored Temple.

On the surface, the issue seems to be one of the protocols governing *berakhot*. Rabbi Tarfon presumably is opposed to the mixing of motifs – *shevaḥ* (praise) and *bakkashah* (petition) – into one *berakhah*, and thus advocates the shorter format. Rambam, in his commentary to the Mishnah, states that the *halakhah* is as Rabbi Akiva held, thereby implying that he disagrees with Rabbi Tarfon. However, in his *Yad ha-Ḥazakah* (*Hilkhot Ḥameẓ u-Maẓẓah* 8:5), Rambam records both versions, at first mentioning the shorter version, and then adding that in contemporary times the *ḥatimah* is recited as well. He does not see the two positions as contradictory

The issue, then, is indeed not one of differing conceptual positions but of differing chronologies. Rabbi Tarfon, as an older contemporary of Rabbi Akiva, was active while the Temple was standing. This is evident from a passage in the Sifre (Num. 75) that discusses the eligibility of one who is blemished to blow the trumpets in the Temple. Rabbi Tarfon reported that he had seen just such an occurence, and Rabbi Akiva, working from logic rather than memory, correctly guided Rabbi Tarfon to a more accurate recollection. Thus, Rabbi Tarfon's advocacy of a short *berakhah* reflects his context. Rabbi Akiva's longer *berakhah*, with its aspirations of redemption, is reflective of his reality following the destruction.

(*Reshimot*)

The Gemara (*Pesaḥim* 108a-b) states that women (normally exempt from time-linked positive *miẓvot*) are obligated in the *miẓvah* of drinking the four cups of wine at the *Seder* because they were included in the miracle of the Exodus. *Tosafot* (*Pesaḥim* 108b, s.v. *hayu be-oto ha-nes*) ask what the distinction is between the *miẓvot* of the four cups of wine, reading *Megillat Ester* on Purim and lighting Ḥanukkah candles, in all of which women are obligated because they were included in the relevant miracles, and the *miẓvah* of dwelling in the *sukkah*, in which women are not obligated, even though they were included in the miraculous divine protection of *Keneset Yisrael* during their sojourn in the desert.

Rabbi Moshe Soloveitchik offered the following answer to *Tosafot*'s question. The principle that women are obligated as to a positive time-linked *miẓvah* that pertains to a miracle in which women were included is an operative principle

us to reach this night to eat *maẓẓah* and *maror*. So too, Lord, our God and God of our ancestors, enable us to reach other holidays and festivals that will come to us in peace with happiness in the

---

only where the *kiyum ha-miẓvah* of the pertinent *miẓvah* consists of *pirsumei nissa*, the publicizing of the miracle. The distinguishing characteristic of the *miẓvot* of the four cups of wine, reading *Megillat Ester* and lighting Ḥanukkah candles is not only that women were included in the miracle of the holiday, but also that the *kiyum ha-miẓvah*, the entire character and essence, of each of these *miẓvot* consists of *pirsumei nissa*. On the other hand, with respect to the *miẓvah* of *sukkah*, although it is true that women were included in the miracle, the *kiyum ha-miẓvah* of the *miẓvah* does not consist of *pirsumei nissa* per se but of dwelling in the *sukkah*.

Continuing his analysis, Rabbi Moshe Soloveitchik further stated that the definitive evidence of whether the *kiyum ha-miẓvah* of a particular *miẓvah* consists of *pirsumei nissa* is whether the *berakhah* of *she-asah nissim* is recited in connection with the performance of the *miẓvah*. This is clearly the case in connection with the *miẓvot* of reading the *Megillah* and lighting Ḥanukkah candles, whose *berakhot* include *she-asah nissim*. As for the *miẓvah* of drinking the four cups of wine at the *Seder*, the *berakhah* of *asher ge'-alanu* is the equivalent of *she-asah nissim*. The view that the *berakhah* of *asher ge'-alanu* is the equivalent of *she-asah nissim* is expressed by Rabbi Yosef Tuv Elem in his *piyut* for *Shabat ha-Gadol*, *Elokei ha-Ruḥot*. In referring to *Kiddush*, he states "*ve-eino omer nes 'adayin*," that the *berakhah* of *she-asah nissim* is not included in *Kiddush* (where we would have expected) because it is properly included in the body of the Haggadah, and, "*ve-ra'u'i le-khaflo ayin*," it would not be appropriate to recite the *berakhah* twice. The *miẓvah* of *sukkah*, on the other hand, is not accompanied by the *berakhah* of *she-asah nissim*, which clearly indicates that the *kiyum ha-miẓvah* of *miẓvat sukkah* does not consist of *pirsumei nissa*.

(*Reshimot*)

כֵּן ה' אֱ-לֹהֵינוּ וֵא-לֹהֵי אֲבוֹתֵינוּ יַגִּיעֵנוּ לְמוֹעֲדִים וְלִרְגָלִים אֲחֵרִים When Maimonides describes the order of events on the fifteenth night of Nisan (*Hilkhot Ḥameẓ u-Maẓẓah* 8:1), he "forgets" temporarily that he is living approximately one thousand years after the destruction of the Temple and paints the image of the service of this holy festival night in the wealth of colors that dazzle the eyes, that reflect the Passover service as it was celebrated thousands of years ago in ancient Jerusalem and as it once again will be celebrated in the era of the Messiah. Our

לְשָׁלוֹם. שְׂמֵחִים בְּבִנְיַן עִירֶךָ, וְשָׂשִׂים בַּעֲבוֹדָתֶךָ, וְנֹאכַל שָׁם מִן הַזְּבָחִים וּמִן הַפְּסָחִים (במוצש"ק יש אומרים: מִן הַפְּסָחִים וּמִן הַזְּבָחִים), אֲשֶׁר יַגִּיעַ דָּמָם עַל קִיר מִזְבַּחֲךָ לְרָצוֹן, וְנוֹדֶה לְךָ שִׁיר חָדָשׁ, עַל גְּאֻלָּתֵנוּ וְעַל פְּדוּת נַפְשֵׁנוּ. בָּרוּךְ אַתָּה יְיָ, גָּאַל יִשְׂרָאֵל:

בָּרוּךְ אַתָּה יְיָ, אֱלֹהֵינוּ מֶלֶךְ הָעוֹלָם, בּוֹרֵא פְּרִי הַגָּפֶן:

שותים בהסיבת שמאל.

---

great master pays no attention to the cruel and bitter present. However, from time to time, he bestirs himself from his ideal dream and romantic vision and finds himself confronted with an exile filled with nightmares and terrors. He states, "So, Lord, our God…bring us to other festivals happy in the building of the city and joyous in Your service…" The present time is only a historical anomaly. The *halakhah* remains in full force, and we hope for and eagerly await the day of Israel's redemption when the ideal world will triumph over the profane reality.

(*Halakhic Man*)

מִן הַזְּבָחִים וּמִן הַפְּסָחִים אֲשֶׁר יַגִּיעַ דָּמָם עַל קִיר מִזְבַּחֲךָ In the *berakhah* at the conclusion of *Maggid,* we pray that we shall return to Jerusalem and eat there from the *zevaḥim* and the *pesaḥim* "whose blood has reached the wall of the altar." The reference to the blood reaching the wall of the altar is significant. There are two ways that blood can be brought onto the altar. Some sacrifices require that the blood be sprinkled on the altar, *zerikah*, while other sacrifices require that blood be poured on the altar, *shefikhah. Zevaḥim* in this blessing refers to the *korban ḥagigah* that is brought on the fourteenth of Nisan and whose blood is required to be sprinkled on the altar. The requirement for the *korban Pesaḥ*, however, is that its blood be poured on the altar. The *berakhah* therefore employs more generic language, "whose blood has reached the wall of the altar," to incorporate both *zerikah* and *shefikhah*.

(*Reshimot*)

rebuilding of Your city, and with rejoicing in Your service [in the *Beit ha-Mikdash*]. Then we shall eat of the sacrifices and of the Passover-offerings [*on a Saturday night some invert the order to "of the Passover-offerings and of the sacrifices"*] whose blood shall be sprinkled on the wall of Your altar for acceptance; and we shall thank You with a new song for our redemption and for the deliverance of our souls. Blessed are You, Lord, who redeemed Israel.

Blessed are You, Lord, our God, King of the universe, who creates the fruit of the vine.

Drink the wine while reclining on the left.

עַל גְּאֻלָּתֵנוּ ועַל פְּדוּת נַפְשֵׁנוּ When we say in the Haggadah, "We shall say before You a new song *al ge'ullatenu ve-al pedut nafshenu*, for our redemption and the freedom of our souls," we refer to the two kinds of slavery. First, *ge'ullatenu* indicates that we were set free from juridic-political slavery. Second, *al pedut nafshenu* means that we have rid ourselves of the very restrictive slave personality. The political-juridic aspect is called in our halakhic terminology *kinyan mamon* – the property rights a master has on the slave. The personalistic aspect is called *kinyan issur*, the limitations imposed upon the slave because of his strange and peculiar personality.

The slave is disqualified from testifying in civil or criminal cases simply because we do not trust the slave personality. First, the slave is a person without options; the possibility of choosing between two alternatives has been denied to him. The greatness of man – his dignity and his creativity – is expressed in his freedom of will and in his ability to choose. A slave is never confronted with two alternatives. He makes no decisions; someone always does it for him. He has no faith in himself, and he is psychologically unable to cope with situations.

(*Festival of Freedom*)

רָחְצָה

נוטלים ידים ומברכים:

בָּרוּךְ אַתָּה יְיָ, אֱלֹהֵינוּ מֶלֶךְ הָעוֹלָם, אֲשֶׁר קִדְּשָׁנוּ בְּמִצְוֹתָיו, וְצִוָּנוּ עַל נְטִילַת יָדָיִם:

מוֹצִיא, מַצָּה

מגביה את שלוש המצות ומברך:

בָּרוּךְ אַתָּה יְיָ, אֱלֹהֵינוּ מֶלֶךְ הָעוֹלָם, הַמּוֹצִיא לֶחֶם מִן הָאָרֶץ:

מוֹצִיא, מַצָּה Raavad (*Hilkhot Ḥamez̧ u-Mazz̧ah* 6:5) maintains that adding flavoring to *maz̧z̧ah* after the completion of the baking process does not change the status of a *maz̧z̧ah* from *leḥem oni* to *maz̧z̧ah ashirah*. *Sha'ar ha-Melekh* notes that the Raavad's position seems to contradict an explicit Gemara. In explaining why the Mishnah disqualifies using the *maz̧z̧ah* of the offering of the *nazir* as *leḥem oni*, the Talmud (*Pesaḥim* 38b) explains, among other considerations, that this *maz̧z̧ah* is "*maz̧z̧ot* spread with oil" (Num. 6:15) and thereby is rendered *maz̧z̧ah ashirah*, even though the oil is spread onto the *maz̧z̧ah* after it is baked.

We may understand Raavad's position by viewing *leḥem oni* as a defining quality of the bread itself. Since the flour and water become bread through the baking process, it is at that time that the *maz̧z̧ah* must be categorized as either *leḥem oni* or *maz̧z̧ah ashirah*. Once it has been categorized as *leḥem oni*, externally spreading oil onto it will not change its essential previously established status. However, in the case of the *nazir* offering, the Torah requires that the *maz̧z̧ah* be brought with the oil, making the latter *mez̧tareif*, associated conceptually – if not physically – with the *maz̧z̧ah* and thereby rendering it *maz̧z̧ah ashirah*.

Rambam writes (*Hilkhot Ḥamez̧ u-Maz̧z̧ah* 5:20) that "on the first day it is forbidden to knead and form the dough with anything but water – not because of a fear of *ḥamez̧*, but rather so that the *maz̧z̧ah* will be *leḥem oni*. And it is only on the first day that we require *zikaron*, a remembrance, of *leḥem oni*." Some commentators (e.g., *Maggid Mishnah*) suggest that this ruling is limited to the single portion of *maz̧z̧ah shel miz̧vah* that is eaten during the *Seder*. However, Rambam is formulating a prohibition against preparing *maz̧z̧ah ashirah* and not saying that such *maz̧z̧ah* cannot be used to fulfill one's obligation. This is clear from Rambam's placement of this *halakhah* – it is only in the next chapter that he discusses the *miz̧vah* of *maz̧z̧ah*. This is an independent requirement

RAḤẒAH

The hands are washed followed by recital of the following blessing:

Blessed are You, Lord, our God, King of the universe, who has sanctified us with His commandments and commanded us concerning the washing of the hands.

MOẒI, MAẒẒAH

The three maẓẓot are raised and the following blessing said:

Blessed are You, Lord, our God, King of the universe, who brings forth bread from the earth.

---

that *zikhron leḥem oni* be maintained beyond the *Seder* night throughout the first day (see *Ḥiddushei Maran Riz ha-Levi* 6:5).

It is clear that the prohibition pertains not simply to preparing *maẓẓah ashirah* but to eating it on the first day. It was therefore the custom of Rav Hayim to not eat *kneidlakh* ("maẓẓah balls") even though he ate *gebrokts* (*maẓẓah* that subsequently came into contact with water) for the rest of the holiday.

(*Reshimot*)

Rambam states (*Hilkhot Ḥameẓ u-Maẓẓah* 6:10), "Everyone is obligated to eat *maẓẓah*, even women and slaves. Children who are able to consume bread must be trained in this *miẓvah*, and we feed them a *ka-zayit* of *maẓẓah*. As for the sick or elderly who cannot eat, we soak a *maẓẓah* and feed it to them." Note that Rambam specifies that the obligation to train a young child in the *miẓvah* of eating *maẓẓah* applies only to a child who is able to consume a *ka-zayit* of *maẓẓah*. Rambam does not rule that the obligation to train a child requires that one soak a *maẓẓah* and feed it to a child who is too young to eat an ordinary *maẓẓah*. The general principle that can be inferred from Rambam's statement is that the *miẓvah* of *ḥinnukh*, the obligation to train a child in the performance of a *miẓvah*, begins at the age when the child is able to perform the *miẓvah* fully.

Similarly, the Gemara's discussion of the *miẓvah* of *lulav* demonstrates the principle that the requirement of *ḥinnukh* applies only once a child is old enough to perform the *miẓvah* in its entirety. The Gemara teaches (*Sukkah* 42a) that the *miẓvah* of *lulav* is fulfilled by merely picking up the *lulav*. Nonetheless,

מניח את המצה התחתונה, ואוחז את העליונה והאמצעית הפרוסה ומברך "על אכילת מצה", ויכוון בברכה זו גם על המצה שבכריכה ובאפיקומן.

בָּרוּךְ אַתָּה יְיָ, אֱלֹהֵינוּ מֶלֶךְ הָעוֹלָם, אֲשֶׁר קִדְּשָׁנוּ בְּמִצְוֹתָיו וְצִוָּנוּ עַל אֲכִילַת מַצָּה:

---

the Gemara goes on to state that the *mizvah* of *ḥinnukh* as to *lulav* applies only once the child understands how to perform the *na'anu'im*, the waving of the *lulav*. The Gemara's statement about *ḥinnukh* is readily understandable if we view the *na'anu'im* as an integral part of the *mizvah* of *lulav*. Even though the child may be capable of picking up the *lulav*, *ḥinnukh* is required only once the child is at the stage where he is able to perform the entire *mizvah* of *lulav*, including the *na'anu'im*. (The view that the *na'anu'im* are an integral part of the *mizvah* of *lulav* is the basis for Rabbi Moshe Soloveitchik's practice of reciting the *berakhah* over the *lulav* immediately before reciting *Hallel*. By so doing, the *berakhah* applies as well to the *na'anu'im*, which are performed during the recitation of *Hallel*. This practice differs from the custom of the Hasidim, who recite the *berakhah* over the *lulav* in the *sukkah* before the *Shaḥarit* service.)

An additional principle pertaining to the *mizvah* of *mazzah* that can be derived from Rambam's statement is that the optimal manner in which to perform the *mizvah* of *mazzah* is to eat *mazzah* that has not been soaked to make it easier to eat. This principle is apparent from Rambam's view, as noted above, that a child who is able to eat only soaked *mazzah* has not yet reached the stage of being obligated in the *mizvah* of *mazzah*. The elderly and infirm, who have already reached the stage of being obligated in the *mizvah* of *mazzah*, are required to eat soaked *mazzah* if that is the only way in which they can perform the *mizvah*, even though eating soaked *mazzah* is not the optimal manner in which the *mizvah* is to be performed.

(*Reshimot*)

The Rabbis (*Yerushalmi Pesaḥim* 10:1) liken a person who eats *mazzah* on *erev Pesaḥ* to a person who has intimate relations with his bride without having completed the *nissu'in* part of the marriage ceremony. Indeed, Or Zaru'a (2:256) points out that just as there are seven blessings in the marriage ceremony, there are seven blessings recited at the *Seder* prior to eating the *mazzah*. There are various ways of counting these seven. For example, *Menorat ha-Ma'or* (chap. 2) lists *ha-gefen*, *she-heḥeyanu*, *al netilat yadayim* prior to the first dipping (in accordance with those who say a *berakhah* for that washing), *bore peri ha-adamah* on the *karpas*, *asher ge'alanu*, not *ha-gefen* on the second cup (following those who do not say a *berakhah* on the second and fourth cup), *al netilat yadayim* prior to the meal, and *al akhilat mazzah*. Others present a different reckoning of the seven blessings.

The bottom maẓẓah is put down and the following blessing
recited over the broken maẓẓah and the top one:
(One should have in mind that this blessing also applies to the korekh which
will be with the third maẓẓah and the eating of the Afikoman.)

Blessed are You, Lord, our God, King of the universe, who has sanctified us with His commandments and commanded us concerning the eating of Maẓẓah.

However we account for these seven *berakhot*, the concept is clear. The groom waits with great emotion for his bride, but halakhically there must be a *matir*, a formal act of sanction, which allows the tension of anticipation to emerge into the reality of their relationship. Eating *maẓẓah* gives us the taste of redemption. We anticipate with a great longing re-enacting our rush to freedom. Just as the *sheva berakhot* under the *ḥupah* act as the *matir* for the groom, the *Seder* and its *berakhot* act as a *matir* for eating the *maẓẓah* and all that it evokes.

(*Reshimot*)

The practice that is generally followed on the night of the *Seder* is to take three *maẓẓot* and split one of them. This is done to fulfill two separate requirements. The first, which relates specifically to the *Seder*, is *leḥem oni* (Deut. 16:3), a phrase that describes the *maẓẓah* as the bread of affliction or poverty. This requires that we break a *maẓẓah* in half, just as a poor person's bread is usually not whole. The second requirement is not specifically related to *Pesaḥ*, but stems from the fact that the night is also a *yom tov*, which calls for *leḥem mishneh*, two whole loaves. This is in accordance with the opinion of *Tosafot* (*Pesaḥim* 116, s.v. *mah* and the *Shulḥan Arukh* (*Oraḥ Ḥayyim* 475:1)).

Rambam (*Hilkhot Ḥamez u-Maẓẓah* 8:6) requires only two *maẓẓot*, one of which is to be broken. Apparently, he is of the view that the *leḥem oni* imperative cancels the requirement for *leḥem mishneh*, in that the two concepts are contradictory. If so, why does he require two *maẓẓot*? The answer is that the broken *maẓẓah* alone will not suffice even though it is *leḥem oni*. A complete *maẓẓah* is also required, because even during the week, it is preferable to make a blessing on a complete loaf and not a broken one (see *Berakhot* 39b and Rambam, *Hilkhot Berakhot* 7:4). The reason for this is that a whole loaf is considered more *ḥashuv*, significant, and it is appropriate to make a blessing on an item that is more *ḥashuv*, if available.

(*Reshimot*)

עַל אֲכִילַת מַצָּה *Ḥamez*, leavened bread, represents the finished, the perfect, the fully grown, the end of the process, the *homo theoreticus* in his full glory and

בוצע כזית מהמצה העליונה וכזית מהפרוסה ואוכל את שני הזיתים יחדיו בהסיבת
שמאל, ויזהר לכתחילה לבלוע לכל הפחות כזית בבת אחת ובדיעבד תוך כדי אכילת
פרס. ואם אינו יכול לאכול את שני הזיתים ביחד יאכל את השלימה תחילה.

☙ מָרוֹר

נוטלים כזית מרור, טובלים בחרוסת ומנערים, ויכוון בברכת
"על אכילת מרור" גם אל המרור שבכריכה.

בָּרוּךְ אַתָּה יְיָ, אֱלֹהֵינוּ מֶלֶךְ הָעוֹלָם, אֲשֶׁר קִדְּשָׁנוּ בְּמִצְוֹתָיו וְצִוָּנוּ עַל
אֲכִילַת מָרוֹר:

ואוכלים בלי הסיבה.

---

majesty. It can never bring man into the presence of God. Adult man is too
practical-minded, too rational to trust his feelings and his intuitive questing,
too impersonal to feel the living experience of fellowship with God. He is too
proud, and his pride consists of the fact that he is involved in the process of
growth, ascent and progress.

Maẓẓah is the symbolic transcript of the intimate experience of childlike
clinging to and longing for God, of finding Him not at the level of noesis but
at the level of naïveté, faith, and feeling. The delivery from all restrictions and
limitations (*Miẓrayim–meẓarim*), the ascent from bondman to freeman, is
attainable through the identification with the root-experience of man, with
his childhood commitments and perceptions, with the uncritical surrender
to and naive trust in God, with the incomplete *ratio*, with the pre-adulthood
notions and verities.

Of course, man does not have to remain in this state of negation of his
intellectual self. Later, he may turn into a heroic adult who translates faith
into terms of a higher knowledge, into categories of a more sensitive intellect.
At the second level of faith, there may be harmony between the knowing I
and the believing I, between the adult and the child, between one's pre-noetic
perceptions of God and his noetic certitudes. One may awaken to the world of
faith united with that of cognition. However, the prelude to the illumination
of one's experiences is the self-denial of the mature person and the emergence
of the child. "When Israel was a child, then I loved him" (Hos. 11:1).

(*Family Redeemed*)

טוֹבְלִים בַּחֲרוֹסֶת The Mishnah (*Pesaḥim* 114a) states, "They brought before him
maẓẓah, *ḥazeret*, and *ḥaroset*, but *ḥaroset* is not a *miẓvah*. Rabbi Eliezer ben

The Seder leader distributes a ka-zayit of each of the two mazzot to each of the assembled; the mazzah is eaten while reclining on the left.

MAROR

Take a ka-zayit of the maror, dip it into the ḥaroset and shake off the ḥaroset. (One should have in mind that this blessing also applies to the maror eaten with the korekh.)

Blessed are You, Lord, our God, King of the universe, who has sanctified us with His commandments and commanded us concerning the eating of *maror*.

Eat the maror without reclining.

Zadok said it is a *mizvah*." The seeming conclusion in the Gemara is that the only purpose of *ḥaroset* is for *kafa*, to counter the sharpness of the *maror*, apparently aligned with the opinion of the Rabbis that *ḥaroset* is not a *mizvah*. Rambam writes in his commentary to the Mishnah that according to Rabbi Eliezer ben Zadok's opinion that *ḥaroset* is a *mizvah*, one is obligated to eat a required measurement – *ka-zayit* – of *ḥaroset* and recite a *berakhah* on its consumption. But the *halakhah* is not in accord with Rabbi Eliezer ben Zadok. However, in *Hilkhot Ḥamez u-Mazzah* (7:11) Rambam writes: *Ḥaroset* is a rabbinic *mizvah* to remember the mortar [used by the Jews when they were slaves in Egypt].... One dips spices into it [the *ḥaroset*] similar to the straw in mortar, and brings it onto the table on the *Seder* night." Despite this characterization of *ḥaroset* as a *mizvah*, Rambam makes no mention here of a requirement to eat a *ka-zayit* or to recite a *berakhah*.

Leḥem Mishneh therefore concludes that Rambam reversed himself on two levels from what he said in the commentary to the Mishnah. First, the *halakhah* is in accordance with Rabbi Eliezer ben Zadok that *ḥaroset* is a *mizvah*; second, despite the fact that it is a *mizvah*, it does not warrant or necessitate either a *berakhah* or *ka-zayit*. However, even *Leḥem Mishneh* acknowledges that this answer does not suffice, because there is no reason why *ḥaroset* should be different from all other rabbinic *mizvot* that require a blessing.

It would seem, therefore, that according to Rambam, *ḥaroset* is a *mizvah* that does not warrant a *berakhah* because there is no specific act associated with it. The *mizvah* is simply to have *ḥaroset* present on the table. Even though, according to Rambam, one must dip the *karpas*, *mazzah*, and *maror* in the *ḥaroset*, the act of dipping is not the *mizvah*; rather it is only a practical way to

כּוֹרֵךְ

נוטלים כזית מהמצה התחתונה וכזית מרור, וכורכם יחד וטובלים בחרוסת (מחבר סי' תע"ה ס"א) ויש נוהגים שלא לטובלו (רמ"א שם), ואומר:

זֵכֶר לְמִקְדָּשׁ כְּהִלֵּל: כֵּן עָשָׂה הִלֵּל בִּזְמַן שֶׁבֵּית הַמִּקְדָּשׁ הָיָה קַיָּם. הָיָה כּוֹרֵךְ (פֶּסַח) מַצָּה וּמָרוֹר וְאוֹכֵל בְּיַחַד, לְקַיֵּם מַה שֶּׁנֶּאֱמַר: עַל־מַצּוֹת וּמְרֹרִים יֹאכְלֻהוּ: (במדבר ט', י"א)

ואוכלים בהסיבת שמאל.

---

include the *ḥaroset* in the context of the meal. No *berakhah* is recited because there is no *ma'aseh mizvah*, an action associated with a *mizvah*; there is only a *kiyum mizvah*, fulfillment of the *mizvah*.

This explains why Rambam wrote, in describing the *mizvah* of *ḥaroset*, "and they bring it onto the table." Rambam was not simply describing how to arrange the *Seder* table; he was detailing and noting that the *mizvah* of *ḥaroset* was performed by simply having it present on the table, to remind the participants of the slavery and redemption from Egypt. In this respect, Rambam changed his position from that in his commentary on the Mishnah, where he maintained that the *mizvah* of *ḥaroset* was a *mizvat akhilah*, a requirement to eat the *ḥaroset*, thus requiring a *ka-zayit* and a *berakhah*.

(*Reshimot*)

כּוֹרֵךְ The Talmud (*Pesaḥim* 115a) presents a dispute between Hillel and the Rabbis as to the proper method for eating the *mazzah* and the *maror* at the *Seder*. Hillel requires *Korekh* and is of the view that in the time of the Temple the *mazzah* and *maror* were required to be wrapped and eaten together. There are two opinions as to the position of the Rabbis: either that the *mazzah* and *maror* must be eaten separately or that they may be eaten either separately or together. The Gemara concludes that nowadays, since it has not been established whether the *halakhah* follows Hillel or the Rabbis, one should first eat the *mazzah* separately with a *berakhah* and then eat the *maror* separately with a *berakhah*; then one should wrap them and eat them together without a *berakhah* as a remembrance to the Temple according to Hillel.

There is a difference of opinion between *Tosafot* and Rambam as to how *Korekh* is to be understood now that the Temple does not exist. According to *Tosafot*, since there is doubt whether the *halakhah* follows the Rabbis or

KOREKH

A ka-zayit of the third mazzah and a ka-zayit of the maror, which is dipped in ḥaroset, are combined like a sandwich. Some do not dip it in the ḥaroset.

In remembrance of the Temple, according to Hillel. Thus did Hillel do at the time of the Temple: He would combine the Passover lamb, *mazzah* and *maror* and eat them together, as it said: "They shall eat it with *mazzah* and bitter herbs."

Eat the korekh while reclining on the left.

Hillel, we follow both opinions, eating the *mazzah* and *maror* separately in accordance with the view of the Rabbis and eating them together as Hillel posits. According to Hillel, the Gemara cites *zekher le-mikdash* as Hillel's "sandwich" consisted of *mazzah, maror,* and *Pesaḥ*. Nowadays, when we do not have the *korban Pesaḥ*, the *mazzah* in *Korekh* serves a dual role, as the *mazzah* itself and also to remind us of the *korban Pesaḥ*. Because *Korekh* is eaten as a result of a doubt as to whether the *halakhah* follows Hillel or the Rabbis, no *berakhah* is recited.

Unlike *Tosafot*, Rambam is of the view that the directive of *Korekh zekher le-mikdash* is not related to the fulfillment of the *mizvah* of *mazzah* and is not an expression of Hillel's position as to the manner in which the *mizvah* of *mazzah* is to be fulfilled. Rambam (*Hilkhot Ḥamez u-Mazzah* 8:6) states that in the time of the Temple one was permitted to eat the *mazzah* and *maror* either together or separately. From this statement, it is apparent that Rambam accepted the position of the Rabbis that once one has eaten the *mazzah* and *maror* independently, one has definitely fulfilled the *mizvah* of *mazzah* and *maror*. According to Rambam, *Korekh* is a new rabbinic directive that was established as a remembrance of the *korban Pesaḥ* and is not a fulfillment of the *mizvot* of *mazzah* and *maror*. Consistent with this view, Rambam (*Hilkhot Ḥamez u-Mazzah* 8:8) refers to *Korekh* as a remembrance to the Temple, but does not cite it as a fulfillment of the position of Hillel. The Gemara's statement that we do not recite a *berakhah* on the *Korekh* is not, as *Tosafot* understood, because of a doubt, but rather that fundamentally the *berakhah* does not relate to *Korekh*, because it is not a fulfillment of the *mizvah* of *mazzah* and *maror*, but only a symbolic remembrance of *korban Pesaḥ*, and thus not susceptible to *berakhah*.

This conceptual argument results in the following practical difference. According to Rambam, because the *mizvah* of *Korekh* is an independent commemoration and is unrelated to the fulfillment of the *mizvot* of *mazzah* and

שֻׁלְחָן עוֹרֵךְ

נוהגים לאכול ביצה בתוך הסעודה, וראוי להדר לאכול הביצה שבקערה. אוכלים ושותים כברכת ה' אשר נתן. ויזהר שלא ימלא כריסו יותר מדי, כדי שיאכל כזית אפיקומן לתיאבון.

---

maror, one is permitted to speak or interrupt between the *berakhot* over the *mazzah* and *maror* and *Korekh*. According to *Tosafot*, however, since *Korekh* constitutes a manner of fulfilling the *mizvah* of *mazzah* and *maror*, and should therefore be included in the *berakhah* on the *mazzah* and *maror*, one should not speak or interrupt from the time one recites the *berakhah* on the *mazzah* until after the completion of *Korekh*. The *Shulḥan Arukh* (*Oraḥ Ḥayyim* 475:1) rules that one should be stringent and not speak or interrupt from the time of the *berakhah* on the *mazzah* until the completion of *Korekh*. *Be'ur Halakhah* (*Oraḥ Ḥayyim* 475, s.v. *ve-omer*) adds that one should not recite *zekher le-mikdash ke-Hillel* before eating the *Korekh* since this, too, is considered an interruption.

(*Reshimot*)

As noted above, there is a dispute in the Talmud (*Pesaḥim* 115a) regarding how a person should properly fulfill the *mizvah* of eating the *mazzah* and *maror*. Hillel was of the view that a person should wrap them together and eat them as a "sandwich," whereas the Rabbis said that a person could eat them together or separately, however one wished. A third opinion, that of Rav Yohanan, is that the Rabbis require that the *mazzah* and *maror* be eaten separately, for if eaten together they would nullify each other. In describing the *Seder* when the Temple still stood, Rambam (*Hilkhot Ḥamez u-Mazzah* 8:6) writes, "he should wrap the *mazzah* and *maror* together...and recite the blessing...'on the eating of *mazzah* and *maror*' and eat them...and if he eats the *mazzah* by itself and the *maror* by itself, he should recite a blessing on this one by itself and on that one by itself." Rambam seemingly rules like the Rabbis, that a person may eat the *mazzah* and *maror* together or separately.

Rambam describes the present-day *Seder*, when the Temple is no longer standing, and states (*Hilkhot Ḥamez u-Mazzah* 8:8) that a person should "recite the blessing regarding the eating of the *mazzah*...and eat it, recite the blessing regarding the eating of the *maror*...and eat it...and then wrap the *mazzah* and *maror*...and eat them without a blessing, as a remembrance to the Temple." However, if Rambam himself writes that in the time of the Temple a person could fulfill his obligation by eating the *mazzah* and *maror* separately, then why today must he also eat them together? As Rambam said, this is an obligation as a remembrance of the Temple, but it was not done at the time of the Temple, so why must one do so today?

SHULḤAN OREKH

Eat a festive meal. Many have the custom to eat an egg with the meal.

The answer to the question is that even the Rabbis who disagreed with Hillel regarding the practical *halakhah* agreed to his fundamental understanding. They, too, felt that the verse "they shall eat it [the *Pesaḥ*] on unleavened bread and bitter herbs" implies that the *maẓẓah* and *maror* should be joined together. However, while Hillel understood that they must be physically wrapped together, the Rabbis believed that the mere fact that both foods came as accompaniments to the *korban Pesaḥ* integrated them and fulfilled the obligation set forth in the verse. Thus, in the time of the Temple one could eat them separately, but today, when the *korban Pesaḥ* no longer exists, the only way to associate and relate them to each other, as Rambam rules, is to physically wrap them together. Nonetheless, the *maẓẓah* and *maror* must also be eaten separately, because if they are eaten together, the *maror* (which nowadays is a rabbinic commandment) would nullify the *maẓẓah* (which is a biblical commandment).

(*Reshimot*)

שֻׁלְחָן עוֹרֵךְ While every meal on *yom tov* is either obligatory or a fulfillment of the *miẓvah* of *simḥat yom tov*, the meal on the night of the *Seder*, beyond the specific obligatory elements, such as *maẓẓah* and *maror*, constitutes its own particular fulfillment. Thus the Rishonim granted it an individual heading in the order of the *Seder*: *Shulḥan Orekh*. On *Pesaḥ* night, there is an obligation to exhibit oneself as an actual, personal beneficiary of the Exodus through overt displays of freedom, *ḥerut* (*Hilkhot Ḥameẓ u-Maẓẓah* 7:6–7). This feeling is created not only by demonstrating the lack of restraints typical of a person in servitude, but also by participating in an active atmosphere of luxury, as typified by the obligation of *haseivah*. We are to demonstrate freedom and not simply relive it internally. If the emotion is too sedate, it is not an experience. The experience should be dynamic, explosive, hypnotic, breaking through the surface and impelling the person to act. "Therefore, when one eats that night, he should eat and drink while he leans in the manner of a free person" (*Hilkhot Ḥameẓ u-Maẓẓah* 7:7). The entire meal, up to and including eating "all that one pleases," joins with the other aspects of the *Seder* night in manifesting *ḥerut* and becomes a vital part of the *miẓvah* of the night. Accordingly, Rama writes (472:7) that ideally we should eat the whole meal in a position of *haseivah*.

This idea may also provide an additional reason for waiting until nightfall before saying *Kiddush* (*Oraḥ Ḥayyim* 472:1). The *Kiddush* that is recited on the

צָפוּן

בגמר הסעודה קודם חצות הלילה נוטלים כזית מהמצה שהצפין לאפיקומן, ולכתחילה שני כזיתים, ואוכלים בהסיבת שמאל.

---

night of *Pesaḥ* has two dimensions. The first is the fulfillment of the requirement to recite *Kiddush* prior to any obligatory Shabbat or *yom tov* meal. The second dimension is that the *Kiddush* of *Pesaḥ* night is an inherent part of *sipur Yeẓi'at Miẓrayim*. *Kiddush* serves as part of the expression of *ḥerut* that the meal accomplishes. It must be recited in the place where the meal is occurring; as implied by Taz, this can be understood not only as the physical place, but also as the chronological place. Thus, just as the meal is an expression of the Exodus and therefore must take place during the actual night of *Pesaḥ*, so, too, is *Kiddush* subject to the same limitation. Further, in describing the obligation of remembering the Exodus, Rambam (*Hilkhot Ḥameẓ u-Maẓẓah* 7:1) explicitly links this *miẓvah* to that of remembering Shabbat. The link between the two is *Kiddush*; just as *Kiddush* is the core fulfillment of the *miẓvah* to remember Shabbat, on *Pesaḥ* night, it becomes integrated into the *miẓvah* of remembering the Exodus.

By extension, any act associated with the meal transcends its usual classification and becomes an event of the *Seder* with its own title. The blessing recited on the *maẓẓah* is not treated simply as a *birkat ha-nehenin* but rather as a *birkat ha-miẓvah* with its own heading: "*Moẓi Maẓẓah*." Likewise, *Birkat ha-Mazon* is not merely that of a typical meal, but is highlighted as "*Barekh*." Indeed, this can explain the Rif's view that it is permitted to recite the *bore peri ha-adamah* on *karpas* on behalf of another person even if one has already recited the *berakhah* himself. One can recite a *birkat ha-nehenin* on behalf of another person only if one will also be eating and thus requires the *berakhah* personally. However, one can recite a *birkat ha-miẓvah* on behalf of another even if one has already fulfilled the obligation. All of the eating on the *Seder* night, and all of the associated activities, attain a special *miẓvah* status on that occasion.

(*Reshimot*)

צָפוּן Rashi (*Pesaḥim* 119b) sees the *afikoman* as the core fulfillment of the *miẓvah* of *maẓẓah*. The fact that the *berakhah* over the *maẓẓah* is not recited on that portion is only a consequence of the fact that the *berakhah* was recited earlier on the initial eating of the *maẓẓah*. Rosh (*Pesaḥim* 10:34), however, sees the *afikoman* as representing the *korban Pesaḥ*; the actual *miẓvah* of *maẓẓah* is fulfilled with the initial eating of *maẓẓah* earlier in the evening.

There is a contradiction in the rulings of Rambam that may reflect an inherent dichotomy within *afikoman*. Rambam rules that *karpas*, *maẓẓah*,

ZAFUN

After the meal, the Afikoman is eaten in the reclining position. Initially, it is preferable to eat two ka-zayit portions. One does not eat or drink after the Afikoman, except for the required cups of wine.

---

and *maror* must be dipped in *ḥaroset* (*Hilkhot Ḥamez̤ u-Maz̤z̤ah* 8:2, 8), but he does not mention *ḥaroset* when speaking of *korban Pesaḥ* and the *afikoman* (*Hilkhot Ḥamez̤ u-Maz̤z̤ah* 8:9). Had he held the view that *afikoman* represents *maz̤z̤ah*, he would have included it among the things to be dipped in *ḥaroset*. He obviously sees *korban Pesaḥ* as representing the redemption; it therefore cannot be dipped in *ḥaroset*, which symbolizes the mortar of slavery. Yet elsewhere (*Hilkhot Ḥamez̤ u-Maz̤z̤ah* 8:9), he subscribes to the position of *Tosafot* that *afikoman* is a fulfillment of *maz̤z̤ah*. Indeed, Rambam (*Hilkhot Ḥamez̤ u-Maz̤z̤ah* 6:11) brings the law of not eating after the *afikoman* in the sixth chapter together with the laws of eating *maz̤z̤ah* and not exclusively in the eighth chapter, which deals with the laws of the *Seder*. This indicates that he considers the obligation to conclude with the taste of *maz̤z̤ah* in one's mouth as a function of the *miz̤vah* of *maz̤z̤ah* and therefore eating after the *afikoman* would create a deficiency in the *miz̤vah* of *maz̤z̤ah*.

Although *maz̤z̤ah* is eaten at the beginning of the meal to ensure that it will be eaten with an appetite, this fulfillment of the *miz̤vah* is deficient. Because *Shulḥan Orekh*, the entire remainder of the meal, is required to be eaten afterwards, the taste of *maz̤z̤ah* does not remain. This creates a deficiency in the *miz̤vah* of *maz̤z̤ah*. Rambam (*Hilkhot Ḥamez̤ u-Maz̤z̤ah* 6:1) writes that there is a biblical obligation to eat *maz̤z̤ah* on the night of the fifteenth of Nisan, and upon eating a *ka-zayit* one has satisfied this obligation. Netziv (preface to *Imrei Shefar*) derives from this that although the minimum amount of *maz̤z̤ah* one is required to eat is *ka-zayit*, any additional *maz̤z̤ah* one eats is also significant and represents a *kiyum*, fulfillment, of the *miz̤vah* of *maz̤z̤ah*. Therefore, the *afikoman* eaten at the end of the meal is a continuation of the original *miz̤vah*. Although the *yom tov* meal canceled the taste of the *maz̤z̤ah* and created a deficiency in the *miz̤vah* of *maz̤z̤ah*, by eating the *afikoman* one is able to retrieve the *miz̤vah* and complete it.

These two perspectives on the *afikoman* affect our understanding of the *halakhah* that it is forbidden to eat any other food after the *afikoman* has been eaten (*Pesaḥim* 119b). If the *afikoman* represents the *korban Pesaḥ*, refraining from other food may be a method of ensuring that the *afikoman* will come at the end of the meal, where it will thus be eaten in a state of satiety (*al hasova*), which is a necessity for the appropriate consumption of sanctified food such as the *korban Pesaḥ*. This is the understanding of Rashbam (s.v. *ke-gon*). Alternatively, if the *afikoman* is essentially the fulfillment of the *miz̤vah* of

בָּרֵךְ:

מוזגים כוס שלישי ונוטלים מים אחרונים.

---

mazzah, the prohibition of eating any further may reflect a requirement inherent in the *mizvah* of *mazzah* (and the *korban Pesaḥ*, when that was practiced) that the taste of the *mazzah* linger in the mouth undiluted. This is the view of *Tosafot* (*Pesaḥim* 120a, *s.v. ein maftirin*).

Furthermore, the two interpretations may impact on the *halakhah* concerning a person who does in fact eat something after the *afikoman*. *Ḥok Ya'akov* (*Oraḥ Ḥayyim* 478:1) states that such a person need not eat the *afikoman* again. *Elyah Rabah* (477:3) disagrees and maintains that if he has not yet said *Birkat ha-Mazon*, he is required to consume another *ka-zayit* of *afikoman*. Apparently, *Elyah Rabah* follows the reasoning that not eating after the *afikoman* is not an independent prohibition but part-and-parcel of the fulfillment of *mazzah* and therefore by eating another *ka-zayit*, one can still retrieve the *mizvah* of *mazzah*. *Ḥok Ya'akov* apparently follows the position of Rosh, namely, that the *afikoman* is representative of the *korban Pesaḥ* and there is an independent prohibition not to eat after the *afikoman* in order to ensure that the *afikoman* is eaten *al ha-sova*. As such, this violation cannot be rectified.

(*Reshimot*)

Rav Hayim would keep the *afikoman* at his side during the entire *Seder* until it was eaten. His reason was that the *afikoman* represents the *korban Pesaḥ*, which, like all sacrifices, becomes disqualified if one is *messi'aḥ da'at*, that is, one's attention is diverted from the *korban* (*Pesaḥim* 34). In this context the *afikoman* is referred to as *zafun* because it is hidden away or guarded.

(*Reshimot*)

קוֹדֶם חֲצוֹת הַלַּיְלָה The Mishnah (*Pesaḥim* 120b) states that after *ḥazot* (midnight) of the *Seder* night, the *korban Pesaḥ* conveys ritual impurity to the hands of those who touch it. The Gemara attributes this ruling to Rabbi Eleazar ben Azariah, who is of the view that the *korban* must be consumed before *ḥazot*. This is extrapolated from the verse "And you shall eat the flesh [of the sacrifice] on this night" (Ex. 12:8). Apparently, when the time for eating the sacrifice has elapsed, it becomes *notar* (sacrificial meat that was not eaten during its allotted time and must be burned). However, *Or Zaru'a* (231) observes that the Tosefta (5:10) seems to contradict this assumption, as it rules that the prohibition of *notar* is violated only if the *korban* is eaten the next day, after dawn.

BAREKH

The third cup is poured and the hands are rinsed with mayim aḥaronim.

Notar, as it exists regarding all sacrifices, stems from the sacred nature of the *korban*, a sanctity that dictates that it will become *notar* the next morning. However, the requirement to eat the *korban Pesaḥ* before *ḥaẓot* is fundamentally distinct from the laws of *notar*; in fact, a separate verse details the application of *notar* to the *Pesaḥ*, "You shall not leave any of it over until the morning" (Ex. 12:10). On the other hand, the deadline of *ḥaẓot* is an independent law associated with the commandment to eat the *korban*. It is not a product of the sanctity of the *korban* but is a condition for the fulfillment of the *miẓvah* of eating the *korban*, similar to the requirement that it be roasted. Accordingly, Rav Hayim explained that the two verses imply two concurrent *miẓvah*-aspect requirements: the obligation to eat this sacrifice on the *Seder* night, as well as the general *miẓvah* that is accomplished when eating the flesh of an offering.

In support of this distinction, we may cite the opinion of Rabbi Eleazar ben Azariah (*Pesaḥim* 120b) that the *maẓẓah* and *maror* must also be eaten before *ḥaẓot*. The Gemara explains that *Ḥazal* derived this law by associating these *miẓvot* with *korban Pesaḥ*. If the deadline of *ḥaẓot* for the *korban* was a result of its inherent sanctity as a sacrifice, it could not have served as a source for the laws of *maẓẓah* and *maror*, which have no sacrificial status. Instead, the requirement of *ḥaẓot* is a stipulation in the fulfillment of the *miẓvah* of eating the *korban Pesaḥ* that is independent of the laws concerning *notar*.

Rabbi Eleazar ben Azariah must also hold that the *korban Pesaḥ* may be eaten only in a manner that fulfills the *miẓvah* to eat it on the *Seder* night (see *Pesaḥim* 41b). This justifies why the *korban* cannot be eaten after *ḥaẓot* in order to fulfill the element that would apply to all sacrifices even after the *miẓvah* of the *Seder* has expired. Touching the *korban* defiles one's hands even at the earlier point of *ḥaẓot*, for the prohibition to eat it applies even before the status of *notar* pertains.

(*Reshimot*)

בָּרֵךְ Man can humanize the physiological and biological function of ingesting nourishment by realizing that the act of eating serves a higher purpose, a more sublime task: sustenance of the body, which is the abode of the spiritual personality. Eating as a means is hallowed by the end, by the goal man pursues. This thought comes to expression in the blessings of *Birkat ha-Mazon*. There is relatedness to an axiological order, to a higher universe.

Eating becomes a worthwhile undertaking, replete in spiritual

שִׁיר הַמַּעֲלוֹת, בְּשׁוּב יְיָ אֶת שִׁיבַת צִיּוֹן הָיִינוּ כְּחֹלְמִים: אָז יִמָּלֵא שְׂחוֹק פִּינוּ וּלְשׁוֹנֵנוּ רִנָּה, אָז יֹאמְרוּ בַגּוֹיִם הִגְדִּיל יְיָ לַעֲשׂוֹת עִם אֵלֶּה: הִגְדִּיל יְיָ לַעֲשׂוֹת עִמָּנוּ הָיִינוּ שְׂמֵחִים: שׁוּבָה יְיָ אֶת שְׁבִיתֵנוּ כַּאֲפִיקִים בַּנֶּגֶב: הַזֹּרְעִים בְּדִמְעָה בְּרִנָּה יִקְצֹרוּ: הָלוֹךְ יֵלֵךְ וּבָכֹה נֹשֵׂא מֶשֶׁךְ הַזָּרַע, בֹּא יָבֹא בְרִנָּה נֹשֵׂא אֲלֻמֹּתָיו: (תהלים קכ"ו)

ויש מוסיפים:

תְּהִלַּת יְיָ יְדַבֶּר־פִּי, וִיבָרֵךְ כָּל־בָּשָׂר שֵׁם קָדְשׁוֹ לְעוֹלָם וָעֶד: (תהלים קמ"ה כ"א) וַאֲנַחְנוּ נְבָרֵךְ יָהּ מֵעַתָּה וְעַד־עוֹלָם הַלְלוּיָהּ: (תהלים קט"ו, י"ח) הוֹדוּ לַייָ כִּי־טוֹב כִּי לְעוֹלָם חַסְדּוֹ: (תהלים קי"ח א') מִי יְמַלֵּל גְּבוּרוֹת יְיָ, יַשְׁמִיעַ כָּל־תְּהִלָּתוֹ: (תהלים ק"ו, ב')

---

meaningfulness and symbolics, if man begins to realize the mystery of organic life, its sustenance through the act of feeding – if one becomes aware of the enigma of the human body, of life in general. Ignorant man is not amazed by anything; nature is a self-explanatory, dynamic system to him, and he does not suspect that the obvious, natural, daily routine constitutes the greatest miracle, defying human imagination and intellectual genius. The term "nature" conveys to the uninitiated the universal answer to all questions. The simplest and the most comprehensible process is the natural one, regulated by unalterable principles. However, to the *homo religiosus* and to the critical scientist, the term "nature," if spelled out correctly, symbolizes the greatest of all problems: the what and the why. It signifies meaningless interdependencies and absurd formal complexities which are determined by laws that, in spite of the fact that we are able in many cases to formulate them mathematically, are bewildering and enigmatic, an eternal mystery.

The recital of the blessings prior to the meal and *Birkat ha-Mazon* after it gives expression to our gratitude to God for His loving-kindness and for the mercy He bestows upon us by sustaining us, lest we vanish into the abyss of nothingness. Wherever God lets His *ḥesed* descend upon us, man stands perplexed and amazed. When man thanks God, he *ipso facto* admits that he did not merit the grace God has showered upon him. In the thanksgiving service, wonder-struck man lifts his hand in reverence and awe, and praises God for the great mystery he experiences, the mystery of being.

(*Festival of Freedom*)

אָז יִמָּלֵא שְׂחוֹק פִּינוּ "Rabbi Yohanan said in the name of Rabbi Shimon the son of Yohai: It is forbidden for a person to fill his mouth with laughter in this

A Song of Ascents. When the Lord will return the exiles of Zion, we will have been like dreamers. Then our mouth will be filled with laughter, and our tongue with joyous song. Then will they say among the nations, "The Lord has done great things for these." The Lord has done great things for us, we were joyful. Lord, return our exiles as streams in the Negev. Those who sow in tears will reap with joyous song. He goes along weeping, carrying the bag of seed; he will surely come [back] with joyous song, carrying his sheaves. (Ps. 126)

Some add:

Now let my mouth declare the Lord's praise and let the whole human race bless his Holy name for all time. (Ps. 145, 21) As for us, we will bless the Lord from now on and forever more: Praise the Lord! (Ps. 115, 18) Give thanks to the Lord for He is good, for His kindness is everlasting. (Ps. 118, 1) Who can describe the mighty deeds of the Lord, or utter all his praise? (Ps. 106, 2)

---

world, for it says (Ps. 126:2), 'Then will our mouth be filled with laughter and our tongue with singing.' When will that be? At the time when 'They shall say among the nations: The Lord has done great things with these' (*Berakhot* 31a)." The Talmud did not intend to recommend suppression of the sense of joy and to replace it with a feeling of gloom. However stately the joy should be at the level of the uncritical emotion, when it is raised to the critical plane (where the awareness commits it to an existential moral order within the personal time experience), the joy cannot endure in isolation from the total life experience of the person about whom this particular emotion centers. The stream of events is reflected not in one state of mind but in the full spectrum of feelings, and the emotional awareness at a certain instant is a microcosm, mirroring not only the dominant emotional motifs – such as joy in the case of a marriage celebration – but the whole range of the emotional cycle. First, the unchecked, reverberating joy passes gradually into calm and quiet, touched with that solemn melancholy which befits one attending a great festival at which two destinies merge into one. Naively, the person surges forward, untarnished and uncontrolled, but immediately the critical awareness intervenes and the withdrawal takes place. The central emotion is joined by its antithesis at the periphery.

(*Out of the Whirlwind*)

כשמברכים בזימון מתחילים כאן:

המזמן אומר:

רַבּוֹתַי נְבָרֵךְ.

המסובים עונים והמזמן חוזר אחריהם:

יְהִי שֵׁם יְיָ מְבֹרָךְ מֵעַתָּה וְעַד עוֹלָם.

המזמן אומר:

בִּרְשׁוּת מָרָנָן וְרַבָּנָן וְרַבּוֹתַי
נְבָרֵךְ (בעשרה אֱלֹהֵינוּ) שֶׁאָכַלְנוּ מִשֶּׁלוֹ.

המסובים עונים:

בָּרוּךְ (בעשרה אֱלֹהֵינוּ) שֶׁאָכַלְנוּ מִשֶּׁלוֹ וּבְטוּבוֹ חָיִינוּ.

וחוזר המזמן:

בָּרוּךְ (בעשרה אֱלֹהֵינוּ) שֶׁאָכַלְנוּ מִשֶּׁלוֹ וּבְטוּבוֹ חָיִינוּ.

יחיד אינו אומר:

בָּרוּךְ הוּא וּבָרוּךְ שְׁמוֹ.

כשאין זימון מתחילים כאן:

בָּרוּךְ אַתָּה יְיָ, אֱלֹהֵינוּ מֶלֶךְ הָעוֹלָם, הַזָּן אֶת הָעוֹלָם כֻּלּוֹ בְּטוּבוֹ בְּחֵן בְּחֶסֶד וּבְרַחֲמִים, הוּא נוֹתֵן לֶחֶם לְכָל בָּשָׂר, כִּי לְעוֹלָם חַסְדּוֹ. וּבְטוּבוֹ הַגָּדוֹל תָּמִיד לֹא חָסַר לָנוּ, וְאַל יֶחְסַר לָנוּ מָזוֹן לְעוֹלָם וָעֶד. בַּעֲבוּר שְׁמוֹ

הַמְזַמֵּן אוֹמֵר Man has the choice to eat either in hiding, alone, like the beast in its lair, or in community, before the Lord. When eating rises to a great service, to an experience of God found and held not by reason but by feeling the discomfort and embarrassment of those who have not, and inviting them to join those who have, a new community is born, a community which consists of master, mistress, servant and pauper. The birth of this community hallows the meal and endows it with sanctity. There is no division into host and guest, into master and servant, into giver and recipient, into a generous philanthropist and an embarrassed individual who is in need.

There is a strange halakhic institution, the *zimmun*, through which the whole *Birkat ha-Mazon* assumes a new dimension. Saying *Birkat ha-Mazon* with a *zimmun*, if truly understood and implemented, represents communal recital of the blessings – one person says them aloud and the rest of the com-

When the zimmun is said before Birkat HaMazzon, begin here.

The Leader says:

Gentlemen let us say the blessing.

The others respond:

May the Name of the Lord be blessed from now and for ever.

The Leader repeats the response and continues:
(If a minyan is present, the phrase "our God" is added)

With the permission of my masters and my teachers
let us bless [our God], He of whose bounty we have eaten.

The others respond:

Blessed be [our God], He of whose bounty we have eaten.

The leader repeats this response and all continue.

(If the zimmun is not said, all begin here.)

Blessed are You, Lord, our God, King of the universe, who, in His goodness, feeds the whole world with grace, with kindness and with mercy. He gives food to all flesh, for His kindness is everlasting. Through His great goodness to us continuously we do not lack food, and may we never lack it, for the sake of His great Name. For He is a [benevolent] God who feeds and sustains all, does good to all, and prepares food for all His creatures whom He has created. (As it is said: You open Your hand and satisfy the desire of every living thing.) Blessed are You, Lord, who provides food for all.

---

pany listens quietly and answers, "Amen." (Such is the ideal practice of *zimmun*, though we do not implement it in this fashion today – see *Mishnah Berurah* 183:27.) The idea which this *halakhah* tried to translate into a ceremonial is that of a community formed by the act of eating. The *se'udah* is designed not only to satisfy man's physical needs, but also to take him out of his sheltered seclusion and loneliness and let him join the thou. Eating becomes a cohesive force bringing together people who were shut up in their own small worlds and coalescing them into a community. The *halakhah* was aware of the fact that a meal partaken together unites people, fosters friendship, and fashions a company of eaters which in the long run may become a community of God-seekers and the God-committed.

(*Festival of Freedom*)

הַגָּדוֹל, כִּי הוּא אֵל זָן וּמְפַרְנֵס לַכֹּל, וּמֵטִיב לַכֹּל, וּמֵכִין מָזוֹן לְכָל בְּרִיּוֹתָיו אֲשֶׁר בָּרָא (כָּאָמוּר: פּוֹתֵחַ אֶת יָדֶךָ, וּמַשְׂבִּיעַ לְכָל חַי רָצוֹן). בָּרוּךְ אַתָּה יְיָ, הַזָּן אֶת הַכֹּל:

נוֹדֶה לְּךָ יְיָ אֱלֹהֵינוּ עַל שֶׁהִנְחַלְתָּ לַאֲבוֹתֵינוּ, אֶרֶץ חֶמְדָּה טוֹבָה וּרְחָבָה, וְעַל שֶׁהוֹצֵאתָנוּ יְיָ אֱלֹהֵינוּ מֵאֶרֶץ מִצְרַיִם, וּפְדִיתָנוּ מִבֵּית עֲבָדִים, וְעַל בְּרִיתְךָ שֶׁחָתַמְתָּ בִּבְשָׂרֵנוּ, וְעַל תּוֹרָתְךָ שֶׁלִּמַּדְתָּנוּ, וְעַל חֻקֶּיךָ שֶׁהוֹדַעְתָּנוּ, וְעַל חַיִּים חֵן וָחֶסֶד שֶׁחוֹנַנְתָּנוּ, וְעַל אֲכִילַת מָזוֹן שָׁאַתָּה זָן וּמְפַרְנֵס אוֹתָנוּ תָּמִיד, בְּכָל יוֹם וּבְכָל עֵת וּבְכָל שָׁעָה:

וְעַל הַכֹּל יְיָ אֱלֹהֵינוּ אֲנַחְנוּ מוֹדִים לָךְ, וּמְבָרְכִים אוֹתָךְ, יִתְבָּרַךְ שִׁמְךָ בְּפִי כָּל חַי תָּמִיד לְעוֹלָם וָעֶד. כַּכָּתוּב: וְאָכַלְתָּ וְשָׂבָעְתָּ, וּבֵרַכְתָּ אֶת יְיָ אֱלֹהֶיךָ עַל הָאָרֶץ הַטֹּבָה אֲשֶׁר נָתַן לָךְ. בָּרוּךְ אַתָּה יְיָ, עַל הָאָרֶץ וְעַל הַמָּזוֹן:

רַחֵם נָא יְיָ אֱלֹהֵינוּ, עַל יִשְׂרָאֵל עַמֶּךָ, וְעַל יְרוּשָׁלַיִם עִירֶךָ, וְעַל צִיּוֹן מִשְׁכַּן

נוֹדֶה לְּךָ The benediction of *Nodeh lekha* in *Birkat ha-Mazon* reflects courage and joy, hope and contentment. Man knows that God is with him; he is confident as to his destiny and his future, and is aware of the significance the Creator attributes to him. The *halakhah* requires that the worshipper bow at the beginning and conclusion of the thanksgiving benediction of the *Amidah* – "*Modim tehillah va-sof*" – but reproaches any kind of bowing at the recital of praise and thanksgiving of *Birkat ha-Mazon* and *Hallel* (*Berakhot* 34b). Prayer is inseparably bound with crisis. Prayer is supplication and begging; it means admitting complete failure, vain hopes and dissipated aspirations. But *Birkat ha-Mazon* is recited on the occasion of full satiety and satisfaction, and *Hallel* on the occasion of a great event which has saved the people from disaster. Instead of feeling that existence is desolate, one is aware of a full and blessed life. The dominant motif is one of abundance. Worthlessness turns into a feeling of centrality, self-esteem and self-respect. Man is not a pauper any more, but rather a king and a magnificent being who is indebted to the King of Kings, his Creator.

(*Out of the Whirlwind*)

וְעַל תּוֹרָתְךָ שֶׁלִּמַּדְתָּנוּ Each meal is transposed into a covenantal feast at which the covenant is renewed and reconfirmed. The individual who ate and was engrossed in a very ordinary activity – the gratification of his physical need – relates himself at the conclusion of the meal to the charismatic community, to

We thank You, Lord, our God, for having given as a heritage to our ancestors a precious, good and spacious land; for having brought us out, Lord our God, from the land of Egypt and redeemed us from the house of slaves; for Your covenant which You have sealed in our flesh; for Your Torah which You have taught us; for Your statutes which You have made known to us; for the life, favor and kindness which You have graciously bestowed upon us; and for the food we eat with which You constantly feed and sustain us every day, at all times, and at every hour.

For all this, Lord our God, we thank You and bless You. May Your Name be blessed by the mouth of every living being, constantly and forever. As it is written: When you have eaten and are satiated, you shall bless the Lord your God, for the good land which He has given you. Blessed are You, Lord, for the land and for the food.

Have mercy, Lord our God, upon Israel Your people, upon Jerusalem Your city, upon Zion the abode of Your glory, upon the kingship of the house of David Your anointed, and upon the great and holy House which is called by Your Name. Our God, our Father, our Shepherd, feed us, sustain us, nourish us and give us comfort;

---

its glorious past, to its covenant, Torah, and great institutions, to its hopes and visions, to the great future and the realization of the messianic kingdom. The individual who a while ago was engaged in a mundane, insensate activity, such as supplying his body with food, rises to the historical, experiential world of the covenant. The meal is transformed into a symposium of generations.

(*Festival of Freedom*)

עַל הָאָרֶץ הַטּוֹבָה אֲשֶׁר נָתַן לָךְ Food plays a minor role in the second *berakhah*. The main emphasis is placed upon *Ereẓ Yisrael*. We are not satisfied to give thanks to God solely for *Ereẓ Yisrael*. It means absolutely nothing to us if *Ereẓ Yisrael* is not associated with the uniqueness of the Jewish people and the fact that God has chosen the Jewish people for His community – "and for Your *berit* which You sealed into our flesh, and for Your Torah which you taught us." God set us up as a unique, singular Jewish community and charged us with a certain task and mission, that of *miẓvot*. *Ereẓ Yisrael* means not only *Ereẓ Yisrael* the state, but also the singularity of the Jewish people.

(*Kol ha-Rav*)

כְּבוֹדֶךָ, וְעַל מַלְכוּת בֵּית דָּוִד מְשִׁיחֶךָ, וְעַל הַבַּיִת הַגָּדוֹל וְהַקָּדוֹשׁ שֶׁנִּקְרָא שִׁמְךָ עָלָיו. אֱלֹהֵינוּ, אָבִינוּ, רְעֵנוּ, זוּנֵנוּ, פַּרְנְסֵנוּ, וְכַלְכְּלֵנוּ, וְהַרְוִיחֵנוּ, וְהַרְוַח לָנוּ יְיָ אֱלֹהֵינוּ מְהֵרָה מִכָּל צָרוֹתֵינוּ. וְנָא אַל תַּצְרִיכֵנוּ יְיָ אֱלֹהֵינוּ, לֹא לִידֵי מַתְּנַת בָּשָׂר וָדָם, וְלֹא לִידֵי הַלְוָאָתָם. כִּי אִם לְיָדְךָ הַמְּלֵאָה, הַפְּתוּחָה, הַקְּדוֹשָׁה וְהָרְחָבָה, שֶׁלֹּא נֵבוֹשׁ וְלֹא נִכָּלֵם לְעוֹלָם וָעֶד:

(בשבת: רְצֵה וְהַחֲלִיצֵנוּ יְיָ אֱלֹהֵינוּ בְּמִצְוֹתֶיךָ, וּבְמִצְוַת יוֹם הַשְּׁבִיעִי הַשַּׁבָּת הַגָּדוֹל וְהַקָּדוֹשׁ הַזֶּה. כִּי יוֹם זֶה גָּדוֹל וְקָדוֹשׁ הוּא לְפָנֶיךָ, לִשְׁבָּת־בּוֹ וְלָנוּחַ בּוֹ בְּאַהֲבָה כְּמִצְוַת רְצוֹנֶךָ. וּבִרְצוֹנְךָ הָנִיחַ לָנוּ יְיָ אֱלֹהֵינוּ, שֶׁלֹּא תְהֵא צָרָה וְיָגוֹן וַאֲנָחָה בְּיוֹם מְנוּחָתֵנוּ. וְהַרְאֵנוּ יְיָ אֱלֹהֵינוּ בְּנֶחָמַת צִיּוֹן עִירֶךָ, וּבְבִנְיַן יְרוּשָׁלַיִם עִיר קָדְשֶׁךָ, כִּי אַתָּה הוּא בַּעַל הַיְשׁוּעוֹת וּבַעַל הַנֶּחָמוֹת:)

אֱלֹהֵינוּ וֵאלֹהֵי אֲבוֹתֵינוּ, יַעֲלֶה וְיָבֹא וְיַגִּיעַ, וְיֵרָאֶה, וְיֵרָצֶה, וְיִשָּׁמַע, וְיִפָּקֵד, וְיִזָּכֵר זִכְרוֹנֵנוּ וּפִקְדוֹנֵנוּ, וְזִכְרוֹן אֲבוֹתֵינוּ, וְזִכְרוֹן מָשִׁיחַ בֶּן דָּוִד עַבְדֶּךָ, וְזִכְרוֹן יְרוּשָׁלַיִם עִיר קָדְשֶׁךָ, וְזִכְרוֹן כָּל עַמְּךָ בֵּית יִשְׂרָאֵל לְפָנֶיךָ, לִפְלֵיטָה לְטוֹבָה לְחֵן וּלְחֶסֶד וּלְרַחֲמִים, לְחַיִּים וּלְשָׁלוֹם בְּיוֹם חַג הַמַּצּוֹת הַזֶּה. זָכְרֵנוּ יְיָ אֱלֹהֵינוּ בּוֹ לְטוֹבָה, וּפָקְדֵנוּ בוֹ לִבְרָכָה, וְהוֹשִׁיעֵנוּ בוֹ לְחַיִּים. וּבִדְבַר יְשׁוּעָה וְרַחֲמִים, חוּס וְחָנֵּנוּ, וְרַחֵם עָלֵינוּ וְהוֹשִׁיעֵנוּ, כִּי אֵלֶיךָ עֵינֵינוּ, כִּי אֵל (מֶלֶךְ) חַנּוּן וְרַחוּם אָתָּה:

וּבְנֵה יְרוּשָׁלַיִם עִיר הַקֹּדֶשׁ בִּמְהֵרָה בְיָמֵינוּ.
בָּרוּךְ אַתָּה יְיָ, בּוֹנֵה בְּרַחֲמָיו יְרוּשָׁלָיִם. אָמֵן.

בָּרוּךְ אַתָּה יְיָ, אֱלֹהֵינוּ מֶלֶךְ הָעוֹלָם, הָאֵל אָבִינוּ, מַלְכֵּנוּ, אַדִּירֵנוּ, בּוֹרְאֵנוּ, גּוֹאֲלֵנוּ, יוֹצְרֵנוּ, קְדוֹשֵׁנוּ, קְדוֹשׁ יַעֲקֹב, רוֹעֵנוּ רוֹעֵה יִשְׂרָאֵל. הַמֶּלֶךְ הַטּוֹב, וְהַמֵּטִיב לַכֹּל, שֶׁבְּכָל יוֹם וָיוֹם הוּא הֵטִיב, הוּא מֵטִיב, הוּא יֵיטִיב לָנוּ. הוּא גְמָלָנוּ, הוּא גוֹמְלֵנוּ, הוּא יִגְמְלֵנוּ לָעַד, לְחֵן וּלְחֶסֶד וּלְרַחֲמִים וּלְרֶוַח, הַצָּלָה וְהַצְלָחָה, בְּרָכָה וִישׁוּעָה, נֶחָמָה, פַּרְנָסָה וְכַלְכָּלָה, וְרַחֲמִים וְחַיִּים וְשָׁלוֹם וְכָל טוֹב, וּמִכָּל טוּב לְעוֹלָם אַל יְחַסְּרֵנוּ:

and speedily, Lord our God, grant us relief from all our afflictions. Lord, our God, please do not make us dependent upon the gifts of mortal men nor upon their loans, but only upon Your full, open, holy and generous hand, that we may not be shamed or disgraced forever and ever.

(*On Shabbat add the following paragraph*: May it please You, Lord, our God, to strengthen us through Your commandments, and through the precept of the Seventh Day, this great and holy Shabbat. For this day is great and holy before You, to refrain from work and to rest thereon with love, in accordance with the commandment of Your will. In Your will, Lord, our God, bestow upon us tranquility, that there shall be no trouble, sadness or grief on the day of our rest. Lord, our God, let us see the consolation of Zion Your city, and the rebuilding of Jerusalem Your holy city, for You are the Master of [all] salvations and the Master of consolations.)

Our God and God of our fathers, may there ascend, come and reach, be seen and accepted, heard, recalled and remembered before You, the remembrance and recollection of us, the remembrance of our fathers, the remembrance of Mashiaḥ the son of David Your servant, the remembrance of Jerusalem Your holy city, and the remembrance of all Your people the House of Israel, for deliverance, well-being, grace, kindness, mercy, good life and peace, on this day of the Festival of *Maẓẓot*, on this Festival of holy convocation. Remember us on this day, Lord, our God, for good; recollect us on this day for blessing; help us on this day for life. With the promise of deliverance and compassion, spare us and be gracious to us; have mercy upon us and deliver us; for our eyes are directed to You, for You, God, are a gracious and merciful King.

Rebuild Jerusalem the holy city speedily in our days. Blessed are You, Lord, who in His mercy rebuilds Jerusalem. Amen.

Blessed are You, Lord, our God, King of the universe, benevolent God, our Father, our King, our Might, our Creator, our Redeemer, our Maker, our Holy One, the Holy One of Jacob, our Shepherd, the Shepherd of Israel, the King who is good and does good to all, each and every day. He has done good for us, He does good for us, and He will do good for us; He has bestowed, He bestows, and He will forever bestow upon us grace,

הָרַחֲמָן, הוּא יִמְלוֹךְ עָלֵינוּ לְעוֹלָם וָעֶד. הָרַחֲמָן, הוּא יִתְבָּרַךְ בַּשָּׁמַיִם וּבָאָרֶץ. הָרַחֲמָן, הוּא יִשְׁתַּבַּח לְדוֹר דּוֹרִים, וְיִתְפָּאַר בָּנוּ לָעַד וּלְנֵצַח נְצָחִים, וְיִתְהַדַּר בָּנוּ לָעַד וּלְעוֹלְמֵי עוֹלָמִים. הָרַחֲמָן, הוּא יְפַרְנְסֵנוּ בְּכָבוֹד. הָרַחֲמָן, הוּא יִשְׁבֹּר עֻלֵּנוּ מֵעַל צַוָּארֵנוּ וְהוּא יוֹלִיכֵנוּ קוֹמְמִיּוּת לְאַרְצֵנוּ. הָרַחֲמָן, הוּא יִשְׁלַח לָנוּ בְּרָכָה מְרֻבָּה בַּבַּיִת הַזֶּה, וְעַל שֻׁלְחָן זֶה שֶׁאָכַלְנוּ עָלָיו. הָרַחֲמָן, הוּא יִשְׁלַח לָנוּ אֶת אֵלִיָּהוּ הַנָּבִיא זָכוּר לַטּוֹב, וִיבַשֶּׂר־לָנוּ בְּשׂוֹרוֹת טוֹבוֹת יְשׁוּעוֹת וְנֶחָמוֹת.

הָרַחֲמָן הוּא יְבָרֵךְ

סמוך על שלחן הוריו או מוסב על שלחן אחרים יאמר:

אֶת (אָבִי מוֹרִי) בַּעַל הַבַּיִת הַזֶּה
וְאֶת (אִמִּי מוֹרָתִי) בַּעֲלַת הַבַּיִת הַזֶּה

סמוך על שלחן עצמו יאמר:

אוֹתִי (וְאֶת אִשְׁתִּי/בַּעְלִי. וְאֶת זַרְעִי)
וְאֶת כָּל אֲשֶׁר לִי

אורח יאמר:

אוֹתָם וְאֶת בֵּיתָם וְאֶת זַרְעָם
וְאֶת כָּל אֲשֶׁר לָהֶם

הכל אומרים:

אוֹתָנוּ וְאֶת כָּל אֲשֶׁר לָנוּ, כְּמוֹ שֶׁנִּתְבָּרְכוּ אֲבוֹתֵינוּ, אַבְרָהָם יִצְחָק וְיַעֲקֹב בַּכֹּל, מִכֹּל, כֹּל, כֵּן יְבָרֵךְ אוֹתָנוּ כֻּלָּנוּ יַחַד בִּבְרָכָה שְׁלֵמָה, וְנֹאמַר אָמֵן:

בַּמָּרוֹם יְלַמְּדוּ עֲלֵיהֶם וְעָלֵינוּ זְכוּת, שֶׁתְּהֵא לְמִשְׁמֶרֶת שָׁלוֹם, וְנִשָּׂא בְרָכָה מֵאֵת יְיָ וּצְדָקָה מֵאֱלֹהֵי יִשְׁעֵנוּ, וְנִמְצָא חֵן וְשֵׂכֶל טוֹב בְּעֵינֵי אֱלֹהִים וְאָדָם:

kindness and mercy, relief, salvation and success, blessing and help, consolation, sustenance and nourishment, compassion, life, peace and all goodness; and may He never cause us to lack any good.

May the Merciful One reign over us forever and ever. May the Merciful One be blessed in heaven and on earth. May the Merciful One be praised for all generations, and be glorified in us forever and all eternity, and honored in us forever and ever. May the Merciful One sustain us with honor. May the Merciful One break the yoke of exile from our neck and may He lead us upright to our land. May the Merciful One send abundant blessing into this house and upon this table at which we have eaten. May the Merciful One send us Elijah the Prophet – may he be remembered for good – and may he bring us good tidings, salvation and consolation.

Add the appropriate phrases in the following paragraph:

May the merciful one bless

Guests and Children at their parents' table recite the following:

(my father, my teacher) the master of this house,
and (my mother, my teacher) lady of this house,

Those eating at their own table recite the following:

Me (my wife/husband and family) and all that is mine,

All guests recite the following:

Them, their house, their family, and all that is theirs,

All continue:

us, and all that is ours. Just as He blessed our forefathers, Abraham, Isaac and Jacob, "in everything," "from everything," "with everything," so may He bless all of us together with a perfect blessing, and let us say, Amen.

From On High, may there be invoked upon them and upon us such merit which will bring a safeguarding of peace. May we receive blessing from the Lord and just kindness from the God of our salvation, and may we find grace and good understanding in the eyes of God and man.

(בְּשַׁבָּת: הָרַחֲמָן, הוּא יַנְחִילֵנוּ יוֹם שֶׁכֻּלּוֹ שַׁבָּת וּמְנוּחָה לְחַיֵּי הָעוֹלָמִים.)

הָרַחֲמָן, הוּא יַנְחִילֵנוּ יוֹם שֶׁכֻּלּוֹ טוֹב, יוֹם שֶׁכֻּלּוֹ אָרוּךְ, יוֹם שֶׁצַּדִּיקִים יוֹשְׁבִים וְעַטְרוֹתֵיהֶם בְּרָאשֵׁיהֶם וְנֶהֱנִים מִזִּיו הַשְּׁכִינָה, וִיהִי חֶלְקֵנוּ עִמָּהֶם:

הָרַחֲמָן, הוּא יְזַכֵּנוּ לִימוֹת הַמָּשִׁיחַ וּלְחַיֵּי הָעוֹלָם הַבָּא.

מִגְדֹּל יְשׁוּעוֹת מַלְכּוֹ, וְעֹשֶׂה חֶסֶד לִמְשִׁיחוֹ, לְדָוִד וּלְזַרְעוֹ עַד עוֹלָם: עֹשֶׂה שָׁלוֹם בִּמְרוֹמָיו, הוּא יַעֲשֶׂה שָׁלוֹם, עָלֵינוּ וְעַל כָּל יִשְׂרָאֵל, וְאִמְרוּ אָמֵן:

יְראוּ אֶת יְיָ קְדֹשָׁיו, כִּי אֵין מַחְסוֹר לִירֵאָיו: כְּפִירִים רָשׁוּ וְרָעֵבוּ, וְדֹרְשֵׁי יְיָ לֹא יַחְסְרוּ כָל טוֹב: הוֹדוּ לַיְיָ כִּי טוֹב, כִּי לְעוֹלָם חַסְדּוֹ: פּוֹתֵחַ אֶת יָדֶךָ, וּמַשְׂבִּיעַ לְכָל חַי רָצוֹן: בָּרוּךְ הַגֶּבֶר אֲשֶׁר יִבְטַח בַּיְיָ, וְהָיָה יְיָ מִבְטַחוֹ: נַעַר הָיִיתִי גַּם זָקַנְתִּי וְלֹא רָאִיתִי צַדִּיק נֶעֱזָב, וְזַרְעוֹ מְבַקֶּשׁ לָחֶם: יְיָ עֹז לְעַמּוֹ יִתֵּן, יְיָ יְבָרֵךְ אֶת עַמּוֹ בַשָּׁלוֹם:

בָּרוּךְ אַתָּה יְיָ, אֱלֹהֵינוּ מֶלֶךְ הָעוֹלָם, בּוֹרֵא פְּרִי הַגָּפֶן:

שׁוֹתִים בַּהֲסִיבַת שְׂמֹאל.

שׁוֹתִים בַּהֲסִיבַת שְׂמֹאל All four cups of wine drunk at the *Seder* are intertwined with and inseparable from *sipur Yeẓi'at Miẓrayim*. This is obvious regarding the second cup, over which *Maggid* is recited. It is also true of *Kiddush*, which has a double function on *Pesaḥ* night: it is related to *yom tov*, as on any other holiday, and also expresses an important aspect of *sipur Yeẓi'at Miẓrayim*, namely, *beḥirat Yisrael*, the election of the Jewish people. *Yeẓi'at Miẓrayim* was not just setting a people free, but setting a people free and elevating them to a priestly and holy nation. Of course, this election was finalized and formalized at Sinai, but it originated in Egypt: "I will take you to Me for a people" (Ex. 6:7).

However, how is the third cup, over which *Birkat ha-Mazon* is recited, part of *sipur Yeẓi'at Miẓrayim*? The same question applies to the fourth cup. *Yeẓi'at Miẓrayim* is mentioned in the first two chapters of *Hallel*, which we recited over the second cup. The concluding chapters of *Hallel*, which are recited over the fourth cup, however, contain no allusion whatsoever to the Exodus. (It is true that after *Hallel Nishmat* mentions *Yeẓi'at Miẓrayim*. But according to Rambam, *Nishmat* is not recited, and even if one does recite *Nishmat*, it mentions *Yeẓi'at Miẓrayim* only parenthetically.)

The answer is that *sipur Yeẓi'at Miẓrayim* is fundamentally inseparable from

(*On Shabbat add the following sentence:* May the Merciful One cause us to inherit that day which will be all Shabbat and rest for life everlasting.)

May the Merciful One cause us to inherit that day which is all good, that everlasting day when the just will sit with crowns on their heads, enjoying the reflection of God's majesty. And may our portion be with them.

May the Merciful One grant us the privilege of reaching the days of the Mashiaḥ and the life of the World to Come.

He is a tower of salvation to His king, and bestows kindness upon His anointed, to David and his descendants forever. He who makes peace in His heights, may He make peace for us and for all Israel; and say, Amen.

Fear the Lord, you His holy ones, for those who fear Him suffer no want. Young lions are in need and go hungry, but those who seek the Lord shall not lack any good. Give thanks to the Lord for He is good, for His kindness is everlasting. You open Your hand and satisfy the desire of every living thing. Blessed is the man who trusts in the Lord, and the Lord will be his trust.

Blessed are You, Lord, our God, King of the universe, who creates the fruit of the vine.

Drink the wine while reclining on the left.

---

the expression of gratitude and indebtedness. Therefore, once we begin to praise God for a certain event that took place, no matter how important and crucial the event was, we have to include all the benefactions and all the acts of grace that God has bestowed upon us. After referring to *Yeẓi'at Miẓrayim* over the second cup, we continue by acknowledging not only the event that precipitated the entire ceremony of *sipur Yeẓi'at Miẓrayim*, but also all the favors that God has done. *Birkat ha-Mazon*, along with its brief mention that God took us out of Egypt, contains a long list of things for which we have to thank God: He has sustained the world, constructed the Temple and Jerusalem, given us life, health, and food, and so forth. All these must be mentioned and included in *sipur Yeẓi'at Miẓrayim*. We have to embrace and encompass everything we know about God's kindness, benevolence, and grace. This is exactly how the four cups are integrated into a single fulfillment.

(*Kol ha-Rav*)

מוזגים כוס רביעי וכוס של אליהו הנביא, פותחים את הדלת ואומרים:

שְׁפֹךְ חֲמָתְךָ אֶל־הַגּוֹיִם אֲשֶׁר לֹא יְדָעוּךָ, וְעַל־מַמְלָכוֹת אֲשֶׁר בְּשִׁמְךָ לֹא קָרָאוּ: כִּי אָכַל אֶת־יַעֲקֹב, וְאֶת־נָוֵהוּ הֵשַׁמּוּ: (תהלים ע"ט, ו–ז) שְׁפָךְ־עֲלֵיהֶם זַעְמֶךָ, וַחֲרוֹן אַפְּךָ יַשִּׂיגֵם: (תהלים ס"ט, כ"ה) תִּרְדֹּף בְּאַף וְתַשְׁמִידֵם, מִתַּחַת שְׁמֵי יְיָ: (איכה ג', ס"ו)

שְׁפֹךְ חֲמָתְךָ The fact that *Hallel* over the fourth cup refers not to *ge'ullat Mizrayim* but to the *ge'ullah atidah*, our future redemption, explains why it is preceded by "*Shefokh ḥamatekha*, Pour out Your wrath upon the nations that refuse to know You." We pray for a future redemption when "we may see soon Your mighty splendor, to remove detestable idolatry from the earth, and false gods will be utterly cut off" (*Aleinu*). Our hope is to see the whole world join *Keneset Yisrael* in accepting God as King. This is the central motif of *Rosh ha-Shanah*'s *Malkhuyyot* prayer: "Let everything that has been made know that You are its Maker."

There are people who are not ready to accept God as Sovereign over the whole world, and they obstruct the realization of our hopes. Indeed, they purposely and tenaciously fight against the ideal of the *ge'ullah ha-atidah*. A single nation should not be able to hold up the *ge'ullah ha-atidah* because it is not ready to accept the truth and participate in *tikkun olam be-malkhut Shadai*, repairing the world under the sovereignty of God. They should simply be removed. We have to combat evil, but evil sometimes does not let itself be defeated. We say, "*Shefokh ḥamatekha*, Pour out Your wrath upon the nations that refuse to know You," and we continue with "*Lo lanu*, Not to us, O Lord, not to us, but to Your name give honor."

(*Festival of Freedom*)

מוזְגִים כּוֹס רְבִיעִי The Torah sets out to teach man how to act. There are two alternatives: either to act like Ahasuerus, or to act the way one would in the presence of God. When one drinks wine in the latter case, the nervous system is stimulated, the sensitivity enhanced, emotions aroused but disciplined. There is a longing for something beautiful and fascinating. Man is under emotional pressure; he wants to release tension. He sings a song to the Almighty: "We

The fourth cup is poured, as is Elijah's Cup. The door is opened and the following said:

Pour out Your wrath upon the nations that do not acknowledge You, and upon the kingdoms that do not call upon Your Name. For they have devoured Jacob and laid waste his habitation. (Ps. 79, 6–7) Pour out Your indignation upon them, and let the wrath of Your anger overtake them. (Ps. 69, 25) Pursue them with anger, and destroy them from beneath the heavens of the Lord. (Lam. 3, 66)

---

do not sanctify except over wine" (*Pesaḥim* 107a). What does a Jew do on Passover night when he fills his fourth cup? Does he engage in idle, coarse talk? No. He recites the *Hallel.*

(*Days of Deliverance*)

כּוֹס שֶׁל אֵלִיָּהוּ There are *arba leshonot shel ge'ullah,* four verbs associated with the promise of redemption: "*Ve-hoẓe'ti,* and I will bring you out from under the burdens of Egypt; *ve-hiẓẓalti,* and I will deliver you out of their bondage; *ve-ga'alti,* and I will redeem you with an outstretched arm and with great judgments; *ve-lakaḥti,* and I will take you to Me for a people, and I will be to you a God" (Ex. 6:6–7). The next verse continues: "*Ve-heve'ti,* and I will bring you into the land which I swore to give to Abraham, to Isaac, and to Jacob" (Ex. 6:8). *Ve-heve'ti* is not counted in the group of four verbs because the grant of the land was not due to a new promise made to Moses. *Ve-heve'ti* is included in the message of redemption revealed to Moses, yet it does not add another dimension to *ge'ullah.* It is a repetition of the word of God addressed to Abraham, Isaac, and Jacob. The closing phrase of the *Arammi oved avi* section read when bringing the *bikurim,* "He brought us to this place, and gave us this land..." (Deut. 26:9), is not included in the section read on *Pesaḥ* night so that we do not give the impression that *Ve-heve'ti* belongs to the group, thus raising the number of *leshonot* from four to five.

The *kos shel Eliyahu* corresponds to the promise of *Ve-heve'ti.* It is Elijah who will announce the future redemption, and this fifth cup of wine is named in his honor.

(*Kol ha-Rav*)

הַלֵּל

יש נוהגים למזוג כוס רביעי אחר שפוך חמתך, קודם שגומרים את ההלל.

לֹא לָנוּ יְיָ, לֹא לָנוּ כִּי לְשִׁמְךָ תֵּן כָּבוֹד, עַל חַסְדְּךָ עַל אֲמִתֶּךָ: לָמָּה יֹאמְרוּ הַגּוֹיִם, אַיֵּה נָא אֱלֹהֵיהֶם: וֵאלֹהֵינוּ בַשָּׁמָיִם, כֹּל אֲשֶׁר חָפֵץ עָשָׂה: עֲצַבֵּיהֶם כֶּסֶף וְזָהָב, מַעֲשֵׂה יְדֵי אָדָם: פֶּה לָהֶם וְלֹא יְדַבֵּרוּ, עֵינַיִם לָהֶם וְלֹא יִרְאוּ: אָזְנַיִם לָהֶם וְלֹא יִשְׁמָעוּ, אַף לָהֶם וְלֹא יְרִיחוּן: יְדֵיהֶם וְלֹא יְמִישׁוּן, רַגְלֵיהֶם וְלֹא יְהַלֵּכוּ, לֹא יֶהְגּוּ בִּגְרוֹנָם: כְּמוֹהֶם יִהְיוּ עֹשֵׂיהֶם, כֹּל אֲשֶׁר בֹּטֵחַ בָּהֶם: יִשְׂרָאֵל בְּטַח בַּייָ, עֶזְרָם וּמָגִנָּם הוּא: בֵּית אַהֲרֹן בִּטְחוּ בַייָ, עֶזְרָם וּמָגִנָּם הוּא: יִרְאֵי יְיָ בִּטְחוּ בַייָ, עֶזְרָם וּמָגִנָּם הוּא:

יְיָ זְכָרָנוּ יְבָרֵךְ, יְבָרֵךְ אֶת בֵּית יִשְׂרָאֵל, יְבָרֵךְ אֶת בֵּית אַהֲרֹן: יְבָרֵךְ יִרְאֵי יְיָ, הַקְּטַנִּים עִם הַגְּדֹלִים: יֹסֵף יְיָ עֲלֵיכֶם, עֲלֵיכֶם וְעַל בְּנֵיכֶם: בְּרוּכִים אַתֶּם

הלל If we analyze the various psalms that make up the *Hallel*, we see that the first two (Ps. 113–114) are purely thanksgiving and hymnal chapters. They consist of praise exclusively; there is not a single petition or request, no kind of intercession or imploring God. We speak about past events which occurred – very important events connected inseparably with our destiny. We describe how a people downtrodden and oppressed, in bondage and in servitude, suddenly rise to a high level of freedom, giving birth to a new nation – a chosen nation, a holy nation, a nation in whose midst God resides. Of course, these two psalms fit beautifully into the context of the Haggadah. But the psalms from *Lo lanu* through *Ahavti*, *Min ha-Meẓar*, and *Anna Hashem* (Ps. 115–118) are very different. The petition motifs are interwoven into the texture of praise. We do not find praise alone in these sections.

The *Hallel* at the *Seder* was divided into its two components. The element of petition was not introduced at all into the first part of the Haggadah, because after we finish the narration of the ten plagues or Rabban Gamliel's dictum, we have only one duty and nothing else: "to thank, praise, extol, bless, exalt and acclaim." We forget for a while that after *Yeẓi'at Miẓrayim* we went through many more experiences – and not all those historical experiences were pleasant. We were slaves quite a number of times, perhaps under conditions much worse than those that prevailed in Egypt. We offered up millions of sacrifices; there was much blood and much martyrdom. We forget all about this and offer only praise.

HALLEL

Some have the custom of pouring the fourth cup after saying "Pour Out Your Wrath," before completing the Hallel.

Not to us, Lord, not to us, but to Your Name give glory, for the sake of Your kindness and Your truth. Why should the nations say, "Where, now, is their God?" Our God is in heaven, whatever He desires, He does. Their idols are of silver and gold, the product of human hands: they have a mouth, but cannot speak; they have eyes, but cannot see; they have ears, but cannot hear; they have a nose, but cannot smell; their hands cannot feel; their feet cannot walk; they can make no sound with their throat. Like them should be their makers, everyone that trusts in them. Israel, trust in the Lord! He is their help and their shield. House of Aaron, trust in the Lord! He is their help and their shield. You who fear the Lord, trust in the Lord! He is their help and their shield.

The Lord, mindful of us, will bless. He will bless the House of Israel; He will bless the House of Aaron; He will bless those who fear the

---

Not so with the subsequent chapters of *Hallel*, the ones recited over the fourth cup. True, there is an outcry of joy, the shouting of the happy person. But at the very instant we achieve the height of bliss and joyousness, we feel how unhappy and insecure we are, and how much help we still need from God. We cry out, "We beseech you, God, save us." We recite not only *Hallel* over the fourth cup, but *Hallel* and *tefillah*, praise and petition. It is not only a shout of joy, but also an outcry of pain. The structural patterns are dialectical; there is an inner contradiction. "This is the day God made; let us rejoice and be glad on it" is the thesis. The antithesis is "We beseech you, God, save us."

Ḥazal chose those psalms for this section because the fourth cup is not related to *Yeẓi'at Miẓrayim*; rather, it is related to the final act of redemption that will usher in the messianic era, when the *ge'ullah*, our redemption, will be complete, when all promises will be consummated and all pledges on the part of God fulfilled. That is why these psalms do not consist of pure praise, but rather include a mixture of praise and petition, joy and fear, happiness and distress.

(*Festival of Freedom*)

לַייָ, עֹשֵׂה שָׁמַיִם וָאָרֶץ: הַשָּׁמַיִם שָׁמַיִם לַייָ, וְהָאָרֶץ נָתַן לִבְנֵי אָדָם: לֹא הַמֵּתִים יְהַלְלוּ יָהּ, וְלֹא כָּל יֹרְדֵי דוּמָה: וַאֲנַחְנוּ נְבָרֵךְ יָהּ, מֵעַתָּה וְעַד עוֹלָם, הַלְלוּיָהּ: (תהלים קט"ו)

אָהַבְתִּי כִּי יִשְׁמַע יְיָ, אֶת קוֹלִי תַּחֲנוּנָי: כִּי הִטָּה אָזְנוֹ לִי, וּבְיָמַי אֶקְרָא: אֲפָפוּנִי חֶבְלֵי מָוֶת, וּמְצָרֵי שְׁאוֹל מְצָאוּנִי, צָרָה וְיָגוֹן אֶמְצָא: וּבְשֵׁם יְיָ אֶקְרָא, אָנָּה יְיָ מַלְּטָה נַפְשִׁי: חַנּוּן יְיָ וְצַדִּיק, וֵאלֹהֵינוּ מְרַחֵם: שֹׁמֵר פְּתָאִים יְיָ, דַּלּוֹתִי וְלִי יְהוֹשִׁיעַ: שׁוּבִי נַפְשִׁי לִמְנוּחָיְכִי, כִּי יְיָ גָּמַל עָלָיְכִי: כִּי חִלַּצְתָּ נַפְשִׁי מִמָּוֶת, אֶת עֵינִי מִן דִּמְעָה, אֶת רַגְלִי מִדֶּחִי: אֶתְהַלֵּךְ לִפְנֵי יְיָ, בְּאַרְצוֹת הַחַיִּים: הֶאֱמַנְתִּי כִּי אֲדַבֵּר, אֲנִי עָנִיתִי מְאֹד: אֲנִי אָמַרְתִּי בְחָפְזִי, כָּל הָאָדָם כֹּזֵב:

There is a disagreement regarding the recitation of *Hallel* in the synagogue on the night of *Pesaḥ*. The *Shulḥan Arukh* (*Oraḥ Ḥayyim* 487:4) rules that it should be said, whereas Rama rules that it should not. The *Shulḥan Arukh* says that the recitation takes place *be-ẓibur*, "with the congregation." Rabbi Moshe Soloveitchik understood the presence of the congregation to be an absolute requirement, and ruled that one who is praying alone should not recite this *Hallel*. We can understand this in light of a comment of Vilna Gaon (*Be'ur ha-Gra* to *Shulḥan Arukh*, *Oraḥ Ḥayyim* 671:7) regarding the practice of lighting *Ḥanukah* candles in shul. Vilna Gaon notes that such lighting is accompanied by a *berakhah*, and supports the practice by comparing it to *Hallel* on *Pesaḥ* night, which is said at the *Seder* table and is nonetheless recited in the synagogue to fully publicize the miracle (*parsumei nissa*). There is a basic obligation performed by an individual – reciting *Hallel* at his *Seder* or lighting candles in his home. Additionally, there is another level, where the *miẓvah* is performed specifically and necessarily in a public context.

However, Rav Hayim had a different understanding of the *Hallel* recited at night in the synagogue. The Talmud (*Arakhin* 10b) derives from the verse "You shall have a song as in the night when the festival is sanctified" (Isa. 30:29) that *Hallel* is recited on a day that is sanctified with a prohibition against *mela'khah*. Thus, *Hallel* is associated with, and a function of, *yom tov* itself. *Pesaḥ* night, as a distinct *yom tov* entity, mandates its own *Hallel* in addition to the *Hallel* at the *Seder* as part of *sipur Yeẓi'at Miẓrayim*.

(*Reshimot*)

Lord, the small with the great. May the Lord increase [blessing] upon you, upon you and upon your children. You are blessed unto the Lord, the Maker of heaven and earth. The heavens are the heavens of the Lord, but the earth He gave to the children of man. The dead do not praise God, nor do those that go down into the silence [of the grave]. But we will bless God, from now to eternity. *Halleluyah*, Praise God. (Ps. 115)

I love the Lord, because He hears my voice, my prayers. For He turned His ear to me; all my days I will call [upon Him]. The pangs of death encompassed me, and the agonies of the grave came upon me, trouble and sorrow I encounter and I call upon the Name of the Lord: Please, Lord, deliver my soul! The Lord is gracious and just, our God is compassionate. The Lord watches over the simpletons; I was brought low and He saved me. Return, my soul, to your rest, for the Lord has dealt kindly with you. For You have delivered my soul from death, my eyes from tears, my foot from stumbling. I will walk before the Lord in the lands of the living. I had faith even when I said, "I am greatly afflicted"; [even when] I said in my haste, "All men are deceitful."

כָּל הָאָדָם כֹּזֵב Man has an inner world; he exists inwardly as well as externally. Man's ontological essence, that is, the essence of his being, is not to be equated with his conduct or routine activities. There is a *homo absconditus*, a "hidden man," whom no one knows. He hardly knows himself. He is a mystery which no one can unravel. "All men are liars," says the psalmist (Ps. 116:11). Not because they want to tell the untruth. They are simply unable to tell the truth. I see my neighbor every morning leave his house at 6:30; I know to where he drives off. I am also familiar with his occupation. I know what he will do when he will arrive at his place of business. I willy-nilly watched his conduct; I am acquainted with his habits and responses to certain challenges. I overhear his conversations with the members of his household. I know his concerns and interests. Do I know? No, he is a mystery to me. The uniqueness of man-*persona* expresses itself in the *mysterium magnum* which no one except God can penetrate.

(*Family Redeemed*)

מָה אָשִׁיב לַיְיָ, כָּל תַּגְמוּלוֹהִי עָלָי: כּוֹס יְשׁוּעוֹת אֶשָּׂא, וּבְשֵׁם יְיָ אֶקְרָא: נְדָרַי לַיְיָ אֲשַׁלֵּם, נֶגְדָה־נָּא לְכָל עַמּוֹ: יָקָר בְּעֵינֵי יְיָ, הַמָּוְתָה לַחֲסִידָיו: אָנָּה יְיָ כִּי אֲנִי עַבְדֶּךָ, אֲנִי עַבְדְּךָ בֶּן אֲמָתֶךָ פִּתַּחְתָּ לְמוֹסֵרָי: לְךָ אֶזְבַּח זֶבַח תּוֹדָה, וּבְשֵׁם יְיָ אֶקְרָא: נְדָרַי לַיְיָ אֲשַׁלֵּם נֶגְדָה נָּא לְכָל עַמּוֹ: בְּחַצְרוֹת בֵּית יְיָ, בְּתוֹכֵכִי יְרוּשָׁלָיִם, הַלְלוּיָהּ: (תהלים קט"ז)

הַלְלוּ אֶת יְיָ, כָּל גּוֹיִם, שַׁבְּחוּהוּ כָּל הָאֻמִּים: כִּי גָבַר עָלֵינוּ חַסְדּוֹ, וֶאֱמֶת יְיָ לְעוֹלָם, הַלְלוּיָהּ: (תהלים קי"ז)

גדול הבית אומר הודו לה' וגו' והמסובים עונים אחריו.

הוֹדוּ לַיְיָ כִּי טוֹב, כִּי לְעוֹלָם חַסְדּוֹ:
יֹאמַר נָא יִשְׂרָאֵל, כִּי לְעוֹלָם חַסְדּוֹ:
יֹאמְרוּ נָא בֵית אַהֲרֹן, כִּי לְעוֹלָם חַסְדּוֹ:
יֹאמְרוּ נָא יִרְאֵי יְיָ, כִּי לְעוֹלָם חַסְדּוֹ:

כִּי אֲנִי עַבְדֶּךָ, אֲנִי עַבְדְּךָ בֶּן אֲמָתֶךָ When we experience the swing back from an illusory eternity to a temporal reality, a new category is discovered, namely, that of service. God summons us to His service; we are called upon to serve Him. We are appointed as the servants of the God. "Hallelujah, praise O you servants of the Lord" (Ps. 113:1), "O Lord, truly I am Thy servant; I am Thy servant the son of Thy handmaid" (Ps. 116:16). There can be no religious experience if it does not entail the element of service. Our existence is not just a coincidence, a mechanical fact, a meaningless caprice on the part of nature or providence, but a meaningful assignment which abounds in responsibility and commitment.

(*Out of the Whirlwind*)

הודו לה' כי טוב – כִּי לְעוֹלָם חַסְדּוֹ After completing the second half of *Hallel*, we continue with Psalm 136, known as *Hallel ha-Gadol*. On Shabbat, we include *Hallel ha-Gadol* in *Pesukei de-Zimrah*. On weekdays, *Pesukei de-Zimrah* was reduced to the psalms from *Ashrei* until *Kol ha-Neshamah* (Ps. 145–150), but fundamentally *Hallel ha-Gadol* is an integral part of *Pesukei de-Zimrah*. Interestingly, the Gemara (*Shabbat* 118b) calls *Pesukei de-Zimrah* "*Hallel*." It is the *Hallel* for the cosmic drama, for organic life and inorganic matter, the astral world, heaven and earth, the seas and forests – essentially, for nature. *Hallel ha-Mizri*, on the other hand, gives expression to our specific relationship with God, to the miracles which took place not in natural processes – the cosmic drama and

What can I repay the Lord for all His kindness to me? I will raise the cup of salvation and call upon the Name of the Lord. I will pay my vows to the Lord in the presence of all His people. Precious in the eyes of the Lord is the death of His pious ones. I thank you, Lord, for I am Your servant. I am Your servant the son of Your handmaid, You have loosened my bonds. To You I will bring an offering of thanksgiving, and I will call upon the Name of the Lord. I will pay my vows to the Lord in the presence of all His people, in the courtyards of the House of the Lord, in the midst of Jerusalem. *Halleluyah*, Praise God. (Ps. 116)

Praise the Lord, all nations! Extol Him, all peoples! For His kindness was mighty over us, and the truth of the Lord is everlasting. *Halleluyah*, Praise God. (Ps. 117)

The senior member of the household recites "Give thanks to the Lord, etc." and those present repeat each phrase responsively.

Give thanks to the Lord, for He is good,
for His kindness is everlasting.
Let Israel say [it],
for His kindness is everlasting.
Let the House of Aaron say [it],
for His kindness is everlasting.
Let those who fear the Lord say [it],
for His kindness is everlasting.

---

the rules of nature – but in specific miracles which defeated cosmic causation. It refers to the miracles responsible for the emergence of the covenantal community and the unique, singular relationship between Israel and God – the Exodus from Egypt and God's revelation throughout our history.

Each of these forms of *Hallel* has its own *ḥatimah*, its own conclusion. *Hallel ha-Mizri* is concluded with *Yehalelukha*, while *Hallel ha-Gadol* is concluded with *Nishmat* and *Yishtabaḥ*. (Essentially, *Nishmat* and *Yishtabaḥ* are one long *ḥatimah*, but on weekdays we do not have time to recite the entire conclusion, so we abridge it to *Yishtabaḥ* alone.) An important idea comes to expression in the section from *Nishmat* through *Yishtabaḥ*: the inadequacy of man to praise God. Words cannot express genuine praise of the Almighty, and a frail,

מִן הַמֵּצַר קָרָאתִי יָּהּ, עָנָנִי בַמֶּרְחָב יָהּ: יְיָ לִי לֹא אִירָא, מַה יַּעֲשֶׂה לִי
אָדָם: יְיָ לִי בְּעֹזְרָי, וַאֲנִי אֶרְאֶה בְשֹׂנְאָי: טוֹב לַחֲסוֹת בַּיְיָ, מִבְּטֹחַ בָּאָדָם:
טוֹב לַחֲסוֹת בַּיְיָ, מִבְּטֹחַ בִּנְדִיבִים: כָּל גּוֹיִם סְבָבֽוּנִי, בְּשֵׁם יְיָ כִּי אֲמִילַם:
סַבּֽוּנִי גַם סְבָבֽוּנִי, בְּשֵׁם יְיָ כִּי אֲמִילַם: סַבּֽוּנִי כִדְבוֹרִים דֹּעֲכוּ כְּאֵשׁ קוֹצִים,
בְּשֵׁם יְיָ כִּי אֲמִילַם: דָּחֹה דְחִיתַֽנִי לִנְפֹּל, וַיְיָ עֲזָרָֽנִי: עׇזִּי וְזִמְרָת יָהּ, וַיְהִי
לִי לִישׁוּעָה: קוֹל רִנָּה וִישׁוּעָה בְּאׇהֳלֵי צַדִּיקִים, יְמִין יְיָ עֹֽשָׂה חָֽיִל: יְמִין
יְיָ רוֹמֵמָה, יְמִין יְיָ עֹֽשָׂה חָֽיִל: לֹא אָמוּת כִּי אֶחְיֶה, וַאֲסַפֵּר מַעֲשֵׂי יָהּ: יַסֹּר
יִסְּרַֽנִּי יָּהּ, וְלַמָּֽוֶת לֹא נְתָנָֽנִי: פִּתְחוּ לִי שַׁעֲרֵי צֶֽדֶק, אָבֹא בָם אוֹדֶה יָהּ: זֶה
הַשַּֽׁעַר לַיְיָ, צַדִּיקִים יָבֹֽאוּ בוֹ: אוֹדְךָ כִּי עֲנִיתָֽנִי, וַתְּהִי לִי לִישׁוּעָה: אוֹדְךָ
כִּי עֲנִיתָֽנִי, וַתְּהִי לִי לִישׁוּעָה: אֶֽבֶן מָאֲסוּ הַבּוֹנִים, הָיְתָה לְרֹאשׁ פִּנָּה:
אֶֽבֶן מָאֲסוּ הַבּוֹנִים, הָיְתָה לְרֹאשׁ פִּנָּה: מֵאֵת יְיָ הָֽיְתָה זֹּאת, הִיא נִפְלָאת
בְּעֵינֵֽינוּ: מֵאֵת יְיָ הָֽיְתָה זֹּאת, הִיא נִפְלָאת בְּעֵינֵֽינוּ: זֶה הַיּוֹם עָשָׂה יְיָ,
נָגִֽילָה וְנִשְׂמְחָה בוֹ: זֶה הַיּוֹם עָשָׂה יְיָ, נָגִֽילָה וְנִשְׂמְחָה בוֹ:

גדול הבית אומר אנא ה' וגו' והמסובים עונים אחריו.

אָנָּא יְיָ הוֹשִֽׁיעָה נָּא: אָנָּא יְיָ הוֹשִֽׁיעָה נָּא:

אָנָּא יְיָ הַצְלִֽיחָה נָּא: אָנָּא יְיָ הַצְלִֽיחָה נָּא:

---

limited, finite human being is incapable of praising God. Whatever he will
say will be insufficient.

Yet we sing praises to God because we cannot do otherwise. If one is filled
with admiration of God for His grace and benevolence, and overflowing with
admiration for God's handiwork, one explodes like a volcano. Thus, *Nishmat*
works with a thesis and antithesis. On the one hand, praise is inadequate; it is
arrogance on the part of man. On the other hand, we can't help ourselves; we
praise Him because we can't restrain ourselves.

However, *Yehalelukha*, which is the general conclusion of *Hallel ha-Mizri*,
does not mention this dichotomy. In *Yehalelukha*, God is not the transcendent
King above our praises, *Kel Melekh gadol ba-tishbaḥot*, whom we mention
in *Yishtabaḥ*. Instead, *Yehalelukha* speaks of the King praised by our singing,
Melekh mehullal ba-tishbaḥot.

We have here two approaches, two philosophies. One viewpoint says that
praising God is perfectly legitimate, provided that each word of praise becomes
an ethical challenge, each hymn a moral code. Each attribute one ascribes to

Out of narrow confines I called to God; God answered me with abounding relief. The Lord is with me, I will not fear; what can man do to me? The Lord is with me, through my helpers, and I can face my enemies. It is better to rely on the Lord than to trust in man. It is better to rely on the Lord than to trust in nobles. All nations surround me, but I cut them down in the Name of the Lord. They surrounded me, they encompassed me, but I cut them down in the Name of the Lord. They surrounded me like bees, yet they are extinguished like a fire of thorns; I cut them down in the Name of the Lord. You [my foes] pushed me again and again to fall, but the Lord helped me. God is my strength and song, and this has been my salvation. The sound of joyous song and salvation is in the tents of the righteous: "The right hand of the Lord performs deeds of valor. The right hand of the Lord is exalted; the right hand of the Lord performs deeds of valor!" I shall not die, but I shall live and relate the deeds of God. God has chastised me, but He did not give me over to death. Open for me the gates of righteousness; I will enter them and give thanks to God. This is the gate of the Lord, the righteous will enter it.

I thank You for You have answered me, and You have been a help to me. *(Repeat this verse.)* The stone scorned by the builders has become the main cornerstone. *(Repeat this verse.)* This was indeed from the Lord, it is wondrous in our eyes. *(Repeat this verse.)* This day the Lord has made, let us be glad and rejoice on it. *(Repeat this verse.)*

The senior member of the household recites "O Lord, please help us!, etc." and those present repeat each phrase responsively.

O Lord, please help us! O Lord, please help us!
O Lord, please grant us success! O Lord, please grant us success!

God must be experienced by man as a commitment, a duty, an obligation. The second viewpoint treats praise as an end in itself, and this gives rise to the question – which comes to expression in *Nishmat* – of whether man should dare to praise God.

(*Festival of Freedom*)

בָּרוּךְ הַבָּא בְּשֵׁם יְיָ, בֵּרַכְנוּכֶם מִבֵּית יְיָ: בָּרוּךְ הַבָּא בְּשֵׁם יְיָ, בֵּרַכְנוּכֶם מִבֵּית יְיָ: אֵל יְיָ וַיָּאֶר לָנוּ, אִסְרוּ חַג בַּעֲבֹתִים, עַד קַרְנוֹת הַמִּזְבֵּחַ: אֵל יְיָ וַיָּאֶר לָנוּ, אִסְרוּ חַג בַּעֲבֹתִים, עַד קַרְנוֹת הַמִּזְבֵּחַ: אֵלִי אַתָּה וְאוֹדֶךָּ, אֱלֹהַי אֲרוֹמְמֶךָּ: אֵלִי אַתָּה וְאוֹדֶךָּ, אֱלֹהַי אֲרוֹמְמֶךָּ: הוֹדוּ לַיְיָ כִּי טוֹב, כִּי לְעוֹלָם חַסְדּוֹ: הוֹדוּ לַיְיָ כִּי טוֹב, כִּי לְעוֹלָם חַסְדּוֹ: (תהלים קי"ח)

יש אומרים כאן יהללוך בלי חתימה (טור סי' ת"פ) ויש אומרים יהללוך אחרי ישתבח (מחבר שם).

יְהַלְלוּךָ יְיָ אֱלֹהֵינוּ (עַל) כָּל מַעֲשֶׂיךָ, וַחֲסִידֶיךָ צַדִּיקִים עוֹשֵׂי רְצוֹנֶךָ, וְכָל עַמְּךָ בֵּית יִשְׂרָאֵל בְּרִנָּה יוֹדוּ וִיבָרְכוּ וִישַׁבְּחוּ וִיפָאֲרוּ וִירוֹמְמוּ וְיַעֲרִיצוּ וְיַקְדִּישׁוּ וְיַמְלִיכוּ אֶת שִׁמְךָ מַלְכֵּנוּ תָּמִיד, כִּי לְךָ טוֹב לְהוֹדוֹת וּלְשִׁמְךָ נָאֶה לְזַמֵּר, כִּי מֵעוֹלָם וְעַד עוֹלָם אַתָּה אֵל.

כִּי מֵעוֹלָם וְעַד עוֹלָם אַתָּה אֵ־ל There is a dispute among the Rishonim regarding the arrangement of the *Seder* immediately after *Hallel*, which is recited over the fourth cup of wine. According to Rashbam (*Pesaḥim* 118a), both *Hallel* and *Hallel ha-Gadol* conclude with a *berakhah*. One recites *Hallel*, which concludes with the *berakhah* of *Yehalelukha*, and then recites *Hallel ha-Gadol*, which concludes with *Yishtabaḥ* together with the concluding *berakhah* of *Yishtabaḥ*.

Tosafot quote Rabbenu Hayim ha-Kohen, who advanced a different opinion as to the order, such that one does not recite any *berakhah* at the conclusion of *Hallel* but instead proceeds directly into *Nishmat* and then recites *Yishtabaḥ* with its concluding *berakhah*. *Nusaḥ Sefard* follows Rashbam's order, and *Nusaḥ Ashkenaz* follows Rabbenu Hayim ha-Kohen's order.

There is another dispute among Rishonim regarding the *ḥatimah*, the form of the concluding *berakhah*, of *Yishtabaḥ* at the *Seder*. Some rule that the regular *ḥatimah* of *Yishtabaḥ* is recited – "*Kel Melekh gadol ba-tishbaḥot…*" while others rule that one concludes *Yishtabaḥ* with the *ḥatimah* of *Hallel* – "*Melekh mehullal ba-tishbaḥot*."

The *minhag* in Volozhin, and that followed by Rav Hayim as well, was to recite these parts of the *Seder* in a manner that fulfilled the opinions of both Rashbam and Rabbenu Hayim ha-Kohen, and although they recited only one *ḥatimah*, they did so in a manner that they held would also be acceptable to

Blessed is he who comes in the Name of the Lord; we bless you from the House of the Lord. *(Repeat this verse.)*
The Lord is Almighty, He gave us light; bind the festival-offering until [you bring it to] the horns of the altar. *(Repeat this verse.)*
You are my God and I will thank You; my God, I will exalt You. *(Repeat this verse.)*
Give thanks to the Lord, for He is good, for His kindness is everlasting. *(Repeat this verse.)*

Some follow the custom to say the following paragraph here. Others defer saying the paragraph until after Yishtabaḥ.

Lord, our God, all Your works shall praise You; Your pious ones, the righteous who do Your will, and all Your people, the House of Israel, with joyous song will thank and bless, laud and glorify, exalt and adore, sanctify and proclaim the sovereignty of Your Name, our King always. For it is good to thank You, and befitting to sing to Your Name, for from the beginning to the end of the world You are Almighty God.

Rashbam. They would recite *Hallel* without a *ḥatimah* (as per the ruling of Rabbenu Hayim ha-Kohen) and then recite *Nishmat* and *Yishtabaḥ*, but before the *ḥatimah*, they would insert the concluding *berakhah* of *Hallel* (*Yehalelukha*), which ends with the *ḥatimah* "*Barukh Ata...Melekh mehullal ba-tishbaḥot*." They would, however, continue the *ḥatimah* with "*Kel ha-hoda'ot Adon ha-nifla'ot, ha-boḥer be-shirei zimrah Melekh Kel Ḥei ha-olamim*," the conclusion of the *ḥatimah* of *Yishtabaḥ*. They were of the opinion that since the *ḥatimah* of *Hallel* (*Melekh mehullal ba-tishbaḥot*) is almost identical to the beginning of the *ḥatimah* of *Yishtabaḥ* (*Kel Melekh gadol ba-tishbaḥot*), they were justified in starting the *ḥatimah* at the *Seder* with the *Hallel ḥatimah*, and appending the ensuing words from the *Yishtabaḥ ḥatimah*. By appending "*Kel ha-hoda'ot Adon ha-nifla'ot...*" they incorporated both *ḥatimot* into one *berakhah* and satisfied the opinion of Rashbam as well as that of Rabbenu Hayim ha-Kohen. (*Reshimot*)

הוֹדוּ לַיְיָ כִּי טוֹב, כִּי לְעוֹלָם חַסְדּוֹ:
הוֹדוּ לֵאלֹהֵי הָאֱלֹהִים, כִּי לְעוֹלָם חַסְדּוֹ:
הוֹדוּ לַאֲדֹנֵי הָאֲדֹנִים, כִּי לְעוֹלָם חַסְדּוֹ:
לְעֹשֵׂה נִפְלָאוֹת גְּדֹלוֹת לְבַדּוֹ, כִּי לְעוֹלָם חַסְדּוֹ:
לְעֹשֵׂה הַשָּׁמַיִם בִּתְבוּנָה, כִּי לְעוֹלָם חַסְדּוֹ:
לְרֹקַע הָאָרֶץ עַל הַמָּיִם, כִּי לְעוֹלָם חַסְדּוֹ:
לְעֹשֵׂה אוֹרִים גְּדֹלִים, כִּי לְעוֹלָם חַסְדּוֹ:
אֶת הַשֶּׁמֶשׁ לְמֶמְשֶׁלֶת בַּיּוֹם, כִּי לְעוֹלָם חַסְדּוֹ:
אֶת הַיָּרֵחַ וְכוֹכָבִים לְמֶמְשְׁלוֹת בַּלָּיְלָה, כִּי לְעוֹלָם חַסְדּוֹ:
לְמַכֵּה מִצְרַיִם בִּבְכוֹרֵיהֶם, כִּי לְעוֹלָם חַסְדּוֹ:
וַיּוֹצֵא יִשְׂרָאֵל מִתּוֹכָם, כִּי לְעוֹלָם חַסְדּוֹ:
בְּיָד חֲזָקָה וּבִזְרוֹעַ נְטוּיָה, כִּי לְעוֹלָם חַסְדּוֹ:
לְגֹזֵר יַם סוּף לִגְזָרִים, כִּי לְעוֹלָם חַסְדּוֹ:
וְהֶעֱבִיר יִשְׂרָאֵל בְּתוֹכוֹ, כִּי לְעוֹלָם חַסְדּוֹ:
וְנִעֵר פַּרְעֹה וְחֵילוֹ בְיַם סוּף, כִּי לְעוֹלָם חַסְדּוֹ:
לְמוֹלִיךְ עַמּוֹ בַּמִּדְבָּר, כִּי לְעוֹלָם חַסְדּוֹ:
לְמַכֵּה מְלָכִים גְּדֹלִים, כִּי לְעוֹלָם חַסְדּוֹ:
וַיַּהֲרֹג מְלָכִים אַדִּירִים, כִּי לְעוֹלָם חַסְדּוֹ:
לְסִיחוֹן מֶלֶךְ הָאֱמֹרִי, כִּי לְעוֹלָם חַסְדּוֹ:
וּלְעוֹג מֶלֶךְ הַבָּשָׁן, כִּי לְעוֹלָם חַסְדּוֹ:
וְנָתַן אַרְצָם לְנַחֲלָה, כִּי לְעוֹלָם חַסְדּוֹ:
נַחֲלָה לְיִשְׂרָאֵל עַבְדּוֹ, כִּי לְעוֹלָם חַסְדּוֹ:
שֶׁבְּשִׁפְלֵנוּ זָכַר לָנוּ, כִּי לְעוֹלָם חַסְדּוֹ:
וַיִּפְרְקֵנוּ מִצָּרֵינוּ, כִּי לְעוֹלָם חַסְדּוֹ:
נֹתֵן לֶחֶם לְכָל בָּשָׂר, כִּי לְעוֹלָם חַסְדּוֹ:
הוֹדוּ לְאֵל הַשָּׁמָיִם, כִּי לְעוֹלָם חַסְדּוֹ: (תהלים קל"ו)

Give thanks to the Lord, for He is good, for His kindness is everlasting;
Give thanks to the God of gods, for His kindness is everlasting;
Give thanks to the Lord of lords, for His kindness is everlasting;
Who alone does great wonders, for His kindness is everlasting;
Who made the heavens with understanding, for His kindness is everlasting;
Who stretched out the earth above the waters, for His kindness is everlasting;
Who made the great lights, for His kindness is everlasting;
The sun, to rule by day, for His kindness is everlasting;
The moon and stars, to rule by night, for His kindness is everlasting;
Who struck Egypt through their first-born, for His kindness is everlasting;
And brought Israel out of their midst, for His kindness is everlasting;
With a strong hand and with an outstretched arm, for His kindness is everlasting;
Who split the Sea of Reeds into sections, for His kindness is everlasting;
And led Israel through it, for His kindness is everlasting;
And cast Pharaoh and his army into the Sea of Reeds, for His kindness is everlasting;
Who led His people through the desert, for His kindness is everlasting;
Who struck great kings, for His kindness is everlasting;
And slew mighty kings, for His kindness is everlasting;
Sihon, king of the Amorites, for His kindness is everlasting;
And Og, king of Bashan, for His kindness is everlasting;
And gave their land as a heritage, for His kindness is everlasting;
A heritage to Israel His servant, for His kindness is everlasting;
Who remembered us in our lowliness, for His kindness is everlasting;
And delivered us from our oppressors, for His kindness is everlasting;
Who gives food to all flesh, for His kindness is everlasting;
Thank the God of heaven, for His kindness is everlasting. (Ps. 136)

נִשְׁמַת כָּל חַי תְּבָרֵךְ אֶת שִׁמְךָ יְיָ אֱלֹהֵינוּ, וְרוּחַ כָּל בָּשָׂר תְּפָאֵר וּתְרוֹמֵם זִכְרְךָ מַלְכֵּנוּ תָּמִיד. מִן הָעוֹלָם וְעַד הָעוֹלָם אַתָּה אֵל, וּמִבַּלְעָדֶיךָ אֵין לָנוּ מֶלֶךְ גּוֹאֵל וּמוֹשִׁיעַ, פּוֹדֶה וּמַצִּיל וּמְפַרְנֵס וּמְרַחֵם, בְּכָל עֵת צָרָה וְצוּקָה. אֵין לָנוּ מֶלֶךְ אֶלָּא אָתָּה: אֱלֹהֵי הָרִאשׁוֹנִים וְהָאַחֲרוֹנִים, אֱלוֹהַּ כָּל בְּרִיּוֹת, אֲדוֹן כָּל תּוֹלָדוֹת, הַמְהֻלָּל בְּרֹב הַתִּשְׁבָּחוֹת, הַמְנַהֵג עוֹלָמוֹ בְּחֶסֶד, וּבְרִיּוֹתָיו בְּרַחֲמִים. וַייָ לֹא יָנוּם וְלֹא יִישָׁן. הַמְעוֹרֵר יְשֵׁנִים וְהַמֵּקִיץ נִרְדָּמִים וְהַמֵּשִׂיחַ אִלְּמִים, וְהַמַּתִּיר אֲסוּרִים, וְהַסּוֹמֵךְ נוֹפְלִים, וְהַזּוֹקֵף כְּפוּפִים לְךָ לְבַדְּךָ אֲנַחְנוּ מוֹדִים.

אִלּוּ פִינוּ מָלֵא שִׁירָה כַּיָּם, וּלְשׁוֹנֵנוּ רִנָּה כַּהֲמוֹן גַּלָּיו, וְשִׂפְתוֹתֵינוּ שֶׁבַח כְּמֶרְחֲבֵי רָקִיעַ, וְעֵינֵינוּ מְאִירוֹת כַּשֶּׁמֶשׁ וְכַיָּרֵחַ, וְיָדֵינוּ פְרוּשׂוֹת כְּנִשְׁרֵי שָׁמָיִם, וְרַגְלֵינוּ קַלּוֹת כָּאַיָּלוֹת, אֵין אֲנַחְנוּ מַסְפִּיקִים, לְהוֹדוֹת לְךָ יְיָ אֱלֹהֵינוּ וֵאלֹהֵי אֲבוֹתֵינוּ, וּלְבָרֵךְ אֶת שְׁמֶךָ עַל אַחַת מֵאָלֶף אֶלֶף אַלְפֵי אֲלָפִים וְרִבֵּי רְבָבוֹת פְּעָמִים הַטּוֹבוֹת שֶׁעָשִׂיתָ עִם אֲבוֹתֵינוּ וְעִמָּנוּ.

מִמִּצְרַיִם גְּאַלְתָּנוּ יְיָ אֱלֹהֵינוּ, וּמִבֵּית עֲבָדִים פְּדִיתָנוּ, בְּרָעָב זַנְתָּנוּ, וּבְשָׂבָע כִּלְכַּלְתָּנוּ, מֵחֶרֶב הִצַּלְתָּנוּ, וּמִדֶּבֶר מִלַּטְתָּנוּ, וּמֵחֳלָיִם רָעִים וְנֶאֱמָנִים דִּלִּיתָנוּ. עַד הֵנָּה עֲזָרוּנוּ רַחֲמֶיךָ, וְלֹא עֲזָבוּנוּ חֲסָדֶיךָ, וְאַל תִּטְּשֵׁנוּ יְיָ אֱלֹהֵינוּ לָנֶצַח. עַל כֵּן אֵבָרִים שֶׁפִּלַּגְתָּ בָּנוּ, וְרוּחַ וּנְשָׁמָה שֶׁנָּפַחְתָּ בְּאַפֵּינוּ, וְלָשׁוֹן אֲשֶׁר שַׂמְתָּ בְּפִינוּ, הֵן הֵם יוֹדוּ וִיבָרְכוּ וִישַׁבְּחוּ וִיפָאֲרוּ וִירוֹמְמוּ וְיַעֲרִיצוּ וְיַקְדִּישׁוּ וְיַמְלִיכוּ אֶת שִׁמְךָ מַלְכֵּנוּ. כִּי כָל פֶּה לְךָ יוֹדֶה, וְכָל לָשׁוֹן לְךָ תִשָּׁבַע וְכָל בֶּרֶךְ לְךָ תִכְרַע, וְכָל קוֹמָה לְפָנֶיךָ תִשְׁתַּחֲוֶה, וְכָל לְבָבוֹת יִירָאוּךָ, וְכָל קֶרֶב וּכְלָיוֹת יְזַמְּרוּ לִשְׁמֶךָ. כַּדָּבָר שֶׁכָּתוּב: כָּל עַצְמוֹתַי תֹּאמַרְנָה יְיָ מִי כָמוֹךָ. מַצִּיל עָנִי מֵחָזָק מִמֶּנּוּ, וְעָנִי וְאֶבְיוֹן מִגֹּזְלוֹ: (תהלים ל״ה, י׳) מִי יִדְמֶה לָּךְ, וּמִי יִשְׁוֶה לָּךְ, וּמִי יַעֲרָךְ לָךְ: הָאֵל הַגָּדוֹל הַגִּבּוֹר

נִשְׁמַת כָּל חַי On Passover night, after we speak of Jewish redemption over the first three cups, we recite the great universal hymn of *Nishmat kol ḥay*, of the salvation of mankind, of every living soul. A Jew is not satisfied with his redemption unless everybody will be redeemed with him; the Jew feels the beat of the heart of the universe. The Jew prays even for the cosmos. Once a month, he prays that God restore the diminution of the moon. The Jewish experience is all-inclusive, all-embracing, sympathetic to all.

(*Days of Deliverance*)

The soul of every living being shall bless Your Name, Lord, our God; and the spirit of all flesh shall always glorify and exalt Your remembrance, our King. From the beginning to the end of the world You are Almighty God; and other than You we have no King, Redeemer and Savior who delivers, rescues, sustains, answers and is merciful in every time of trouble and distress; we have no King but You. [You are] the God of the first and of the last [generations], God of all creatures, Lord of all events, who is extolled with manifold praises, who directs His world with kindness and His creatures with compassion. Behold, the Lord neither slumbers nor sleeps. He arouses the sleepers and awakens the slumberous, gives speech to the mute, releases the bound, supports the falling and raises up those who are bowed. To You alone we give thanks.

Even if our mouths were filled with song as the sea, and our tongues with joyous singing like the multitudes of its waves, and our lips with praise like the expanse of the sky; and our eyes shining like the sun and the moon, and our hands spread out like the eagles of heaven, and our feet swift like deer we would still be unable to thank You Lord, our God and God of our fathers, and to bless Your Name, for even one of the thousands of millions, and myriads of myriads, of favors, miracles and wonders which You have done for us and for our ancestors before us.

Lord, our God, You have redeemed us from Egypt, You have freed us from the house of bondage, You have fed us in famine and nourished us in plenty; You have saved us from the sword and delivered us from pestilence, and raised us from evil and lasting maladies. Until now Your mercies have helped us, and Your kindnesses have not forsaken us; and do not abandon us, Lord our God, forever! Therefore, the limbs which You have arranged within us, and the spirit and soul which You have breathed into our nostrils, and the tongue which You have placed in our mouth they all shall thank, bless, praise, glorify, exalt, adore, sanctify and proclaim the sovereignty of Your Name, our King. For every mouth shall offer thanks to You, every tongue shall swear by You, every eye shall look to You, every knee shall bend to You, all who stand erect shall, bow

וְהַנּוֹרָא, אֵל עֶלְיוֹן, קֹנֵה שָׁמַיִם וָאָרֶץ: נְהַלֶּלְךָ וּנְשַׁבֵּחֲךָ וּנְפָאֶרְךָ וּנְבָרֵךְ אֶת־שֵׁם קָדְשֶׁךָ. כָּאָמוּר: לְדָוִד, בָּרְכִי נַפְשִׁי אֶת יְיָ, וְכָל קְרָבַי אֶת שֵׁם קָדְשׁוֹ: (תהלים ק"ג, א')

הָאֵל בְּתַעֲצֻמוֹת עֻזֶּךָ, הַגָּדוֹל בִּכְבוֹד שְׁמֶךָ, הַגִּבּוֹר לָנֶצַח וְהַנּוֹרָא בְּנוֹרְאוֹתֶיךָ, הַמֶּלֶךְ הַיּוֹשֵׁב עַל כִּסֵּא רָם וְנִשָּׂא:

שׁוֹכֵן עַד, מָרוֹם וְקָדוֹשׁ שְׁמוֹ. וְכָתוּב: רַנְּנוּ צַדִּיקִים בַּייָ, לַיְשָׁרִים נָאוָה תְהִלָּה.

בְּפִי יְשָׁרִים תִּתְהַלָּל.
וּבְדִבְרֵי צַדִּיקִים תִּתְבָּרַךְ.
וּבִלְשׁוֹן חֲסִידִים תִּתְרוֹמָם.
וּבְקֶרֶב קְדוֹשִׁים תִּתְקַדָּשׁ:

וּבְמַקְהֲלוֹת רִבְבוֹת עַמְּךָ בֵּית יִשְׂרָאֵל, בְּרִנָּה יִתְפָּאַר שִׁמְךָ מַלְכֵּנוּ בְּכָל דּוֹר וָדוֹר. שֶׁכֵּן חוֹבַת כָּל הַיְצוּרִים, לְפָנֶיךָ יְיָ אֱלֹהֵינוּ, וֵאלֹהֵי אֲבוֹתֵינוּ, לְהוֹדוֹת לְהַלֵּל לְשַׁבֵּחַ, לְפָאֵר לְרוֹמֵם לְהַדֵּר, לְבָרֵךְ לְעַלֵּה וּלְקַלֵּס, עַל כָּל דִּבְרֵי שִׁירוֹת וְתִשְׁבְּחוֹת דָּוִד בֶּן יִשַׁי, עַבְדְּךָ מְשִׁיחֶךָ:

יִשְׁתַּבַּח שִׁמְךָ לָעַד מַלְכֵּנוּ, הָאֵל הַמֶּלֶךְ הַגָּדוֹל וְהַקָּדוֹשׁ בַּשָּׁמַיִם וּבָאָרֶץ, כִּי לְךָ נָאֶה, יְיָ אֱלֹהֵינוּ וֵאלֹהֵי אֲבוֹתֵינוּ, שִׁיר וּשְׁבָחָה, הַלֵּל וְזִמְרָה, עֹז

יִשְׁתַּבַּח שִׁמְךָ The *Pesukei de-Zimrah* section of the morning *tefillah* commences with the *berakhah* of *Barukh she-amar*, in which we confidently declare, "and with the songs of your servant David, we will praise You and honor You." *Pesukei de-Zimrah* concludes, however, on a more realistic note. On Shabbat and *yom tov*, *Pesukei de-Zimrah* draws to a close with the *Nishmat* prayer, in which we recite, "and if our mouths were full of song as the sea and our tongues with music as the multitude of its waves, and our lips with praise as the expanses of the heavens…we could not suffice to give thanks to You…and to bless Your name…." *Pesukei de-Zimrah* finally concludes with our declaration: "*Yishtabaḥ shimkha la-ad Malkenu*, may Your name, our King, be praised forever" as if to say, "as far as *we* are concerned – it is impossible for us to praise You properly; but may Your name be praised – by *itself* and not by *us*, as praise by mere mortals is inadequate." Even on weekdays, when we do not recite the extensive language of the *Nishmat* prayer, the same intent is, nevertheless, expressed by the language "*Yishtabaḥ* – may Your name be praised by *itself*" as opposed to

down before You, all hearts shall fear You, and every innermost part shall sing praise to Your Name, as it is written: "All my bones will say, Lord, who is like You; You save the poor from one stronger than he, the poor and the needy from one who would rob him!" (Ps. 35, 10) Who can be likened to You, who is equal to You, who can be compared to You, the great, mighty, awesome God, God most high, Possessor of heaven and earth! We will laud You, praise You and glorify You, and we will bless Your holy Name, as it is said: "[A Psalm] by David; bless the Lord, O my soul, and all that is within me [bless] His holy Name." (Ps. 103, 1)

You are the Almighty God in the power of Your strength; the Great in the glory of Your Name; the Mighty forever, and the Awesome in Your awesome deeds; the King who sits upon a lofty and exalted throne.

He who dwells for eternity, lofty and holy is His Name. And it is written: "Sing joyously to the Lord, you righteous; it befits the upright to offer praise."

By the mouth of the upright You are exalted; by the lips of the righteous You are blessed; by the tongue of the pious You are exalted; and among the holy ones You are sanctified.

In the assemblies of the myriads of Your people, the House of Israel, Your Name, our King, shall be glorified with song in every generation. For such is the obligation of all creatures before You, Lord, our God and God of our ancestors, to thank, to laud, to praise, to glorify, to exalt, to adore, to bless, to elevate and to honor You, even beyond all the words of songs and praises of David son of Yishai, Your anointed servant.

May Your Name be praised forever, our King, the great and holy God and King in heaven and on earth. For to You, Lord, our God

---

that which we said at the beginning of *Pesukei de-Zimrah* in *Barukh she-amar*, that *we* will praise You. We have just concluded expressing praise after praise, and we have come to the realization that it is impossible for finite human beings to praise the Almighty properly.

(*Shi'urim le-Zekher Abba Mori*)

וּמֶמְשָׁלָה, נֶצַח, גְּדֻלָּה וּגְבוּרָה, תְּהִלָּה וְתִפְאֶרֶת, קְדֻשָּׁה וּמַלְכוּת, בְּרָכוֹת וְהוֹדָאוֹת מֵעַתָּה וְעַד עוֹלָם.

אלו שאמרו "יהללוך" לפני "הלל הגדול," אינם חוזרים
עליה אלא חותמים "ישתבח" בברכה דלהלן:

בָּרוּךְ אַתָּה יְיָ, אֵל מֶלֶךְ גָּדוֹל בַּתִּשְׁבָּחוֹת, אֵל הַהוֹדָאוֹת, אֲדוֹן הַנִּפְלָאוֹת, הַבּוֹחֵר בְּשִׁירֵי זִמְרָה, מֶלֶךְ (יָחִיד), אֵל, חֵי הָעוֹלָמִים:

אלו שלא אמרו "יהללוך" לפני "הלל הגדול" ו"ישתבח" כדלעיל, אומרים "יהללוך" כאן.

יְהַלְלוּךְ יְיָ אֱלֹהֵינוּ (עַל) כָּל מַעֲשֶׂיךָ, וַחֲסִידֶיךָ צַדִּיקִים עוֹשֵׂי רְצוֹנֶךָ, וְכָל עַמְּךָ בֵּית יִשְׂרָאֵל בְּרִנָּה יוֹדוּ וִיבָרְכוּ וִישַׁבְּחוּ וִיפָאֲרוּ וִירוֹמְמוּ וְיַעֲרִיצוּ וְיַקְדִּישׁוּ וְיַמְלִיכוּ אֶת שִׁמְךָ מַלְכֵּנוּ תָּמִיד, כִּי לְךָ טוֹב לְהוֹדוֹת וּלְשִׁמְךָ נָאֶה לְזַמֵּר, כִּי מֵעוֹלָם וְעַד עוֹלָם אַתָּה אֵל. בָּרוּךְ אַתָּה יְיָ, מֶלֶךְ מְהֻלָּל בַּתִּשְׁבָּחוֹת:

בָּרוּךְ אַתָּה יְיָ, אֱלֹהֵינוּ מֶלֶךְ הָעוֹלָם, בּוֹרֵא פְּרִי הַגָּפֶן:

שׁוֹתִים בַּהֲסִיבַת שְׂמֹאל.

שׁוֹתִים בַּהֲסִיבַת שְׂמֹאל The fifteenth night of Nisan is a night of ecstasy, love, and gratitude. Hence, we thank God not only for the ḥesed He has bestowed upon us, for this would be a limited way of expressing thanks and indebtedness. On this night, the Jew is God-aware and God-loving; he suddenly reminds himself of the many acts of endless kindness for which he is indebted to his Maker. Everything he is and everything he has belongs to God. God created him; God sustains and feeds him; God gives him whatever makes life worthwhile. As we say in *Birkat ha-Mazon*, "Through His great goodness, we have never lacked, and may we never lack nourishment for all eternity."

We express gratitude for everyone, for humanity as a whole. We acknowledge our indebtedness for all flesh, for every plant, for the flowering bush in the garden, and for the flying seagull over the water. The *shirah ḥadashah* embraces everyone and everything. It expresses thanks on behalf of the universe to its Creator. "He gives nourishment to all flesh, for His grace is eternal" (*Birkat ha-Mazon* and Ps. 136:25). The fourth cup represents the destiny of humanity

and God of our ancestors, forever befits song and praise, laud and hymn, strength and dominion, victory, greatness and might, glory, splendor, holiness and sovereignty; blessings and thanksgivings for now and forever.

Those who have already recited the Yehalelukha paragraph conclude:

Blessed are You, Lord, Almighty God, King, great and extolled in praises, God of thanksgivings, Lord of wonders, Creator of all souls, Master of all creatures, who takes pleasure in songs of praise; the only King, the Life of all worlds.

Those who did not recite the Yehalelukha paragraph above after Hallel conclude with the following:

Lord, our God, all Your works shall praise You; Your pious ones, the righteous who do Your will, and all Your people, the House of Israel, with joyous song will thank and bless, laud and glorify, exalt and adore, sanctify and proclaim the sovereignty of Your Name, our King always. For it is good to thank You, and befitting to sing to Your Name, for from the beginning to the end of the world You are Almighty God. Blessed are You, Lord, King extolled in praises.

Blessed are You, Lord, our God, King of the universe, who creates the fruit of the vine.

Drink the wine while reclining on the left.

---

and of the world. We begin with thanks for ourselves, for the lonely Jew whom everyone dislikes; we finish with thanks for everyone.

The *shirah ḥadashah* reaches out beyond the present into the future. We thank God not only for what He has done for us, but also for what He will do. Whether *aḥarit ha-yamim*, the end of days, is far or near, we say *shirah* for something that has not yet happened. These portions add a glorious eschatological dimension to the praise and thanksgiving sections so essential to the Haggadah.

(*Kol ha-Rav*)

בָּרוּךְ אַתָּה יְיָ, אֱלֹהֵינוּ מֶלֶךְ הָעוֹלָם, עַל הַגֶּפֶן וְעַל פְּרִי הַגֶּפֶן, וְעַל תְּנוּבַת הַשָּׂדֶה, וְעַל אֶרֶץ חֶמְדָּה טוֹבָה וּרְחָבָה, שֶׁרָצִיתָ וְהִנְחַלְתָּ לַאֲבוֹתֵינוּ, לֶאֱכֹל מִפִּרְיָהּ וְלִשְׂבֹּעַ מִטּוּבָהּ. רַחֵם (נָא) יְיָ אֱלֹהֵינוּ עַל יִשְׂרָאֵל עַמֶּךָ, וְעַל יְרוּשָׁלַיִם עִירֶךָ, וְעַל צִיּוֹן מִשְׁכַּן כְּבוֹדֶךָ, וְעַל מִזְבְּחֶךָ וְעַל הֵיכָלֶךָ. וּבְנֵה יְרוּשָׁלַיִם עִיר הַקֹּדֶשׁ בִּמְהֵרָה בְיָמֵינוּ, וְהַעֲלֵנוּ לְתוֹכָהּ, וְשַׂמְּחֵנוּ בְּבִנְיָנָהּ, וְנֹאכַל מִפִּרְיָהּ וְנִשְׂבַּע מִטּוּבָהּ, וּנְבָרֶכְךָ עָלֶיהָ בִּקְדֻשָּׁה וּבְטָהֳרָה (בשבת: וּרְצֵה וְהַחֲלִיצֵנוּ בְּיוֹם הַשַּׁבָּת הַזֶּה). וְשַׂמְּחֵנוּ בְּיוֹם חַג הַמַּצּוֹת הַזֶּה, כִּי אַתָּה יְיָ טוֹב וּמֵטִיב לַכֹּל, וְנוֹדֶה־לְּךָ עַל הָאָרֶץ וְעַל פְּרִי הַגֶּפֶן. בָּרוּךְ אַתָּה יְיָ, עַל הָאָרֶץ וְעַל פְּרִי הַגֶּפֶן: (על יין של א"י: פְּרִי גַפְנָהּ)

נִרְצָה

חֲסַל סִדּוּר פֶּסַח כְּהִלְכָתוֹ, כְּכָל מִשְׁפָּטוֹ וְחֻקָּתוֹ. כַּאֲשֶׁר זָכִינוּ לְסַדֵּר אוֹתוֹ, כֵּן נִזְכֶּה לַעֲשׂוֹתוֹ. זָךְ שׁוֹכֵן מְעוֹנָה, קוֹמֵם קְהַל עֲדַת מִי מָנָה. בְּקָרוֹב נַהֵל נִטְעֵי כַנָּה, פְּדוּיִם לְצִיּוֹן בְּרִנָּה.

נִרְצָה The central portion of the biblical *Seder* focused on the eating of the *korban Pesaḥ*. The sacrificial service contained an aspect of pleasing God and receiving His acceptance, as the verse (Lev. 1:4) states: "*vi-nirẓah lo*, and it will be considered pleasing on his behalf." Hence, the blessing over the second cup of wine on *Pesaḥ* night speaks of "the blood will be sprinkled on the sides of Your altar for gracious acceptance, *le-raẓon*."

Rav Hayim noted that inherent in *Tefillah* – that is, the *Amidah* – is a biblical *kiyum* of *korban*. It is that *kiyum* which generates the obligation of *Birkat Kohanim*, for the Priestly Blessing is linked to *korban* by the verse "Aaron lifted his hands toward the people and blessed them, and he stepped down after

Blessed are You, Lord our God, King of the universe, for the vine and the fruit of the vine, for the produce of the field, and for the precious, good and spacious land which You have favored to give as an heritage to our ancestors, to eat of its fruit and be satiated by its goodness. Have mercy, Lord our God, on Israel Your people, on Jerusalem Your city, on Zion the abode of Your glory, on Your altar and on Your Temple. Rebuild Jerusalem, the holy city, speedily in our days, and bring us up into it, and make us rejoice in it, and we will bless You in holiness and purity (on Shabbat add: May it please You to strengthen us on this Shabbat day) and gladden us on this day of the Festival of M*aẓẓot*. For You, Lord, are good and do good to all, and we thank You for the land and for the fruit of the vine. Blessed are You, Lord, for the land and for the fruit of the vine [if the wine was from Israel, conclude: and for the fruit of her vine].

NIRẒAH

The order of the Pesah service is now completed in accordance with all its laws, ordinances and statutes. Just as we were worthy to perform it, so may we be worthy to do it in the future. O Pure One who dwells on high, raise up the congregation which is without number. Soon lead offshoots of the stock You have planted, redeemed to Zion, rejoicing in song.

---

offering the sin offering, the burnt offering, and the offering of well-being" (Lev. 9:25). Thus, we find that the blessing of *Avodah* in the *Amidah* begins with the word "*Reẓeh* – Be favorable," and later continues with the words: "And May the service of Your people Israel always be favorable to You," reflecting the *riẓẓu'i ha-korban* inherent in *Tefillah*.

As we bring the *Pesaḥ Seder* to a conclusion according to all its laws, we, too, close with *Nirẓah*, with the prayer that our service be accepted favorably before God.

(*Reshimot*)

לְשָׁנָה הַבָּאָה בִּירוּשָׁלָיִם

סְפִירַת הָעוֹמֶר

בחו"ל יש נוהגים בלילה השני לספור כאן ספירת העומר.

הִנְנִי מוּכָן וּמְזֻמָּן לְקַיֵּם מִצְוַת עֲשֵׂה שֶׁל סְפִירַת הָעוֹמֶר כְּמוֹ שֶׁכָּתוּב בַּתּוֹרָה. וּסְפַרְתֶּם לָכֶם מִמָּחֳרַת הַשַּׁבָּת מִיּוֹם הֲבִיאֲכֶם אֶת עוֹמֶר הַתְּנוּפָה

לְשָׁנָה הַבָּאָה בִּירוּשָׁלָיִם The daily *Kedushah* draws from the words of different prophets. Isaiah saw the Master of the Universe in the Temple when the priests performed the service and the Levites sang their song. It was a time of blessing and success. Everyone could see the resting of the Divine Presence, *hashra'at ha-Shekhinah*, and angels called to one another: "Holy, holy, holy…the whole earth is full of His glory" (Isa. 6:3). Ezekiel's prophecy, on the other hand, was at a time of *hester panim*, hiding of the Divine face. The word of God came to Ezekiel not in Israel, but in exile; he was in mourning, a prisoner of war. Standing on the banks of the river Chebar, he saw a fierce wind come from the north, a great cloud, and a blazing fire. Instead of priests and Levites, he beheld war and destruction. He does not declare that "the whole earth is full of His glory," that every detail bears witness to the Holy One. Rather, God is hidden in the seven firmaments, and Ezekiel hears a voice of a great rushing say: "Blessed be the glory of the Lord from His place" (Ezek. 3:12).

Sometimes we need not search for the Holy One; we see His presence in the whole world. At other times, we must search for Him at great length. When it is a time of favor and grace, when we can see Him in the world, He is praised as *Kadosh* – the *Kadosh Barukh Hu*. When the Divine Presence is not evident, when there is *hester panim*, we say that His glory is blessed from His place, wherever it may be.

The path of the Jew is neither a straight road nor an easy one; it twists and turns, up and down, over seas and deserts. True, in the end, the Holy One kept His promise and "calculated the end" of the bondage. God ultimately took our forefathers out of Egypt, but in the beginning the realization of His promise was hidden from view.

"The Jew has taught me how to wait" – so wrote the famous playwright Henrik Ibsen (*Peer Gynt*, act IV, sc. i), a gentile and a very sensitive person. Waiting

Next Year In Jerusalem!

COUNTING THE OMER

Outside of Israel, some count the Omer here on the second night.

Behold, I am ready and prepared to fulfill the positive commandment of counting the Omer, as it is written in the Torah: "You shall count from the day following the day of rest, from the day you

---

is the art which a Jew knows best; no other nation knows how to wait like the Jew. "Next year in Jerusalem!" "This year, we are here; next year – in the Land of Israel!" "This year, we are slaves; next year – free men!" This is a characteristic trait of the Jew. The Messiah is a little slow in coming; nevertheless, we are still waiting. If he will knock on our door, we will open it for him.

(*Festival of Freedom*)

There are two instances during the year that we say "*Le-shanah ha-ba'ah bi-Yerushalayim*, Next year in Jerusalem" – at the conclusion of the *Seder* and at the conclusion of *Yom Kippur*. These are the times that we feel most keenly the loss of the *Beit ha-Mikdash*, for we are not able to fulfill the *mizvah* of the *korban Pesaḥ* or experience the *Avodah* on *Yom Kippur*. It is therefore entirely appropriate that the *Seder* culminates with the prayer for our return to Jerusalem, may it happen speedily in our day.

(*Reshimot*)

סְפִירַת הָעֹמֶר Counting is symbolic of our halakhic thinking, in that both demand precision and continuity. The mathematical series is a continuous one. There is a systematic transition from one to another; one cannot leap from position to position. Our halakhic thinking behaves in a similar manner; it is orderly, precise cognition. There is no arbitrariness and no haphazard conclusions; logical necessity reigns supreme. An erroneous count, or omission of one position, suspends the whole count. One cannot jump from three to five; one must move through position four. In a word, halakhic thinking is like mathematical thinking. The detail is extremely important.

שֶׁבַע שַׁבָּתוֹת תְּמִימֹת תִּהְיֶינָה. עַד מִמָּחֳרַת הַשַּׁבָּת הַשְּׁבִיעִת תִּסְפְּרוּ

The Jew who approaches Mount Sinai to receive the Torah is rooted in the ancient past, while he or she is at the same time committed to a future which is pre-experienced as a reality. One's mind is precise and exact, pedantic as to the component parts, and also beholds an exalted vision of the whole. All this is symbolized by counting the *omer.*

(*Family Redeemed*)

Tosafot (*Megillah* 20b) cite the famous ruling of Behag that one who fails to count *sefirah* at night should do so during the next day without a *berakhah*, after which he may resume his normal count. However, one who misses a complete day of *sefirah* may no longer count, because *sefirat ha-omer in toto* must be "*temimot*, complete." Behag clearly believes that the *miẓvah* cannot be fulfilled during the day; thus he does not allow counting during the day with a *berakhah*. The common understanding of the rule that one who completely misses a day forfeits the ability to continue counting *sefirah* is that the complete *sefirah*, all forty-nine days, constitutes a single *miẓvah*. We make a *berakhah* each night because the single *kiyum ha-miẓvah* has forty-nine distinct *ma'asei miẓvah*, to which each *berakhah* relates. When any portion of the total *kiyum* is lacking, there is an irreparable deficiency in the *miẓvah*, rendering its fulfillment impossible. If so, why is an ineffectual utterance the next day sufficient to permit one to continue to count with a *berakhah*?

It would, therefore, seem more correct to say that we make a *berakhah* each night because *sefirat ha-omer* actually consists of forty-nine separate *kiyumim*. The reason, then, that a single failure to count can affect the *sefirah* of the subsequent nights would be that skipping even one day undermines the count. The very nature of counting implies wholeness and continuity. Counting during the day constitutes a *ma'aseh sefirah* in that it is a count, but it is not a *kiyum* of the *miẓvah* that would allow for a *berakhah*. That day's *miẓvah* was lost, but with the count restored, *sefirah* may continue. Any gap in the count produces a list of numbers that is no longer ordinal, and the flaw in the count cannot be repaired. The notion of a complete count also enables us resolve the question raised by *Minḥat Ḥinnukh* (*Miẓvah* 306) regarding whether someone who reaches the age of *miẓvot* in the middle of *sefirah* may continue counting with a *berakhah*. He may, because while he was not obligated before reaching *bar miẓvah* age, his actions certainly constituted an actual continuous count, a *ma'aseh sefirah*.

Tur (*Oraḥ Ḥayyim* 489) quotes the opinion of Rav Saadiah Gaon against Behag, that a person who forgets an entire day may continue to count with

brought the Omer offering, seven complete weeks shall be counted,

---

a *berakhah*, but if he misses the first day, he may not recite any *berakhah* at all for the rest of *sefirah*. Why should that night be different from any other night? If all the days of *sefirah* constitute a single *mizvah*, then any deficiency should preclude subsequent *berakhot*. If they are forty-nine separate *mizvot*, then even the failure to count the first night should have no impact on the remaining forty-eight *mizvot*. If, however, the problem is that an incomplete *sefirah* does not qualify as "counting," we can understand an opinion that a gap from twenty-two to twenty-four is implicitly filled in, but a count that starts with the number two is not a count.

Mishnah Berurah (*Oraḥ Ḥayyim* 489:8) quotes yet another opinion on the subject. He rules that a person who misses an entire day should count the next night with a *berakhah*, but say, "Yesterday was day x, today is day $x + 1$." While this language cannot turn back the clock and reconstitute the *sefirah* of a past day, perhaps it can serve as a make-up to fill in the missing day and continue the counting as if uninterrupted.

Sefer ha-Ḥinnukh (*Mizvah* 306) repeats Behag's ruling and adds, "but the halakhic authorities of our generation did not concede his theory; rather, one who forgets one day counts the others along with the rest of Israel." This concluding phrase is difficult to understand. Are not most *mizvot* performed with the rest of the community? Rather, *Sefer ha-Ḥinnukh* is explaining why the other opinions are not concerned with Behag's problem: Even though this individual did not count that night, he is a member of the Jewish people, who did count, and thus kept his count alive.

Finally, this insight allows us to explain the practice of Rashi (quoted in *Maḥzor Vitry*, see Beit Yosef, *Oraḥ Ḥayyim* 489), who would count *sefirah* after *pelag minḥah*, but before nightfall without a *berakhah*, and then repeat it at night with a *berakhah*. Rashba (see Magen Avraham, ibid.) is puzzled by this custom. If the first counting is proper, how can he count again later with a *berakhah* after the *mizvah* has already been fulfilled? And if the first counting is not effective, why do it at all?

While *pelag minḥah* does not signify nightfall, it is the earliest time that *halakhah* can attach to the next day, as we see with *tosefet Shabbat*, starting Shabbat early on Friday afternoon, which may be done only after *pelag minḥah*. Therefore, concerned that he may later forget to count *sefirah*, and, in accordance with the rule of Behag, lose the ability to recite a *berakhah* for the rest of the year, Rashi would register a count of the day, even one that does not qualify as a fulfillment of his *mizvah*, in order to keep his ordinal count intact.

(*Reshimot*)

חֲמִישִּׁים יוֹם וְהִקְרַבְתֶּם מִנְחָה חֲדָשָׁה לַיְיָ. וִיהִי נוֹעַם אֲדֹנָי אֱלֹהֵינוּ עָלֵינוּ
וּמַעֲשֵׂה יָדֵינוּ כּוֹנְנָה עָלֵינוּ, וּמַעֲשֵׂה יָדֵינוּ כּוֹנְנֵהוּ:

The basic criterion which distinguishes free man from slave is the kind of relationship each has with time and its experience. Freedom is identical with a rich, colorful, creative time-consciousness. Bondage is identical with passive intuition and reception of an empty, formal time-stream.

When the Jews were delivered from the Egyptian oppression and Moses rose to undertake the almost impossible task of metamorphosing a tribe of slaves into a nation of priests, he was told by God that the path leading from the holiday of Passover to *Shavu'ot*, from initial liberation to consummate freedom, leads through the medium of time. The commandment of *sefirah* was entrusted to the Jew; the wondrous test of counting forty-nine successive days was put to him. These forty-nine days must be whole. If one day is missed, the act of enumeration is invalidated.

A slave who is capable of appreciating each day, of grasping its meaning and worth, of weaving every thread of time into a glorious fabric, quantitatively stretching over the period of seven weeks but qualitatively forming the warp and woof of centuries of change, is eligible for Torah. He has achieved freedom.

(*Sacred and Profane*)

We recite the blessing of *She-heḥeyanu* before performing most *miẓvot* that are applicable only at certain times during the year, thereby expressing our excitement and gratitude to God for allowing and helping us to reach this moment. *Sefirat ha-omer* stands out as an exception to this rule in that we do not recite *She-heḥeyanu*. Ba'al ha-Ma'or (*Pesaḥim* 28a) offers an explanation for this omission. *Sefirat ha-omer* as it is performed today is *zekher la-Mikdash*, but only a general remembrance of the original practice in the *Beit ha-Mikdash*, not one that is meant to remind us of the actual past practice. This is demonstrated by Ameimar's custom (*Menaḥot* 66a) of counting only the days and not both the days and weeks, as were counted in the time of the Temple. This general remembrance does not rise to the level of a performance that requires a *She-heḥeyanu*.

There are two types of such remembrances, one that recalls the glory of the *Beit ha-Mikdash* (such as taking the *lulav* for seven days, which reflects the ritual in the Temple when it was standing) and another that reminds us of its destruction (such as putting ashes on the head of a groom under the *ḥupah*). Since *sefirat ha-omer* is not of the first type, it is therefore meant to remind us

you shall count fifty days, to the day following the seventh week you shall count fifty days; and then you shall offer a new meal offering to the Lord."

---

of the destruction of the Temple. That is why we do not recite *She-heḥeyanu*, which is an expression of joy. This may also serve as a source for the mourning nature of the *sefirah* period. It is not only a remembrance of the death of Rabbi Akiva's students but an expression of the intrinsic nature of the contemporary *miẓvah*. According to this rationale, mourning should extend throughout the entire *sefirah* period, which is in fact the opinion of the Ari.

Rambam, however, assumes that the *miẓvah* of *sefirat ha-omer* is still biblically mandated today and does not differ in this sense from its status at the time of the *Beit ha-Mikdash*. It is possible to explain the lack of *She-heḥeyanu* even according to Rambam based on the understanding of the *Sefer ha-Ḥinnukh* (*Miẓvah* 306). The *Ḥinnukh* explains that the count expresses a sense of longing and anticipation for the ultimate goal of accepting the Torah at Sinai, and therefore indicates that we have not yet reached the goal. This is antithetical to the nature of *She-heḥeyanu*, which is recited to express gratitude for having reached a particular goal.

This understanding may also explain why the Torah has us wait until after the first day of *Pesaḥ* to begin counting *sefirat ha-omer*. The *Ḥinnukh* explains that the first day of *Pesaḥ* is singled out for the specific purpose of remembering the miraculous Exodus, which in itself was a testament to God's dual role as Creator and Controller of History. Since *sefirat ha-omer* is an expression of our not having yet attained our intended goal, it is inappropriate to perform this *miẓvah* on the first day of *Pesaḥ* and mitigate our happiness and joy over the actual Exodus. It is also perhaps for this reason that some people outside the Land of Israel follow the custom of reciting *sefirat ha-omer* on the second night only after completing the *Seder* so as not to mitigate the joy of the *Seder* with our feelings of sadness for not yet having attained the ultimate goal of accepting the Torah.

(*Reshimot*)

There is a long-standing question as to the preferred text one should recite when counting the *omer*. Should one recite "*ba-omer*," which connotes that one is counting the days in the period of the *omer*, or should one recite "*la-omer*,"

בָּרוּךְ אַתָּה יְיָ אֱלֹהֵינוּ מֶלֶךְ הָעוֹלָם, אֲשֶׁר קִדְּשָׁנוּ בְּמִצְוֹתָיו וְצִוָּנוּ עַל סְפִירַת הָעוֹמֶר:

הַיּוֹם יוֹם אֶחָד לָעוֹמֶר.

הָרַחֲמָן הוּא יַחֲזִיר לָנוּ עֲבוֹדַת בֵּית הַמִּקְדָּשׁ לִמְקוֹמָהּ, בִּמְהֵרָה בְיָמֵינוּ אָמֵן סֶלָה:

---

which connotes that one is counting the days from the bringing of the *omer*? The *omer* was an offering of barley that was brought on the morning of the sixteenth day of Nisan. There is a dispute among Rishonim as to whether the *mizvah* of *sefirat ha-omer* nowadays is biblical or rabbinic. Those who consider it to be biblical understand that the *mizvah* of counting the *omer* is not directly connected to the bringing of the *korban omer*, the *omer* offering. Although we do not bring the *korban omer* nowadays, the *mizvah* of counting is nonetheless biblical. This is the opinion of Rambam (*Temidim u-Musafim* 7:22). However, *Tosafot* (*Megillah* 20b *s.v. Kol*) are of the opinion that nowadays the *mizvah* of counting the *omer* is only a rabbinic enactment that serves as a remembrance for what once was in the days of the Temple, with a view to the rebuilding of the Temple. Apparently, *Tosafot* understand that the *mizvah* of counting the *omer* is contingent on the bringing of the *korban*.

If we count "*ba-omer*," we are stating that it is the period of the *omer* which establishes the requirement to count. "*Ba-omer*" should be the correct text in accordance with the ruling of Rambam. If we count "*la–omer*," we are stating that we are counting from the bringing of the *korban*, which is the cause of the obligation. "*La-omer*" should thus be the correct text according to *Tosafot*.

It is worth noting that, surprisingly, given his view that even nowadays *sefirat ha-omer* is a biblical obligation, Rambam records the *mizvah* of *sefirat ha-omer* in *Hilkhot Temidim u-Musafim*, which deals with the *korban omer*. This implies that Rambam felt that while the *mizvah* of *sefirat ha-omer* is independent of the *korban omer*, there is, nonetheless, a *kiyum*, an additional dimension of the *mizvah*, when the counting is linked to the *korban*.

Ramban (*Pesaḥim* 7b) expresses the concept that the *korban omer* is a fundamental aspect of the counting of the *omer* with his statement that we recite the blessing "*Al sefirat ha-omer*" and not "*Li-sefirat ha-omer*" because

Blessed are You, Lord our God, King of the Universe, who has sanctified us with His commandments and commanded us concerning the counting of the Omer.

Today is one day of the Omer.

May the merciful One return for us the service of the Holy Temple to its place, speedily in our days, Amen Selah.

---

the *korban omer* has been brought before the counting commenced. Ramban's view is based on the passage in the Gemara (ibid.) that when a *berakhah* for a *miẓvah* is recited after the performance of the *miẓvah* has begun but before the *miẓvah* has been fully performed, the text of the *berakhah* is "*al*" rather than "*le*," as in the case of the four species, for which the *berakhah* is "*al netilat lulav*" – as soon as one picks up the *lulav* and *etrog* one has fulfilled a part of the *miẓvah*. From Ramban, we see that the offering of the *korban omer* is part of the *miẓvah* of *sefirat ha-omer*; when one counts the *omer*, the *miẓvah* has already begun with the bringing of the *korban omer*.

If one counts and recites "*ba-omer*" and then counts again and recites "*la-omer*" and then recites the *Yehi Raẓon*, the prayer for the rebuilding of the Temple, then the prayer for the rebuilding of the Temple is connected with the version of "*la-omer*" according to which the *miẓvah* was indeed enacted as a remembrance to the Temple.

(*Reshimot*)

Tosafot (*Megillah* 20b) note that after counting the *omer* we say, "*Yehi Raẓon*, may it be Your will that the Temple be speedily rebuilt," but we make no similar declaration after shaking the *lulav*, which after the first day is also *zekher le-mikdash*. *Tosafot* differentiate between the two by saying that *sefirah* is only a *zekher le-mikdash* whereas *lulav* has a specific action associated with it. Both *lulav* and *sefirah* are remembrances, but they represent two kinds of *zekher le-mikdash*. *Lulav* was instituted as a remembrance, but it represents the fulfillment, the *kiyum*, of the *miẓvah* of *lulav*. On the other hand, both the institution and fulfillment of *sefirah* are *zekher le-mikdash per se*.

(*Reshimot*)

בחו"ל אומרים רק בלילה הראשון:

וּבְכֵן "וַיְהִי בַּחֲצִי הַלַּיְלָה"

אָז רֹב נִסִּים הִפְלֵאתָ בַּלַּיְלָה, בְּרֹאשׁ אַשְׁמוּרוֹת זֶה הַלַּיְלָה, גֵּר צֶדֶק נִצַּחְתּוֹ כְּנֶחֱלַק לוֹ לַיְלָה,

וַיְהִי בַּחֲצִי הַלַּיְלָה.

דַּנְתָּ מֶלֶךְ גְּרָר בַּחֲלוֹם הַלַּיְלָה, הִפְחַדְתָּ אֲרַמִּי בְּאֶמֶשׁ לַיְלָה, וַיָּשַׂר יִשְׂרָאֵל לְמַלְאָךְ וַיּוּכַל לוֹ לַיְלָה,

וַיְהִי בַּחֲצִי הַלַּיְלָה.

זֶרַע בְּכוֹרֵי פַתְרוֹס מָחַצְתָּ בַּחֲצִי הַלַּיְלָה, חֵילָם לֹא מָצְאוּ בְּקוּמָם בַּלַּיְלָה, טִיסַת נְגִיד חֲרֹשֶׁת סִלִּיתָ בְכוֹכְבֵי לַיְלָה,

וַיְהִי בַּחֲצִי הַלַּיְלָה.

יָעַץ מְחָרֵף לְנוֹפֵף אִוּוּי, הוֹבַשְׁתָּ פְגָרָיו בַּלַּיְלָה, כָּרַע בֵּל וּמַצָּבוֹ בְּאִישׁוֹן לַיְלָה, לְאִישׁ חֲמוּדוֹת נִגְלָה רָז חֲזוֹת לַיְלָה,

וַיְהִי בַּחֲצִי הַלַּיְלָה.

מִשְׁתַּכֵּר בִּכְלֵי קֹדֶשׁ נֶהֱרַג בּוֹ בַּלַּיְלָה, נוֹשַׁע מִבּוֹר אֲרָיוֹת פּוֹתֵר בִּעֲתוּתֵי לַיְלָה, שִׂנְאָה נָטַר אֲגָגִי וְכָתַב סְפָרִים בַּלַּיְלָה,

וַיְהִי בַּחֲצִי הַלַּיְלָה.

עוֹרַרְתָּ נִצְחֲךָ עָלָיו בְּנֶדֶד שְׁנַת לַיְלָה, פּוּרָה תִדְרוֹךְ לְשׁוֹמֵר מַה מִּלַּיְלָה, צָרַח כַּשּׁוֹמֵר וְשָׂח אָתָא בֹקֶר וְגַם לַיְלָה,

וַיְהִי בַּחֲצִי הַלַּיְלָה.

קָרֵב יוֹם אֲשֶׁר הוּא לֹא יוֹם וְלֹא לַיְלָה, רָם הוֹדַע כִּי לְךָ הַיּוֹם אַף לְךָ הַלַּיְלָה, שׁוֹמְרִים הַפְקֵד לְעִירְךָ כָּל הַיּוֹם וְכָל הַלַּיְלָה, תָּאִיר כְּאוֹר יוֹם חֶשְׁכַּת לַיְלָה,

וַיְהִי בַּחֲצִי הַלַּיְלָה:

Outside of Israel, the following piyut is recited only on the first night.

Va-Yehi Be-Ḥaẓi Ha-Lailah

It came to pass, at midnight.

You made many miracles at night, at the beginning of the watches of this night. The righteous convert prevailed when he divided his company at night.

It came to pass at midnight.

You judged the king of Gerar in a dream at night. The Aramean was struck with terror in the dark of the night. Israel strove with an angel and prevailed at night.

It came to pass at midnight.

The first-born of the Egyptians were struck by You at midnight. They did not find their host when they arose at night. The army of the Prince of Haroshet You swept away with the stars of night.

It came to pass at midnight.

The blasphemer planned to raise his hand against Jerusalem, and you defeated him by night. The idol Bel and its pedestal were overthrown in the darkness of the night. To the much beloved was the secret vision revealed at night.

It came to pass at midnight.

He who caroused from the holy vessels was slain that same night. He who was rescued from the lion's den interpreted the awesome dreams of night. The Agagite who cherished hatred wrote letters at night.

It came to pass at midnight.

You roused Your power against him when sleep fled at night. You will tread the winepress for he who asks, Watchman, what of the night. He shall answer like a watchman and say, The morning will come after this night.

It came to pass at midnight.

Bring near the day which is neither day nor night! Make known, Most High, that Yours is the day as well as the night. Appoint watchmen to Your city by day and night. Make shine as with the light of the day the darkness of the night.

It came to pass at midnight.

בחו"ל אומרים רק בלילה השני:

וּבְכֵן "וַאֲמַרְתֶּם זֶבַח פֶּסַח"

אֹמֶץ גְּבוּרוֹתֶיךָ הִפְלֵאתָ בַּפֶּסַח, בְּרֹאשׁ כָּל מוֹעֲדוֹת נִשֵּׂאתָ פֶּסַח, גִּלִּיתָ לְאֶזְרָחִי חֲצוֹת לֵיל פֶּסַח,

וַאֲמַרְתֶּם זֶבַח פֶּסַח.

דְּלָתָיו דָּפַקְתָּ כְּחֹם הַיּוֹם בַּפֶּסַח, הִסְעִיד נוֹצְצִים עֻגוֹת מַצּוֹת בַּפֶּסַח, וְאֶל הַבָּקָר רָץ זֵכֶר לְשׁוֹר עֵרֶךְ פֶּסַח,

וַאֲמַרְתֶּם זֶבַח פֶּסַח.

זֹעֲמוּ סְדוֹמִים וְלֹהֲטוּ בָּאֵשׁ בַּפֶּסַח, חֻלַּץ לוֹט מֵהֶם, וּמַצּוֹת אָפָה בְּקֵץ פֶּסַח, טִאטֵאתָ אַדְמַת מֹף וְנֹף בְּעָבְרְךָ בַּפֶּסַח,

וַאֲמַרְתֶּם זֶבַח פֶּסַח.

יָהּ, רֹאשׁ כָּל אוֹן מָחַצְתָּ בְּלֵיל שִׁמּוּר פֶּסַח, כַּבִּיר, עַל בֵּן בְּכוֹר פָּסַחְתָּ בְּדַם פֶּסַח, לְבִלְתִּי תֵּת מַשְׁחִית לָבֹא בִּפְתָחַי בַּפֶּסַח,

וַאֲמַרְתֶּם זֶבַח פֶּסַח.

מְסֻגֶּרֶת סֻגָּרָה בְּעִתּוֹתֵי פֶּסַח, נִשְׁמְדָה מִדְיָן בִּצְלִיל שְׂעוֹרֵי עֹמֶר פֶּסַח, שֹׂרְפוּ מִשְׁמַנֵּי פּוּל וְלוּד בִּיקַד יְקוֹד פֶּסַח,

וַאֲמַרְתֶּם זֶבַח פֶּסַח.

עוֹד הַיּוֹם בְּנֹב לַעֲמֹד, עַד גָּעָה עוֹנַת פֶּסַח, פַּס יַד כָּתְבָה לְקַעֲקֵעַ צוּל בַּפֶּסַח, צָפֹה הַצָּפִית עָרוֹךְ הַשֻּׁלְחָן בַּפֶּסַח,

וַאֲמַרְתֶּם זֶבַח פֶּסַח.

קָהָל כִּנְּסָה הֲדַסָּה צוֹם לְשַׁלֵּשׁ בַּפֶּסַח, רֹאשׁ מִבֵּית רָשָׁע מָחַצְתָּ בְּעֵץ חֲמִשִּׁים בַּפֶּסַח, שְׁתֵּי אֵלֶּה רֶגַע, תָּבִיא לְעוּצִית בַּפֶּסַח, תָּעֹז יָדְךָ וְתָרוּם יְמִינְךָ, כְּלֵיל הִתְקַדֵּשׁ חַג פֶּסַח,

וַאֲמַרְתֶּם זֶבַח פֶּסַח.

Outside of Israel, the following is recited only on the second night.

Va-Amartem Zevaḥ Pesaḥ

And you shall say, It is the sacrifice of Pesaḥ.

You showed Your power on Pesaḥ. You made our first festival Pesaḥ. You revealed to the Ezrehite [Abraham] the wondrous midnight of Pesaḥ.

And you shall say, It is the sacrifice of Pesaḥ.

You knocked at his door in the midday heat on Pesaḥ. He fed the angels unleavened cakes on Pesaḥ. He ran to the herd – a memorial of the sacrifice of Pesaḥ.

And you shall say, It is the sacrifice of Pesaḥ.

The Sodomites angered God and were consumed with fire on Pesaḥ. Lot, saved from them, baked unleavened cakes at the end of Pesaḥ. You swept clean the land of Moph and Noph when You passed through on Pesaḥ.

And you shall say, It is the sacrifice of Pesaḥ.

God, You destroyed the first-born on the night of Pesaḥ. Master, You spared Your first-born because of the blood of the sacrifice of Pesaḥ. You did not let the destoyer enter my doors on Pesaḥ.

And you shall say, It is the sacrifice of Pesaḥ.

The beleaguered city was besieged on Pesaḥ. Midian was destroyed by a barley cake, the offering on Pesaḥ. The Princes of Pul and Lud were consumed in a great fire on Pesaḥ.

And you shall say, It is the sacrifice of Pesaḥ.

He was to be that day in Nob towards Pesaḥ. The hand wrote prophesying the destruction of Zul on Pesaḥ. "The watch was set, the table spread" on Pesaḥ.

And you shall say, It is the sacrifice of Pesaḥ.

Hadassah assembled the people for a three-day fast on Pesaḥ. The chief of an evil house You did hang on a fifty-cubit gallows on Pesaḥ. "Both of these" will You bring in one moment on Utz on Pesaḥ. Your hand will be strong, Your right hand uplifted as on the night you sanctified Pesaḥ.

And you shall say, It is the sacrifice of Pesaḥ.

כִּי לוֹ נָאֶה, כִּי לוֹ יָאֶה

אַדִּיר בִּמְלוּכָה, בָּחוּר כַּהֲלָכָה, גְּדוּדָיו יֹאמְרוּ לוֹ: לְךָ וּלְךָ, לְךָ כִּי לְךָ, לְךָ אַף לְךָ, לְךָ יְיָ הַמַּמְלָכָה. כִּי לוֹ נָאֶה, כִּי לוֹ יָאֶה.

דָּגוּל בִּמְלוּכָה, הָדוּר כַּהֲלָכָה, וָתִיקָיו יֹאמְרוּ לוֹ: לְךָ וּלְךָ, לְךָ כִּי לְךָ, לְךָ אַף לְךָ, לְךָ יְיָ הַמַּמְלָכָה. כִּי לוֹ נָאֶה, כִּי לוֹ יָאֶה.

זַכַּאי בִּמְלוּכָה, חָסִין כַּהֲלָכָה, טַפְסְרָיו יֹאמְרוּ לוֹ: לְךָ וּלְךָ, לְךָ כִּי לְךָ, לְךָ אַף לְךָ, לְךָ יְיָ הַמַּמְלָכָה. כִּי לוֹ נָאֶה, כִּי לוֹ יָאֶה.

יָחִיד בִּמְלוּכָה, כַּבִּיר כַּהֲלָכָה, לִמּוּדָיו יֹאמְרוּ לוֹ: לְךָ וּלְךָ, לְךָ כִּי לְךָ, לְךָ אַף לְךָ, לְךָ יְיָ הַמַּמְלָכָה. כִּי לוֹ נָאֶה, כִּי לוֹ יָאֶה.

מוֹשֵׁל בִּמְלוּכָה, נוֹרָא כַּהֲלָכָה, סְבִיבָיו יֹאמְרוּ לוֹ: לְךָ וּלְךָ, לְךָ כִּי לְךָ, לְךָ אַף לְךָ, לְךָ יְיָ הַמַּמְלָכָה. כִּי לוֹ נָאֶה, כִּי לוֹ יָאֶה.

עָנָיו בִּמְלוּכָה, פּוֹדֶה כַּהֲלָכָה, צַדִּיקָיו יֹאמְרוּ לוֹ: לְךָ וּלְךָ, לְךָ כִּי לְךָ, לְךָ אַף לְךָ, לְךָ יְיָ הַמַּמְלָכָה. כִּי לוֹ נָאֶה, כִּי לוֹ יָאֶה.

קָדוֹשׁ בִּמְלוּכָה, רַחוּם כַּהֲלָכָה, שִׁנְאַנָּיו יֹאמְרוּ לוֹ: לְךָ וּלְךָ, לְךָ כִּי לְךָ, לְךָ אַף לְךָ, לְךָ יְיָ הַמַּמְלָכָה. כִּי לוֹ נָאֶה, כִּי לוֹ יָאֶה.

תַּקִּיף בִּמְלוּכָה, תּוֹמֵךְ כַּהֲלָכָה, תְּמִימָיו יֹאמְרוּ לוֹ: לְךָ וּלְךָ, לְךָ כִּי לְךָ, לְךָ אַף לְךָ, לְךָ יְיָ הַמַּמְלָכָה. כִּי לוֹ נָאֶה, כִּי לוֹ יָאֶה.

Ki Lo Na'eh

Powerful in kingship, truly chosen, His troops sing to Him: To You and to You; to You, surely to You; to You, only to You; to You, Lord, is the sovereignty; to Him it is becoming; to Him it is fitting.

Famous in kingship, truly glorious, His faithful sing to Him: To You and to You; to You, surely to You; to You, only to You; to You, Lord, is the sovereignty; to Him it is becoming; to Him it is fitting.

Guiltless in kingship, truly strong, His angels sing to Him: To You and to You; to You, surely to You; to You, only to You; to You, Lord, is the sovereignty; to Him it is becoming; to Him it is fitting.

Alone in kingship, truly powerful, His scholars sing to Him: To You and to You; to You, surely to You; to You, only to You; to You, Lord, is the sovereignty; to Him it is becoming; to Him it is fitting.

Commanding in kingship, truly revered, His near ones sing to Him: To You and to You; to You, surely to You; to You, only to You; to You, Lord, is the sovereignty; to Him it is becoming; to Him it is fit-ting.

Humble in kingship, truly redeeming, His righteous sing to Him: To You and to You; to You, surely to You; to You, only to You; to You, Lord, is the sovereignty; to Him it is becoming; to Him it is fitting

Holy in kingship, truly merciful, His angels sing to Him: To You and to You; to You, surely to You; to You, only to You; to You, Lord, is the sovereignty; to Him it is becoming; to Him it is fitting

Indomitable in kingship, truly sustaining, His innocent sing to Him: To You and to You; to You, surely to You; to You, only to You; to You, Lord, is the sovereignty; to Him it is becoming; to Him it is fitting.

אַדִּיר הוּא

אַדִּיר הוּא, יִבְנֶה בֵיתוֹ בְּקָרוֹב, בִּמְהֵרָה בִּמְהֵרָה, בְּיָמֵינוּ בְּקָרוֹב. אֵל בְּנֵה, אֵל בְּנֵה, בְּנֵה בֵיתְךָ בְּקָרוֹב.

בָּחוּר הוּא, גָּדוֹל הוּא, דָּגוּל הוּא, יִבְנֶה בֵיתוֹ בְּקָרוֹב, בִּמְהֵרָה בִּמְהֵרָה, בְּיָמֵינוּ בְקָרוֹב. אֵל בְּנֵה, אֵל בְּנֵה, בְּנֵה בֵיתְךָ בְּקָרוֹב.

הָדוּר הוּא, וָתִיק הוּא, זַכַּאי הוּא, חָסִיד הוּא, יִבְנֶה בֵיתוֹ בְּקָרוֹב, בִּמְהֵרָה בִּמְהֵרָה, בְּיָמֵינוּ בְקָרוֹב. אֵל בְּנֵה, אֵל בְּנֵה, בְּנֵה בֵיתְךָ בְּקָרוֹב.

טָהוֹר הוּא, יָחִיד הוּא, כַּבִּיר הוּא, לָמוּד הוּא, מֶלֶךְ הוּא, נוֹרָא הוּא, סַגִּיב הוּא, עִזּוּז הוּא, פּוֹדֶה הוּא, צַדִּיק הוּא, יִבְנֶה בֵיתוֹ בְּקָרוֹב, בִּמְהֵרָה בִּמְהֵרָה, בְּיָמֵינוּ בְקָרוֹב. אֵל בְּנֵה, אֵל בְּנֵה, בְּנֵה בֵיתְךָ בְּקָרוֹב.

קָדוֹשׁ הוּא, רַחוּם הוּא, שַׁדַּי הוּא, תַּקִּיף הוּא, יִבְנֶה בֵיתוֹ בְּקָרוֹב, בִּמְהֵרָה בִּמְהֵרָה, בְּיָמֵינוּ בְקָרוֹב. אֵל בְּנֵה, אֵל בְּנֵה, בְּנֵה בֵיתְךָ בְּקָרוֹב.

Adir Hu

Mighty is He. May He soon rebuild His House. Rapidly, rapidly! Soon, in our days. God, rebuild; God, rebuild. Speedily rebuild Your House.

Choice is He. Great is He. Foremost is He. May He soon rebuild His House. Rapidly, rapidly! Soon, in our days. God, rebuild; God, rebuild. Speedily rebuild Your House.

Glorious is He. Worthy is He. Faultless is He. Righteous is He. May He soon rebuild His House. Rapidly, rapidly! Soon, in our days. God, rebuild; God, rebuild. Speedily rebuild Your House.

Pure is He. One is He. Mighty is He. Wise is He. Sovereign is He. Awe-inspiring is He. Exalted is He. Powerful is He. Redeeming is He. Just is He. May He soon rebuild His House. Rapidly, rapidly! Soon, in our days. God, rebuild; God, rebuild. Speedily rebuild Your House.

Holy is He. Compassionate is He. Almighty is He. Omnipotent is He. May He soon rebuild His House. Rapidly, rapidly! Soon, in our days. God, rebuild; God, rebuild. Speedily rebuild Your House.

אֶחָד מִי יוֹדֵעַ

אֶחָד מִי יוֹדֵעַ? אֶחָד אֲנִי יוֹדֵעַ:
אֶחָד אֱלֹהֵינוּ שֶׁבַּשָּׁמַיִם וּבָאָרֶץ.

שְׁנַיִם מִי יוֹדֵעַ? שְׁנַיִם אֲנִי יוֹדֵעַ:
שְׁנֵי לֻחוֹת הַבְּרִית, אֶחָד אֱלֹהֵינוּ שֶׁבַּשָּׁמַיִם וּבָאָרֶץ.

שְׁלֹשָׁה מִי יוֹדֵעַ? שְׁלֹשָׁה אֲנִי יוֹדֵעַ:
שְׁלֹשָׁה אָבוֹת, שְׁנֵי לֻחוֹת הַבְּרִית, אֶחָד אֱלֹהֵינוּ שֶׁבַּשָּׁמַיִם וּבָאָרֶץ.

אַרְבַּע מִי יוֹדֵעַ? אַרְבַּע אֲנִי יוֹדֵעַ:
אַרְבַּע אִמָּהוֹת, שְׁלֹשָׁה אָבוֹת, שְׁנֵי לֻחוֹת הַבְּרִית, אֶחָד אֱלֹהֵינוּ שֶׁבַּשָּׁמַיִם וּבָאָרֶץ.

חֲמִשָּׁה מִי יוֹדֵעַ? חֲמִשָּׁה אֲנִי יוֹדֵעַ:
חֲמִשָּׁה חֻמְשֵׁי תוֹרָה, אַרְבַּע אִמָּהוֹת, שְׁלֹשָׁה אָבוֹת, שְׁנֵי לֻחוֹת הַבְּרִית, אֶחָד אֱלֹהֵינוּ שֶׁבַּשָּׁמַיִם וּבָאָרֶץ.

שִׁשָּׁה מִי יוֹדֵעַ? שִׁשָּׁה אֲנִי יוֹדֵעַ:
שִׁשָּׁה סִדְרֵי מִשְׁנָה, חֲמִשָּׁה חֻמְשֵׁי תוֹרָה, אַרְבַּע אִמָּהוֹת, שְׁלֹשָׁה אָבוֹת, שְׁנֵי לֻחוֹת הַבְּרִית, אֶחָד אֱלֹהֵינוּ שֶׁבַּשָּׁמַיִם וּבָאָרֶץ.

שִׁבְעָה מִי יוֹדֵעַ? שִׁבְעָה אֲנִי יוֹדֵעַ:
שִׁבְעָה יְמֵי שַׁבַּתָּא, שִׁשָּׁה סִדְרֵי מִשְׁנָה, חֲמִשָּׁה חֻמְשֵׁי תוֹרָה, אַרְבַּע אִמָּהוֹת, שְׁלֹשָׁה אָבוֹת, שְׁנֵי לֻחוֹת הַבְּרִית, אֶחָד אֱלֹהֵינוּ שֶׁבַּשָּׁמַיִם וּבָאָרֶץ.

שְׁמוֹנָה מִי יוֹדֵעַ? שְׁמוֹנָה אֲנִי יוֹדֵעַ:
שְׁמוֹנָה יְמֵי מִילָה, שִׁבְעָה יְמֵי שַׁבַּתָּא, שִׁשָּׁה סִדְרֵי מִשְׁנָה, חֲמִשָּׁה חֻמְשֵׁי תוֹרָה, אַרְבַּע אִמָּהוֹת, שְׁלֹשָׁה אָבוֹת, שְׁנֵי לֻחוֹת הַבְּרִית, אֶחָד אֱלֹהֵינוּ שֶׁבַּשָּׁמַיִם וּבָאָרֶץ.

Eḥad Mi Yode'a?

Who knows one? I know one:

One is our God in heaven and earth.

Who knows two? I know two:

Two stone tablets of the Law; One is our God in heaven and earth.

Who knows three? I know three:

Three Patriarchs; Two stone tablets of the Law; One is our God in heaven and earth.

Who knows four? I know four:

Four Matriarchs; Three Patriarchs; Two stone tablets of the Law; One is our God in heaven and earth.

Who knows five? I know five:

Five the Books of the Torah; Four Matriarchs; Three Patriarchs; Two stone tablets of the Law; One is our God in heaven and earth.

Who knows six? I know six:

Six sections of Mishnah; Five the Books of the Torah; Four Matriarchs; Three Patriarchs; Two stone tablets of the Law; One is our God in heaven and earth.

Who knows seven? I know seven:

Seven days of the week; Six sections of Mishnah; Five the Books of the Torah; Four Matriarchs; Three Patriarchs; Two stone tablets of the Law; One is our God in heaven and earth.

Who knows eight? I know eight:

Eight days to the *brit milah*; Seven days of the week; Six sections of Mishnah; Five the Books of the Torah; Four Matriarchs; Three Patriarchs; Two stone tablets of the Law; One is our God in heaven and earth.

תִּשְׁעָה מִי יוֹדֵעַ? תִּשְׁעָה אֲנִי יוֹדֵעַ:

תִּשְׁעָה יַרְחֵי לֵדָה, שְׁמוֹנָה יְמֵי מִילָה, שִׁבְעָה יְמֵי שַׁבְּתָא, שִׁשָּׁה סִדְרֵי מִשְׁנָה, חֲמִשָּׁה חֻמְשֵׁי תוֹרָה, אַרְבַּע אִמָּהוֹת, שְׁלֹשָׁה אָבוֹת, שְׁנֵי לֻחוֹת הַבְּרִית, אֶחָד אֱלֹהֵינוּ שֶׁבַּשָּׁמַיִם וּבָאָרֶץ.

עֲשָׂרָה מִי יוֹדֵעַ? עֲשָׂרָה אֲנִי יוֹדֵעַ:

עֲשָׂרָה דִבְּרַיָּא, תִּשְׁעָה יַרְחֵי לֵדָה, שְׁמוֹנָה יְמֵי מִילָה, שִׁבְעָה יְמֵי שַׁבְּתָא, שִׁשָּׁה סִדְרֵי מִשְׁנָה, חֲמִשָּׁה חֻמְשֵׁי תוֹרָה, אַרְבַּע אִמָּהוֹת, שְׁלֹשָׁה אָבוֹת, שְׁנֵי לֻחוֹת הַבְּרִית, אֶחָד אֱלֹהֵינוּ שֶׁבַּשָּׁמַיִם וּבָאָרֶץ.

אַחַד עָשָׂר מִי יוֹדֵעַ? אַחַד עָשָׂר אֲנִי יוֹדֵעַ:

אַחַד עָשָׂר כּוֹכְבַיָּא, עֲשָׂרָה דִבְּרַיָּא, תִּשְׁעָה יַרְחֵי לֵדָה, שְׁמוֹנָה יְמֵי מִילָה, שִׁבְעָה יְמֵי שַׁבְּתָא, שִׁשָּׁה סִדְרֵי מִשְׁנָה, חֲמִשָּׁה חֻמְשֵׁי תוֹרָה, אַרְבַּע אִמָּהוֹת, שְׁלֹשָׁה אָבוֹת, שְׁנֵי לֻחוֹת הַבְּרִית, אֶחָד אֱלֹהֵינוּ שֶׁבַּשָּׁמַיִם וּבָאָרֶץ.

שְׁנֵים עָשָׂר מִי יוֹדֵעַ? שְׁנֵים עָשָׂר אֲנִי יוֹדֵעַ:

שְׁנֵים עָשָׂר שִׁבְטַיָּא, אַחַד עָשָׂר כּוֹכְבַיָּא, עֲשָׂרָה דִבְּרַיָּא, תִּשְׁעָה יַרְחֵי לֵדָה, שְׁמוֹנָה יְמֵי מִילָה, שִׁבְעָה יְמֵי שַׁבְּתָא, שִׁשָּׁה סִדְרֵי מִשְׁנָה, חֲמִשָּׁה חֻמְשֵׁי תוֹרָה, אַרְבַּע אִמָּהוֹת, שְׁלֹשָׁה אָבוֹת, שְׁנֵי לֻחוֹת הַבְּרִית, אֶחָד אֱלֹהֵינוּ שֶׁבַּשָּׁמַיִם וּבָאָרֶץ.

שְׁלֹשָׁה עָשָׂר מִי יוֹדֵעַ? שְׁלֹשָׁה עָשָׂר אֲנִי יוֹדֵעַ:

שְׁלֹשָׁה עָשָׂר מִדַּיָּא, שְׁנֵים עָשָׂר שִׁבְטַיָּא, אַחַד עָשָׂר כּוֹכְבַיָּא, עֲשָׂרָה דִבְּרַיָּא, תִּשְׁעָה יַרְחֵי לֵדָה, שְׁמוֹנָה יְמֵי מִילָה, שִׁבְעָה יְמֵי שַׁבְּתָא, שִׁשָּׁה סִדְרֵי מִשְׁנָה, חֲמִשָּׁה חֻמְשֵׁי תוֹרָה, אַרְבַּע אִמָּהוֹת, שְׁלֹשָׁה אָבוֹת, שְׁנֵי לֻחוֹת הַבְּרִית, אֶחָד אֱלֹהֵינוּ שֶׁבַּשָּׁמַיִם וּבָאָרֶץ.

Who knows nine? I know nine:

Nine months of pregnancy; Eight days to the *brit milah*; Seven days of the week; Six sections of Mishnah; Five the Books of the Torah; Four Matriarchs; Three Patriarchs; Two stone tablets of the Law; One is our God in heaven and earth.

Who knows ten? I know ten:

Ten, the Ten Commandments; Nine months of pregnancy; Eight days to the *brit milah*; Seven days of the week; Six sections of Mishnah; Five the Books of the Torah; Four Matriarchs; Three Patriarchs; Two stone tablets of the Law; One is our God in heaven and earth.

Who knows eleven? I know eleven:

Eleven stars in Joseph's dream; Ten, the Ten Commandments; Nine months of pregnancy; Eight days to the *brit milah*; Seven days of the week; Six sections of Mishnah; Five the Books of the Torah; Four Matriarchs; Three Patriarchs; Two stone tablets of the Law; One is our God in heaven and earth.

Who knows twelve? I know twelve:

Twelve tribes of Israel; Eleven stars in Joseph's dream; Ten, the Ten Commandments; Nine months of pregnancy; Eight days to the *brit milah*; Seven days of the week; Six sections of Mishnah; Five the Books of the Torah; Four Matriarchs; Three Patriarchs; Two stone tablets of the Law; One is our God in heaven and earth.

Who knows thirteen? I know thirteen:

Thirteen attributes of God; Twelve tribes of Israel; Eleven stars in Joseph's dream; Ten, the Ten Commandments; Nine months of pregnancy; Eight days to the *brit milah*; Seven days of the week; Six sections of Mishnah; Five the Books of the Torah; Four Matriarchs; Three Patriarchs; Two stone tablets of the Law; One is our God in heaven and earth.

חַד גַּדְיָא

חַד גַּדְיָא, חַד גַּדְיָא,דְּזַבִּין אַבָּא בִּתְרֵי זוּזֵי, חַד גַּדְיָא, חַד גַּדְיָא.

וְאָתָא שֻׁנְרָא,וְאָכְלָה לְגַדְיָא, דְּזַבִּיןאַבָּא בִּתְרֵי זוּזֵי, חַד גַּדְיָא, חַד גַּדְיָא.

וְאָתָא כַלְבָּא, וְנָשַׁךְ לְשֻׁנְרָא, דְּאָכְלָה לְגַדְיָא, דְּזַבִּין אַבָּא בִּתְרֵי זוּזֵי, חַד גַּדְיָא, חַד גַּדְיָא.

וְאָתָא חֻטְרָא, וְהִכָּה לְכַלְבָּא, דְּנָשַׁךְ לְשֻׁנְרָא, דְּאָכְלָה לְגַדְיָא, דְּזַבִּין אַבָּא בִּתְרֵי זוּזֵי, חַד גַּדְיָא, חַד גַּדְיָא.

וְאָתָא נוּרָא, וְשָׂרַף לְחֻטְרָא,דְּהִכָּה לְכַלְבָּא, דְּנָשַׁךְ לְשֻׁנְרָא, דְּאָכְלָה לְגַדְיָא, דְּזַבִּין אַבָּא בִּתְרֵי זוּזֵי, חַד גַּדְיָא, חַד גַּדְיָא.

וְאָתָא מַיָּא, וְכָבָה לְנוּרָא, דְּשָׂרַף לְחֻטְרָא, דְּהִכָּה לְכַלְבָּא, דְּנָשַׁךְ לְשֻׁנְרָא, דְּאָכְלָה לְגַדְיָא, דְּזַבִּין אַבָּא בִּתְרֵי זוּזֵי, חַד גַּדְיָא, חַד גַּדְיָא.

וְאָתָא תּוֹרָא, וְשָׁתָא לְמַיָּא,דְּכָבָה לְנוּרָא, דְּשָׂרַף לְחֻטְרָא, דְּהִכָּה לְכַלְבָּא, דְּנָשַׁךְ לְשֻׁנְרָא, דְּאָכְלָה לְגַדְיָא, דְּזַבִּין אַבָּא בִּתְרֵי זוּזֵי, חַד גַּדְיָא, חַד גַּדְיָא.

וְאָתָא הַשּׁוֹחֵט, וְשָׁחַט לְתוֹרָא, דְּשָׁתָא לְמַיָּא, דְּכָבָה לְנוּרָא,דְּשָׂרַף לְחֻטְרָא, דְּהִכָּה לְכַלְבָּא, דְּנָשַׁךְ לְשֻׁנְרָא, דְּאָכְלָה לְגַדְיָא, דְּזַבִּין אַבָּא בִּתְרֵי זוּזֵי, חַד גַּדְיָא, חַד גַּדְיָא.

וְאָתָא מַלְאַךְ הַמָּוֶת, וְשָׁחַט לְשׁוֹחֵט, דְּשָׁחַט לְתוֹרָא, דְּשָׁתָא לְמַיָּא, דְּכָבָה לְנוּרָא, דְּשָׂרַף לְחֻטְרָא, דְּהִכָּה לְכַלְבָּא, דְּנָשַׁךְ לְשֻׁנְרָא, דְּאָכְלָה לְגַדְיָא,דְּזַבִּין אַבָּא בִּתְרֵי זוּזֵי, חַד גַּדְיָא, חַד גַּדְיָא.

וְאָתָא הַקָּדוֹשׁ בָּרוּךְ הוּא, וְשָׁחַט לְמַלְאַךְ הַמָּוֶת, דְּשָׁחַט לְשׁוֹחֵט, דְּשָׁחַט לְתוֹרָא, דְּשָׁתָא לְמַיָּא, דְּכָבָה לְנוּרָא,דְּשָׂרַף לְחֻטְרָא, דְּהִכָּה לְכַלְבָּא, דְּנָשַׁךְ לְשֻׁנְרָא, דְּאָכְלָה לְגַדְיָא, דְּזַבִּין אַבָּא בִּתְרֵי זוּזֵי, חַד גַּדְיָא, חַד גַּדְיָא.

Ḥad Gadya

One kid, One kid, that father bought for two zuzim. One kid, One kid.

A cat passed by and ate the kid, that father bought for two zuzim. One kid, One kid.

A dog arrived and bit the cat, that ate the kid, that father bought for two zuzim. One kid, One kid.

A heavy stick then beat the dog, that bit the cat, that ate the kid, that father bought for two zuzim. One kid, One kid.

A fire burned the heavy stick, that beat the dog, that bit the cat, that ate the kid, that father bought for two zuzim. One kid, One kid.

Water doused the fire, that burned the stick, that beat the dog that bit the cat, that ate the kid, that father bought for two zuzim. One kid, One kid.

An ox drank the water, that doused the fire, that burned the stick, that beat the dog, that bit the cat, that ate the kid, that father bought for two zuzim. One kid, One kid.

A butcher slaughtered the ox, that drank the water, that doused the fire, that burned the stick, that beat the dog, that bit the cat, that ate the kid, that father bought for two zuzim. One kid, One kid.

The Angel of Death slew the butcher who slaughtered the ox, that drank the water, that doused the fire, that burned the stick, that beat the dog, that bit the cat, that ate the kid, that father bought for two zuzim. One kid, One kid.

Then the Holy One Blessed be He killed the Angel of Death, who slew the butcher who slaughtered the ox, that drank the water, that doused the fire, that burned the stick, that beat the dog, that bit the cat, that ate the kid, that father bought for two zuzim. One kid, One kid.

עניני ערב פסח

MATTERS CONCERNING EREV PESAḤ

Destruction of Ḥameẓ בעור חמץ

The Mishnah (*Temurah* 33b) divides *issurei hana'ah*, objects from which benefit is prohibited and thus must be disposed of, into two categories: *nikbarin*, those which are to be buried, and *nisrafin*, those which are to be burned. *Nikbarin* includes any such prohibited object that the Torah does not require us to eliminate through burning. The Mishnah then states that the method of disposal of these two kinds of objects may not be reversed: one may neither bury *nisrafin* nor burn *nikbarin*. According to the Rabbis (Mishnah, *Pesaḥim* 21a), *bi'ur ḥameẓ*, the elimination of *ḥameẓ*, may be done in any fashion. *Ḥameẓ* would thus seem to belong to the category of *nikbarin*. How then, asks Magen Avraham (*Oraḥ Ḥayyim* 445:1), is it permissible to burn *ḥameẓ*?

Gra (*Oraḥ Ḥayyim* 445:1) maintains that even the Rabbis are of the view that ideally one should burn the *ḥameẓ*. In fact, this is implied by the language in the Mishnah, which states that one may even ("*af*") eliminate the *ḥameẓ* through other means, implying that it is a secondary option; furthermore, there is frequent mention at the beginning of *Pesaḥim* of the rules regarding the burning of the *ḥameẓ* without any indication that the majority opinion does not specifically require burning at all. Evidently, then, *ḥameẓ* is different from other *nikbarin* in that it is preferable to burn it, even though secondary options certainly exist. *Ḥameẓ*, therefore, not only may be burned but should be burned.

We can utilize this idea to explain another *halakhah* as well. The Gemara (*Pesaḥim* 21b) states that *ḥameẓ* that is singed before it becomes prohibited on *Erev Pesaḥ* is permitted on *Pesaḥ*. Some of the Rishonim (*Tosafot, Pesaḥim* 21b, s.v. *ḥorkho kodem zemano*) are of the view that the statement of the Gemara deals with the case where the *ḥameẓ* has been rendered inedible; only then is it permitted to eat this *ḥameẓ* on *Pesaḥ*; others (Rashi, *Pesaḥim* 21b, s.v. *lo ẓerikha*) require the *ḥameẓ* to have been transformed to the point that it no longer appears or tastes like *ḥameẓ*. Rambam, however, does not specify any of these requirements. He might very well believe that since it is preferable for one to fulfill the *miẓvah* of *tashbitu*, eliminating the *ḥameẓ*, by burning the *ḥameẓ*, as opposed to other methods of destruction, it becomes permitted after it has been burned sufficiently, even if it is still edible and recognizable. This is due to the principle of *na'aseit miẓvato*: once one performs the specific *miẓvah* that is applicable to a particular prohibited item (if there is one), the prohibition is no longer in effect. It would be for this reason that Rambam records this *halakhah* in his discussion of the details of the *miẓvah* of *bi'ur ḥameẓ* (*Hilkhot Ḥameẓ u-Maẓẓah* 3:11) and not while discussing the *halakhot* of inedible and ruined *ḥameẓ* (ibid. 4:8–12).

There is, however, one caveat which must be added. It is explicit in the same

Gemara that according to the Rabbis, this burning is effective in permitting the *ḥameẓ* to be eaten only if it is done before the onset of the prohibition of *ḥameẓ* on *Erev Pesaḥ*; if it is done afterwards, the *ḥameẓ* remains prohibited. According to Rabbi Judah, however, it becomes permitted if burned at any time. Now, if the Rabbis indeed apply the principle of *na'aseit miẓvato*, and allow the burned *ḥameẓ* to be eaten, because they agree that ideally one must burn the *ḥameẓ*, then they should allow the *ḥameẓ* – no matter when it was burned. We must, therefore, conclude that according to Rambam (see *Hilkhot Ḥameẓ u-Maẓẓah* 2:1), since the *miẓvah* of *tashbitu*, destroying one's *ḥameẓ*, is in effect only before the *ḥameẓ* becomes prohibited, only then is there a preference to eliminate it specifically through burning. After it becomes prohibited, one is required to dispose of the *ḥameẓ* simply so as not to violate *bal yera'eh* (the prohibition of possessing *ḥameẓ* on *Pesaḥ*) – but there is no longer a requirement to specifically burn the *ḥameẓ*, because there is no *kiyum aseh* of *tashbitu*, to destroy the *ḥameẓ*. Since there is no preference to destroy the *ḥameẓ* by burning, no permissibility to consume the *ḥameẓ* is created by *na'aseit miẓvato*. Rabbi Judah, however, derives the obligation to burn *ḥameẓ* from the *miẓvah* of burning *notar* (sacrificial meat that was not eaten during its allotted time), and therefore, the *miẓvah* applies specifically after the prohibition sets in; he thus maintains that when one burns the *ḥameẓ*, even at that point it becomes permitted.

Rama (*Oraḥ Ḥayyim* 445:1) writes that the custom is specifically to burn the *ḥameẓ* and not use other means of destruction. Gra comments that the reason why this is only a custom is that even Rabbi Judah actually requires burning only after the time that *ḥameẓ* is prohibited (except according to Rashi), and since our practice is to eliminate the *ḥameẓ* earlier, there is no real obligation to burn it according to any opinion in the Gemara. Yet Gra himself maintains, as noted above, that before the *ḥameẓ* becomes prohibited, everyone agrees that at least ideally one must burn it! We must perforce conclude that even though one indeed fulfills a *miẓvah* by specifically burning the *ḥameẓ* on *Erev Pesaḥ* while it is still permitted, and that is why one may derive benefit from the burnt *ḥameẓ* even on *Pesaḥ*, it is still not in any sense obligatory to do so. Therefore, it is only a custom to burn the *ḥameẓ*. (*Reshimot*)

On the fourteenth of Nisan, *Erev Pesaḥ*, there is a *miẓvah* to destroy all *ḥameẓ* found in one's domain. When the fourteenth of Nisan occurs on a Shabbat, Rabbi Meir (*Pesaḥim* 49a) states, all *ḥameẓ* must be destroyed before Shabbat (on the thirteenth of Nisan), except for *ḥameẓ* that will be needed for two Shabbat meals. Rambam (*Hilkhot Ḥameẓ u-Maẓẓah* 3:3) and the *Shulḥan Arukh* (*Oraḥ Ḥayyim* 444) follow Rabbi Meir's opinion. With respect to *ḥameẓ* that is left over on Shabbat, Rambam and *Shulḥan Arukh* state that one must nullify

the remaining *ḥameẓ* and cover it until after the first days of *yom tov*, at which time one is to destroy any leftover *ḥameẓ*. Rabbi Akiva Eiger, in his glosses to the *Shulḥan Arukh*, wonders why one must one wait until after *yom tov* to burn the *ḥameẓ* instead of discarding the remaining *ḥameẓ* on Shabbat itself, prior to the time that the prohibition against *ḥameẓ* goes into effect. Rabbi Akiva Eiger suggests that there may be a prohibition of handling *ḥameẓ* that must be destroyed, and states that the matter requires additional investigation.

The question posed by Rabbi Akiva Eiger can be resolved as follows. According to Rambam, Rabbi Meir, in requiring that *ḥameẓ* must be destroyed on the thirteenth of Nisan prior to Shabbat, is of the view that one is not permitted to perform the *miẓvah* of destroying the *ḥameẓ* on Shabbat. One may set aside the amount of bread that will be needed for the two Shabbat meals. One may not, however, destroy the leftover bread on Shabbat because that would violate a rabbinic prohibition of destroying *ḥameẓ* on Shabbat.

The concept that destruction of *ḥameẓ* on Shabbat violates a prohibition is analogous to the destruction of *ḥallah* that has become impure. The Mishnah (*Beiẓah* 27b) states that *ḥallah* that has become impure may not be moved during a *yom tov*. Rashi states that although feeding one's animal on a *yom tov* is permitted, and ordinarily, one may feed impure *ḥallah* to his animals, one may not feed impure *ḥallah* to his animals on a *yom tov*, because there is a prohibition against the destruction on a *yom tov* of *kodshim* (consecrated items) that have become impure. Rashi explains that the fact that the Torah requires one to destroy impure *kodshim* indicates that the destruction of such items is considered a *mela'khah* (work), and performing a *mela'khah* on a *yom tov* is not permitted. Rashi's rationale may similarly apply to the destruction of *ḥameẓ*. The fact that the Torah requires us to destroy *ḥameẓ* before *Pesaḥ* indicates that such destruction is rabbinically equivalent to a *mela'khah*. Consequently, we are not permitted to destroy *ḥameẓ* on Shabbat. (*Reshimot*)

The punishment of lashes is not imposed for violation of a prohibition that is *nitak la-aseh*, that is, associated with and mitigated by fulfilling a positive commandment. The Gemara (*Pesaḥim* 95a) states that a person who did not remove his *ḥameẓ* from his possession before *Pesaḥ* is not liable for lashes, because the negative prohibitions of *bal yera'eh* – "*lo yera'eh lekha se'or*, no leaven shall be found in all your territory" (Ex. 13:7) and *bal yimmaẓe* – "*se'or lo yimmaẓe be-bateikhem*, no leaven shall be found in your houses" (Ex. 12:19) are each considered *nitak* to the positive commandment of "*tashbitu se'or mi-bateikhem*, eliminate leavening from your property" (Ex. 12:15). The ruling of Rambam (*Hilkhot Ḥameẓ u-Maẓẓah* 1:3), that a person who purchases *ḥameẓ* on *Pesaḥ* is punished with lashes, seems to be inconsistent with the Gemara. To resolve this inconsistency, Rav Hayim of Brisk explained that in this case the positive

commandment actually acts as an implied prohibition. Although the *mizvah* of *tashbitu* is phrased in the active form, it does not, according to Rav Hayim, constitute a *ma'aseh mizvah*. Rather, the verse implies an injunction against owning *ḥamez*, with the requirement to destroy it being merely a preventive measure (*issur aseh*). Consequently, the aforementioned prohibitions are not considered *nitak la-aseh*, because the positive commandment of *tashbitu* is not an ordinary *aseh*.

The Mishnah (*Pesaḥim* 2:1) records a dispute between Rabbi Judah and the Rabbis as to the correct method of eliminating *ḥamez* from one's possession. Rabbi Judah states that the only acceptable method for destroying *ḥamez* is with fire. The Rabbis hold that any method may be employed, including grinding the *ḥamez* and casting it to the wind. According to Rabbi Judah, burning *ḥamez* is more than just a means to ensure that one will not violate the prohibitions of *bal yera'eh* and *bal yimmaze*, for if that were the case, he should agree that any method of destruction would suffice. Rather, burning *ḥamez*, according to Rabbi Judah, must be considered a *kiyum mizvah*, and as such, mitigates the prohibitions of *bal yera'eh* and *bal yimmaze*, and lashes would not be administered for their violation. According to the Rabbis, however, the desired result is the elimination of the *ḥamez*. The purpose of destroying the *ḥamez* is to preclude one from being in violation of the negative prohibitions and not to facilitate a *kiyum mizvah*; the method of destruction is thus immaterial. As such, according to the Rabbis, there is no positive commandment to offset the negative commandments, and a violator would thus be liable for lashes. The ruling of the Gemara (*Pesaḥim* 95a) that one does not receive lashes for either of these prohibitions is based upon the opinion of Rabbi Judah, while Rambam (*Hilkhot Ḥamez u-Mazzah* 3:11), who states that one is liable for lashes if he commits these transgressions, accepts the ruling of the Rabbis.

If, however, according to Rav Hayim, *tashbitu* is only an implied prohibition, one may ask why it is that on *Erev Pesaḥ* we recite a blessing on *bedikat ḥamez*, the act which is a prelude to destroying the *ḥamez*, as this would appear to violate the principle that one does not recite a blessing on a *mizvah* that is designed to avoid a prohibition.

The answer lies in the important distinction between the nature of the *mizvah* of *tashbitu* before midday of the fourteenth of Nisan, when *ḥamez* is still permitted to be in one's possession, and after that time. Ramban (beginning of *Pesaḥim*) explains that just as we learn from the word "*akh*, however" (Ex. 12:15) that we are to split the day in terms of the prohibition of owning *ḥamez*, meaning that it is permissible to own *ḥamez* until midday and only forbidden after that time, so, too, we learn that we are obligated to remove *ḥamez* from our possession before midday. Therefore, until midday, *tashbitu* is a *kiyum aseh*, representing a fulfillment of the *mizvah*, and hence, it is appropriate to recite a blessing on this *kiyum*, because the *bedikah* and *bi'ur* are done before

midday. However, the prohibitions of *bal yera'eh* and *bal yimmaze*, and hence the possibility of considering them *nitak la-aseh*, came into force only on *Pesaḥ*, and at that point the *mizvah* of *tashbitu* has already been transformed into an *issur aseh*, a prohibition derived from a positive commandment.

Alternatively, even if we were to assume that the prohibitions of *bal yera'eh* and *bal yimmaze* are *nitak la-aseh*, it is possible to suggest another reason why one would receive lashes for owning *ḥamez*, despite the fact that this prohibited act can be mitigated by a positive commandment. Rambam (*Hilkhot Temurah* 1:1) writes that one receives lashes for violating the prohibition of *temurah*, transferring the *kedushah* from an animal designated as a *korban* to another animal. He explains that one gets lashes even though *temurah* can be rectified by fulfillment of the positive commandment that the sanctity devolves on both animals "*ve-hayah hu u-temurato yihyeh kodesh*" (Lev. 27:10), because *temurah* actually constitutes two negative commandments, "*lo yah'alifennu*, you shall not change it" (Lev. 27:10) and "*ve-lo yamir oto*, you shall not replace it" (Lev. 27:10). The positive commandment can rectify only one negative commandment; thus one receives lashes for violating the second negative commandment. Owning *ḥamez* also entails two negative commandments, *lo yera'eh* and *lo yimmaze*. Since the positive commandment of *tashbitu* can mitigate only one prohibition, one receives lashes for purchasing *ḥamez*.

This approach is still difficult, because the Gemara (*Pesaḥim* 95a) clearly states that one is not liable for lashes for either prohibition, as they are associated with a positive commandment. Rabbenu Hananel presents an alternative text for this Gemara. His text reads, "One does not receive lashes for owning *ḥamez* on *Pesaḥ*, because this violation does not involve an activity." This undoubtedly was the text that Rambam had as well. This text implies that a person who does take an active role in the violation of the prohibitions of *bal yera'eh* and *bal yimmaze*, such as by purchasing *ḥamez* on *Pesaḥ*, would indeed be liable to receive lashes. (*Reshimot*)

Kashering Utensils for Pesaḥ — הכשר כלים

Using utensils that are kosher for *Pesaḥ* is not simply a matter of using utensils that have no *ta'am* (taste) of *ḥamez*. Rather it is part of a requirement of using utensils that have a status related to *Pesaḥ*. We can see this from the fact that Rambam (*Hilkhot Ḥamez u-Mazzah* 5:23) states that after a vessel has been immersed in boiling water to kasher it for *Pesaḥ*, it should then be rinsed in cold water, a process Rambam does not mention when discussing kashering utensils in other circumstances. *Haga'ot Maimoniot* (ibid.) explains in the name of the Gaonim that this *halakhah* is modeled after the process of kashering utensils that have absorbed the flavor of *korbanot*. These vessels must be purged

in hot water and then rinsed in cold water (*merikah u-shetifah*). Based on this comparison, we may understand that the process of kashering for *Pesaḥ* is different from the regular process of kashering vessels, which is derived from the section in the Torah that discusses *gi'ulei kelei Midyan* (Num. 31:22), which does not mention rinsing in cold water. Normally, it is necessary to simply extract the prohibited *ta'am* absorbed by the vessel; when kashering for *Pesaḥ*, however, one must change the status of the utensil from a *ḥamez̧* vessel to a non-*ḥamez̧* one. Similarly, when kashering vessels that have absorbed the *ta'am* of *korbanot*, it is necessary to do more than just extract the prohibited *ta'am*; in fact, the Gemara (*Zevaḥim* 95b) presents the possibility that one must purge these vessels even if they have not absorbed *ta'am*. In both cases, the goal of the process is not simply to extract the prohibited *ta'am*, but to change the utensil's status.

This point explains other unique *halakhot* of *Pesaḥ*. Quoting the Gemara (*Pesaḥim* 30b) and a line in the *yoz̧er* of *Shabbat ha-Gadol*, Magen Avraham (*Oraḥ Ḥayyim* 451:6) rules that it is preferable to buy new vessels for *Pesaḥ* rather than to kasher old ones, a *halakhah* not found regarding general kashering requirements. Through kashering the utensil, the *yoz̧er* states, it becomes like new. We see again that it is not enough to merely remove the *ḥamez̧* from a vessel, for there would then be no preference to obtain new vessels over kashered old ones. Rather, there is a unique *halakhah* to change the status of the vessel from a *ḥamez̧* one to a non-*ḥamez̧* one, and it is as if a new vessel emerges through the kashering. Similarly, Rambam (*Hilkhot Ḥamez̧ u-Maz̧z̧ah* 5:24) rules that even a *keli sheni* (a pot not itself heated over a fire, but that has hot water poured into it from a pot that was heated on the fire) that had cooked *ḥamez̧* in it must be kashered for *Pesaḥ*. Rambam does not mention this requirement with respect to any other prohibition, because a *keli sheni* will not absorb *ta'am*. On *Pesaḥ*, however, all vessels used for *ḥamez̧* are prohibited, even if they do not have prohibited *ta'am*, because they lack the status of being a *Pesaḥ* utensil.

After stating that the kashered utensils must be washed with cold water, Rambam adds "and then use them for *maz̧z̧ah*," a phrase that is seemingly unnecessary because that is obviously the point of the whole process. Yet Rambam stresses this line, repeating it several times when describing each different type of vessel. In this phrase, Rambam suggests that for *Pesaḥ*, rabbinically, it is not enough to merely extract the *ḥamez̧* from the vessel's walls, as is normally the case when removing prohibited flavors. For *Pesaḥ*, there is a special requirement to positively change the status of the vessel, from *ḥamez̧* to *maz̧z̧ah*.

Most years, *Shabbat ha-Gadol* coincides with *Parashat Z̧av*, the *parashah* that contains the *halakhot* of kashering vessels that were used for *korbanot* (*merikah u-shetifah*). It is therefore fitting that we should read *Parshat Z̧av* just

before *Pesaḥ* as we are preparing for the holiday, because this *parashah* serves as the model of the special process in kashering utensils for *Pesaḥ*. (*Reshimot*)

Prohibition of Eating on Erev Pesaḥ אסור אכילה בערב פסח

The Mishnah (*Pesaḥim* 10:1) states that eating is prohibited on the eve of Passover from the time that is "close to *minḥah*" until nightfall. Rashi (*Pesaḥim* 99b) explains that refraining from eating in the afternoon enables us to fulfill the *miẓvah* of eating the *maẓẓah* at night with greater appetite and enthusiasm, and that is considered a *hiddur miẓvah*, a "beautification of the commandment."

The concept of *hiddur miẓvah* is derived from the verse (Ex. 15:2) "*Zeh Keli ve-anvehu*, This is my Lord and I will adorn Him." *Hiddur miẓvah* is frequently associated with the physical objects through which a *miẓvah* is fulfilled. For example, the Talmud, quoting this verse, states, "Make a beautiful *sukah* in His honor, a beautiful *lulav*, a beautiful *shofar*, beautiful *ẓiẓit*, and a beautiful Torah scroll" (*Shabbat* 133b).

The prohibition of eating on the eve of Passover teaches us, according to Rashi, that *hiddur miẓvah* also applies to the manner in which one performs a *miẓvah*. This is similar to the *miẓvah* of *kissu'i ha-dam*, the "covering of the blood" with earth when certain animals and fowl are slaughtered. One should place the earth to cover the blood in a respectful manner, using one's hand or an instrument but not one's foot (*Ḥullin* 87a). Thus, we see that not only is one required to beautify the object through which a *miẓvah* is fulfilled, but one must as well beautify the manner in which a *miẓvah* is performed. (*Reshimot*)

Baking Maẓẓah on Erev Pesaḥ אפיית מצה בערב פסח

Tur (*Oraḥ Ḥayyim* 458) recommends that one should bake *maẓẓah* on the afternoon of the fourteenth of Nisan, at the time the *korban Pesaḥ* may be slaughtered. This is based on the comparison Rava makes between *maẓẓah* and the *korban Pesaḥ*, which is offered on the afternoon of the fourteenth (see *Pesaḥim* 120b). In the event the fourteenth of Nisan occurs on Shabbat, when one offers the *korban Pesaḥ* but is not permitted to bake, *Mordekhai* (*Pesaḥim* 543) quotes the opinion of Rabbi Samson of Sens, that one should not bake the *maẓẓah* on Friday; rather, one should bake it on Saturday night, the fifteenth of Nisan, after the conclusion of Shabbat. This view requires explanation, because the *korban Pesaḥ* may no longer be brought on the night of the fifteenth of Nisan, at the time the *maẓẓah* is baked. What advantage is there in baking the *maẓẓah* at night, when the *korban Pesaḥ* could not be brought?

We learn from the verse "*u-shemartem et ha-maẓẓot*, and you shall guard the

mazzot" (Ex. 12:17) that *mazzah* needs to have *shimur* (i.e., it must be guarded from becoming *ḥamez*, and it must be baked *li-shemah*, with the specific intent to use it for the *mizvah*). *Shimur* can only apply to *mazzah*, and the identity of *mazzah* can only emerge in contradistinction to the prohibition of *ḥamez*.

The verse states, "You shall not offer the blood of My sacrifice with leavened bread" (Ex. 34:25). This verse indicates that the prohibition of *ḥamez* is connected to the offering of the *korban Pesaḥ*. Accordingly, the distinction between *ḥamez* and *mazzah* commences on the afternoon of the fourteenth of Nisan, at the time when one may offer the *korban Pesaḥ*. Prior to the afternoon of the fourteenth, when there is no practical distinction between *ḥamez* and *mazzah*, the identity of *mazzah* cannot emerge. Therefore, if the fourteenth of Nisan occurs on a Shabbat, one cannot prepare *mazzah* on Friday, because at that time, the distinction between *ḥamez* and *mazzah* has not yet come into existence. One must wait until after Shabbat ends, at a time when the distinction between *ḥamez* and *mazzah* has already commenced, in order to create the status of *mazzah*. The comparison between *mazzah* and the *korban Pesaḥ*, according to Rabbi Samson, teaches us that it is only after the prohibition of *ḥamez*, derivative of the time of the slaughtering of the *korban Pesaḥ*, arises that the identity and status of *mazzah* can be established. (*Reshimot*)

שיר השירים

The allegorical character of the Song of Songs is a firm principle of the *halakhah* upon which are founded both the physical sanctity of the scroll of the Song of Songs as not to be touched (it "defiles the hands" [*Yadayim* 3:5]), and the sanctity of the name Shelomoh (Solomon), occurrences of which in the Song of Songs are interpreted allegorically as appellations for God (*Shelomoh* = "*Melekh she-ha-shalom shelo*, the King to whom peace belongs"). The aggadic tradition interprets the Song of Songs symbolically.

The *halakhah* asserts, "All the Scriptures are holy, but the Song of Songs is the holy of holies" (*Yadayim* 3:6). The Song of Songs is the most wonderful and most astonishing poem of the divine ontic dialectics. It is the poem of the creation and the Creator in general, and of the Jewish nation and its God in particular.

The sun-blackened Shulamite — the creation — in her lowly, turbid state yearns for her heart's choice: God.

The lover/Creator loves His beloved/creation.

The Creator has captured the heart of His creation; the Eternal has captivated the spirit of every living thing.

The Creator has promised the creation that He will never abandon her. The creation has drawn the Creator's heart with one of her eyes that gaze upon the face of eternity. Finitude has drawn the heart of infinitude with one coil of her necklace.

The Creator loves His creation, yet He nevertheless rests in a hidden place, in the shade.

The creation craves her Creator, yet she nevertheless refuses to open the doors of her dwelling!

(*From There You Shall Seek*)

פרק א

א שִׁיר הַשִּׁירִים אֲשֶׁר לִשְׁלֹמֹה. **ב** יִשָּׁקֵנִי מִנְּשִׁיקוֹת פִּיהוּ כִּי טוֹבִים
דֹּדֶיךָ מִיָּיִן. **ג** לְרֵיחַ שְׁמָנֶיךָ טוֹבִים שֶׁמֶן תּוּרַק שְׁמֶךָ עַל כֵּן עֲלָמוֹת
אֲהֵבוּךָ. **ד** מָשְׁכֵנִי אַחֲרֶיךָ נָּרוּצָה. הֱבִיאַנִי הַמֶּלֶךְ חֲדָרָיו נָגִילָה
וְנִשְׂמְחָה בָּךְ נַזְכִּירָה דֹדֶיךָ מִיַּיִן מֵישָׁרִים אֲהֵבוּךָ. **ה** שְׁחוֹרָה אֲנִי
וְנָאוָה בְּנוֹת יְרוּשָׁלָם כְּאָהֳלֵי קֵדָר כִּירִיעוֹת שְׁלֹמֹה. **ו** אַל תִּרְאוּנִי
שֶׁאֲנִי שְׁחַרְחֹרֶת שֶׁשֱּׁזָפַתְנִי הַשָּׁמֶשׁ בְּנֵי אִמִּי נִחֲרוּ בִי שָׂמֻנִי נֹטֵרָה
אֶת הַכְּרָמִים כַּרְמִי שֶׁלִּי לֹא נָטָרְתִּי. **ז** הַגִּידָה לִּי שֶׁאָהֲבָה נַפְשִׁי
אֵיכָה תִרְעֶה אֵיכָה תַּרְבִּיץ בַּצָּהֳרָיִם שַׁלָּמָה אֶהְיֶה כְּעֹטְיָה עַל עֶדְרֵי
חֲבֵרֶיךָ. **ח** אִם לֹא תֵדְעִי לָךְ הַיָּפָה בַּנָּשִׁים צְאִי לָךְ בְּעִקְבֵי הַצֹּאן וּרְעִי
אֶת גְּדִיֹּתַיִךְ עַל מִשְׁכְּנוֹת הָרֹעִים. **ט** לְסֻסָתִי בְּרִכְבֵי פַרְעֹה דִּמִּיתִיךְ
רַעְיָתִי. **י** נָאווּ לְחָיַיִךְ בַּתֹּרִים צַוָּארֵךְ בַּחֲרוּזִים. **יא** תּוֹרֵי זָהָב נַעֲשֶׂה

מָשְׁכֵנִי אַחֲרֶיךָ נָּרוּצָה *Draw me, we will run after you* There is no hidden corner of the natural or spiritual world which man's consciousness, pining for its divine beloved, does not peer into and scrutinize. Human consciousness carefully investigates the buds of transcendence that appear every so often in the spiritual desert. This search is not the romantic yearning of fugitives from the monotonous secularism of the everyday. Rather, it is rooted in the general cultural consciousness. Flesh-and-blood man longs to escape from the straits of the limited, bounded, and contingent world and go out into the limitless, independent, wide-open spaces. This search is an act of self-transcendence, which is truly the essence of man's cultural ascent.

(*From There You Shall Seek*)

שְׁחוֹרָה אֲנִי וְנָאוָה *I am black but comely* A person is unable to repent if he lacks the courage to blame and to condemn himself. Regret is impossible without recognition of sin. On the other hand, one cannot imagine recognition of sin and commitment for the future unless man believes in his creative faculties and abilities, and in the powers of his soul that can help him to sacrifice himself.

If a person thinks that he is beyond saving and hence subject to natural, mechanical forces, if he is not convinced of human freedom of action, then it is impossible for him to feel guilt and there is no reason to expect him to change. Every expression expresses itself in the call: "I am black but comely." If we do not see the comely, we cannot discern the black. The sinner must see himself from two antithetical viewpoints — the nullity of self and the greatness of self. Hence man's praise, like his shame, is part of confession.

(*Hamesh Derashot*)

לָךְ עִם נְקֻדּוֹת הַכָּסֶף. **יב** עַד שֶׁהַמֶּלֶךְ בִּמְסִבּוֹ נִרְדִּי נָתַן רֵיחוֹ. **יג**
צְרוֹר הַמֹּר דּוֹדִי לִי בֵּין שָׁדַי יָלִין. **יד** אֶשְׁכֹּל הַכֹּפֶר דּוֹדִי לִי בְּכַרְמֵי
עֵין גֶּדִי. **טו** הִנָּךְ יָפָה רַעְיָתִי הִנָּךְ יָפָה עֵינַיִךְ יוֹנִים. **טז** הִנְּךָ יָפֶה
דוֹדִי אַף נָעִים אַף עַרְשֵׂנוּ רַעֲנָנָה. **יז** קֹרוֹת בָּתֵּינוּ אֲרָזִים רחיטנו
(רַהִיטֵנוּ) בְּרוֹתִים.

פרק ב

א אֲנִי חֲבַצֶּלֶת הַשָּׁרוֹן שׁוֹשַׁנַּת הָעֲמָקִים. **ב** כְּשׁוֹשַׁנָּה בֵּין הַחוֹחִים כֵּן
רַעְיָתִי בֵּין הַבָּנוֹת. **ג** כְּתַפּוּחַ בַּעֲצֵי הַיַּעַר כֵּן דּוֹדִי בֵּין הַבָּנִים בְּצִלּוֹ
חִמַּדְתִּי וְיָשַׁבְתִּי וּפִרְיוֹ מָתוֹק לְחִכִּי. **ד** הֱבִיאַנִי אֶל בֵּית הַיָּיִן וְדִגְלוֹ
עָלַי אַהֲבָה. **ה** סַמְּכוּנִי בָּאֲשִׁישׁוֹת רַפְּדוּנִי בַּתַּפּוּחִים כִּי חוֹלַת אַהֲבָה
אָנִי. **ו** שְׂמֹאלוֹ תַּחַת לְרֹאשִׁי וִימִינוֹ תְּחַבְּקֵנִי. **ז** הִשְׁבַּעְתִּי אֶתְכֶם

הַגִּידָה לִּי שֶׁאָהֲבָה נַפְשִׁי *Tell me, You whom my soul loves* Maimonides writes (*Hilkhot Teshuvah* 10:3) that all of *Shir ha-Shirim* is a parable for the longing of man for God. In this verse, God is the shepherd, and His beloved is full of longing for Him. His beloved asks, "Can you tell me where to find You? I need protection and shelter, and You are the only one who can help me. Where do You keep Your flock in the scorching noon sun?" When the burning sun is above, we seek the shade and protection of God. The sheep should be with the shepherd, but here there is a very strange situation. Here is the Shepherd, tall and visible, not far from us at all, but nevertheless, when His flock comes closer to Him, He disappears. Why, asks *Kenesset Yisrael*, should I be like the *otyah,* the wandering widow who has no one to show her any compassion?

(*The Lord Is Righteous in All His Ways*)

כִּי חוֹלַת אַהֲבָה אָנִי *For I am lovesick* For the Jew there is no such thing as routine. Everything is a wondrous miracle. He is excited by everything, from the novel and unknown to the everyday and the ordinary. In everything he sees the glory of God; over everything he utters a benediction. The beloved goes out always — at each dawn with the radiance of the morning star, and at every twilight with the winking of the evening star, when her drowsy eyelids droop each night and when she opens her eyes every morning — to greet her ruddy lover, who peers out from the radiant dawn and the starlight, and from tiredness and rest! The benediction always signifies a moment of grace, a great, sublime moment for the utterer of the benediction, in which he attains a deep vision and acute look through the miraculous portal torn open by a hidden hand to reveal a world that is entirely good and pleasant, and entirely miraculous. The *halakhah*

בְּנוֹת יְרוּשָׁלַם בִּצְבָאוֹת אוֹ בְּאַיְלוֹת הַשָּׂדֶה אִם תָּעִירוּ וְאִם תְּעוֹרְרוּ
אֶת הָאַהֲבָה עַד שֶׁתֶּחְפָּץ. **ח** קוֹל דּוֹדִי הִנֵּה זֶה בָּא מְדַלֵּג עַל הֶהָרִים
מְקַפֵּץ עַל הַגְּבָעוֹת. **ט** דּוֹמֶה דוֹדִי לִצְבִי אוֹ לְעֹפֶר הָאַיָּלִים הִנֵּה זֶה
עוֹמֵד אַחַר כָּתְלֵנוּ מַשְׁגִּיחַ מִן הַחַלֹּנוֹת מֵצִיץ מִן הַחֲרַכִּים. **י** עָנָה
דוֹדִי וְאָמַר לִי קוּמִי לָךְ רַעְיָתִי יָפָתִי וּלְכִי לָךְ. **יא** כִּי הִנֵּה הַסְּתָו עָבָר
הַגֶּשֶׁם חָלַף הָלַךְ לוֹ. **יב** הַנִּצָּנִים נִרְאוּ בָאָרֶץ עֵת הַזָּמִיר הִגִּיעַ וְקוֹל
הַתּוֹר נִשְׁמַע בְּאַרְצֵנוּ. **יג** הַתְּאֵנָה חָנְטָה פַגֶּיהָ וְהַגְּפָנִים סְמָדַר נָתְנוּ
רֵיחַ קוּמִי לכי (לָךְ) רַעְיָתִי יָפָתִי וּלְכִי לָךְ. **יד** יוֹנָתִי בְּחַגְוֵי הַסֶּלַע
בְּסֵתֶר הַמַּדְרֵגָה הַרְאִינִי אֶת מַרְאַיִךְ הַשְׁמִיעִנִי אֶת קוֹלֵךְ כִּי קוֹלֵךְ
עָרֵב וּמַרְאֵיךְ נָאוֶה. **טו** אֶחֱזוּ לָנוּ שֻׁעָלִים שֻׁעָלִים קְטַנִּים מְחַבְּלִים
כְּרָמִים וּכְרָמֵינוּ סְמָדַר. **טז** דּוֹדִי לִי וַאֲנִי לוֹ הָרֹעֶה בַּשּׁוֹשַׁנִּים. **יז** עַד
שֶׁיָּפוּחַ הַיּוֹם וְנָסוּ הַצְּלָלִים סֹב דְּמֵה לְךָ דוֹדִי לִצְבִי אוֹ לְעֹפֶר הָאַיָּלִים
עַל הָרֵי בָתֶר.

פרק ג

א עַל מִשְׁכָּבִי בַּלֵּילוֹת בִּקַּשְׁתִּי אֵת שֶׁאָהֲבָה נַפְשִׁי בִּקַּשְׁתִּיו וְלֹא

---

says: Fortunate is the creature who encounters the Creator along the pathways of the world from time to time, when he takes a sip of water or tastes a bit of bread. Fortunate is the man for whom God is the Lord whenever he uses his senses and derives enjoyment from them.

(*From There You Shall Seek*)

There is a dispute between Rashi and Maimonides as to how one interprets the metaphor of the Song of Songs. Maimonides (*Hilkhot Teshuvah* 10:3) views it as a metaphor for the individual ecstatic religious experience, for the degree of love that the individual is required to feel for God. He states, "One is required to be constantly obsessed with love of God just as one is lovesick for a particular woman and cannot remove her from his thoughts and yearns for her constantly, while he is at rest or up and about, while eating and drinking; even greater than this must be the love of God, as we are commanded to love Him with all one's heart and soul; and this is what Solomon said metaphorically, 'for I am lovesick' (2:5); and the entirety of the Song of Songs is a metaphor for this theme."

Rashi, however, in his introduction to the Song of Songs, explains that the Song of Songs is a metaphor for the history of the relationship between the Children of Israel and God. For example, Rashi explains the verse "Who is ascending from the wilderness" (3:6) as a reference to *Benei Yisrael* when they

מְצָאתִיו. **ב** אָקוּמָה נָּא וַאֲסוֹבְבָה בָעִיר בַּשְּׁוָקִים וּבָרְחֹבוֹת אֲבַקְשָׁה
אֵת שֶׁאָהֲבָה נַפְשִׁי בִּקַּשְׁתִּיו וְלֹא מְצָאתִיו. **ג** מְצָאוּנִי הַשֹּׁמְרִים
הַסֹּבְבִים בָּעִיר אֵת שֶׁאָהֲבָה נַפְשִׁי רְאִיתֶם. **ד** כִּמְעַט שֶׁעָבַרְתִּי מֵהֶם
עַד שֶׁמָּצָאתִי אֵת שֶׁאָהֲבָה נַפְשִׁי אֲחַזְתִּיו וְלֹא אַרְפֶּנּוּ עַד שֶׁהֲבֵיאתִיו
אֶל בֵּית אִמִּי וְאֶל חֶדֶר הוֹרָתִי. **ה** הִשְׁבַּעְתִּי אֶתְכֶם בְּנוֹת יְרוּשָׁלִַם
בִּצְבָאוֹת אוֹ בְּאַיְלוֹת הַשָּׂדֶה אִם תָּעִירוּ וְאִם תְּעוֹרְרוּ אֶת הָאַהֲבָה
עַד שֶׁתֶּחְפָּץ. **ו** מִי זֹאת עֹלָה מִן הַמִּדְבָּר כְּתִימְרוֹת עָשָׁן מְקֻטֶּרֶת מֹר
וּלְבוֹנָה מִכֹּל אַבְקַת רוֹכֵל. **ז** הִנֵּה מִטָּתוֹ שֶׁלִּשְׁלֹמֹה שִׁשִּׁים גִּבֹּרִים
סָבִיב לָהּ מִגִּבֹּרֵי יִשְׂרָאֵל. **ח** כֻּלָּם אֲחֻזֵי חֶרֶב מְלֻמְּדֵי מִלְחָמָה אִישׁ
חַרְבּוֹ עַל יְרֵכוֹ מִפַּחַד בַּלֵּילוֹת. **ט** אַפִּרְיוֹן עָשָׂה לוֹ הַמֶּלֶךְ שְׁלֹמֹה
מֵעֲצֵי הַלְּבָנוֹן. **י** עַמּוּדָיו עָשָׂה כֶסֶף רְפִידָתוֹ זָהָב מֶרְכָּבוֹ אַרְגָּמָן תּוֹכוֹ
רָצוּף אַהֲבָה מִבְּנוֹת יְרוּשָׁלִָם. **יא** צְאֶינָה וּרְאֶינָה בְּנוֹת צִיּוֹן בַּמֶּלֶךְ
שְׁלֹמֹה בָּעֲטָרָה שֶׁעִטְּרָה לּוֹ אִמּוֹ בְּיוֹם חֲתֻנָּתוֹ וּבְיוֹם שִׂמְחַת לִבּוֹ.

פרק ד

א הִנָּךְ יָפָה רַעְיָתִי הִנָּךְ יָפָה עֵינַיִךְ יוֹנִים מִבַּעַד לְצַמָּתֵךְ שַׂעְרֵךְ כְּעֵדֶר

---

followed God in the desert after the Exodus, and the verse "on the day of his wedding" (3:11) as referring to the special relationship forged between God and *Benei Yisrael* upon their acceptance of the Torah.

In truth, both interpretations refer to the same basic idea: the relationship between God and the world. This connection, however, is expressed in two ways. Just as God longs to cleave to the individual, He also desires to perpetuate His dwelling within a singular collective, a chosen community and a unique nation.

(*Reshimot*)

אַחַר כָּתְלֵנוּ *Behind our wall* Neither the Babylonian nor the Jerusalem Talmud mentions the Western Wall, and the *Rishonim* hardly mention it. For example, Maimonides' letter describing his arrival in Jerusalem writes only, "And I entered into the large and holy house, and I prayed in it." There is a reference to the Western Wall in the Midrash on the verse from Song of Songs, "Behold, He stands behind our wall, He looks in through the windows, He peers through the lattice" (2:9). Says the Midrash (*Exodus Rabbah* 2:2), the wall here refers to the *Kotel ha-Ma'aravi*. The *Shekhinah* is behind the *Kotel*; She never left the *Har ha-Bayit*.

(*The Lord Is Righteous in All His Ways*)

הָעִזִּים שֶׁגָּלְשׁוּ מֵהַר גִּלְעָד. **ב** שִׁנַּיִךְ כְּעֵדֶר הַקְּצוּבוֹת שֶׁעָלוּ מִן הָרַחְצָה
שֶׁכֻּלָּם מַתְאִימוֹת וְשַׁכֻּלָה אֵין בָּהֶם. **ג** כְּחוּט הַשָּׁנִי שִׂפְתוֹתַיִךְ וּמִדְבָּרֵךְ
נָאוֶה כְּפֶלַח הָרִמּוֹן רַקָּתֵךְ מִבַּעַד לְצַמָּתֵךְ. **ד** כְּמִגְדַּל דָּוִיד צַוָּארֵךְ בָּנוּי
לְתַלְפִּיּוֹת אֶלֶף הַמָּגֵן תָּלוּי עָלָיו כֹּל שִׁלְטֵי הַגִּבֹּרִים. **ה** שְׁנֵי שָׁדַיִךְ
כִּשְׁנֵי עֳפָרִים תְּאוֹמֵי צְבִיָּה הָרוֹעִים בַּשּׁוֹשַׁנִּים. **ו** עַד שֶׁיָּפוּחַ הַיּוֹם
וְנָסוּ הַצְּלָלִים אֵלֶךְ לִי אֶל הַר הַמּוֹר וְאֶל גִּבְעַת הַלְּבוֹנָה. **ז** כֻּלָּךְ
יָפָה רַעְיָתִי וּמוּם אֵין בָּךְ. **ח** אִתִּי מִלְּבָנוֹן כַּלָּה אִתִּי מִלְּבָנוֹן תָּבוֹאִי
תָּשׁוּרִי מֵרֹאשׁ אֲמָנָה מֵרֹאשׁ שְׂנִיר וְחֶרְמוֹן מִמְּעֹנוֹת אֲרָיוֹת מֵהַרְרֵי
נְמֵרִים. **ט** לִבַּבְתִּנִי אֲחֹתִי כַלָּה לִבַּבְתִּנִי באחד (בְּאַחַת) מֵעֵינַיִךְ
בְּאַחַד עֲנָק מִצַּוְּרֹנָיִךְ. **י** מַה יָּפוּ דֹדַיִךְ אֲחֹתִי כַלָּה מַה טֹּבוּ דֹדַיִךְ מִיַּיִן
וְרֵיחַ שְׁמָנַיִךְ מִכָּל בְּשָׂמִים. **יא** נֹפֶת תִּטֹּפְנָה שִׂפְתוֹתַיִךְ כַּלָּה דְּבַשׁ

כְּמִגְדַּל דָּוִיד צַוָּארֵךְ בָּנוּי לְתַלְפִּיּוֹת *Your neck is like the tower of David built with talpiot* The Talmud's interpretation of the word *talpiyot* is a "*tel she-kol piyot ponim bo*, a mount to which all mouths [that pray] face." Accordingly, one is required to face the Temple in Jerusalem when praying (*Berakhot* 30a).

Rav Hayim of Brisk infers from Maimonides that this is biblically mandated. Maimonides' discussion of the prayer laws begins with the biblical requirements of the *mizvah* of prayer (*Hilkhot Tefillah* 1:1–3), and then he discusses Ezra's enactments pertaining to prayer (ibid. 1:4). Specifically, Maimonides states that there is a biblical requirement to pray each day, and, among other things, "wherever one is located, one should pray in the direction of the Temple, as practiced from the times of Moses until Ezra" (ibid. 1:3). Thus, according to Maimonides, the requirement to face the Temple is a biblical requirement that preceded the later enactments instituted by Ezra.

(*Reshimot*)

קוֹל דּוֹדִי דוֹפֵק *My beloved knocks* Years ago, in the midst of a night of terror filled with the horrors of Maidanek, Treblinka, and Buchenwald, in a night of gas chambers and crematoria, in a night of absolute divine self-concealment, in a night ruled by the satan of doubt and apostasy which sought to sweep the maiden from her house into the Christian church, in a night of continuous searching, of questing for the Beloved — in that very night the Beloved appeared. "God who conceals Himself in His dazzling hiddenness" suddenly manifested Himself and began to knock at the tent of His despondent and disconsolate love, twisting convulsively on her bed, suffering the pains of hell.

וְחָלָב תַּחַת לְשׁוֹנֵךְ וְרֵיחַ שַׂלְמֹתַיִךְ כְּרֵיחַ לְבָנוֹן. **יב** גַּן נָעוּל אֲחֹתִי
כַלָּה גַּל נָעוּל מַעְיָן חָתוּם. **יג** שְׁלָחַיִךְ פַּרְדֵּס רִמּוֹנִים עִם פְּרִי מְגָדִים
כְּפָרִים עִם נְרָדִים. **יד** נֵרְדְּ וְכַרְכֹּם קָנֶה וְקִנָּמוֹן, עִם כָּל עֲצֵי לְבוֹנָה
מֹר וַאֲהָלוֹת עִם, כָּל רָאשֵׁי בְשָׂמִים. **טו** מַעְיַן גַּנִּים בְּאֵר מַיִם חַיִּים
וְנֹזְלִים מִן לְבָנוֹן. **טז** עוּרִי צָפוֹן וּבוֹאִי תֵימָן הָפִיחִי גַנִּי יִזְּלוּ בְשָׂמָיו
יָבֹא דוֹדִי לְגַנּוֹ וְיֹאכַל פְּרִי מְגָדָיו.

פרק ה

א בָּאתִי לְגַנִּי אֲחֹתִי כַלָּה אָרִיתִי מוֹרִי עִם בְּשָׂמִי אָכַלְתִּי יַעְרִי עִם
דִּבְשִׁי שָׁתִיתִי יֵינִי עִם חֲלָבִי אִכְלוּ רֵעִים שְׁתוּ וְשִׁכְרוּ דּוֹדִים. **ב** אֲנִי
יְשֵׁנָה וְלִבִּי עֵר קוֹל דּוֹדִי דוֹפֵק פִּתְחִי לִי אֲחֹתִי רַעְיָתִי יוֹנָתִי תַמָּתִי
שֶׁרֹּאשִׁי נִמְלָא טָל קְוֻצּוֹתַי רְסִיסֵי לָיְלָה. **ג** פָּשַׁטְתִּי אֶת כֻּתָּנְתִּי

As a result of the knocks on the door of the maiden, wrapped in mourning, the State of Israel was born!

How many times did the Beloved knock on the door of the tent of His love? It appears to me that we can count at least six knocks. First, the knock of the Beloved was heard in the political arena. No one can deny that from the standpoint of international relations, the establishment of the State of Israel, in a political sense, was an almost supernatural occurrence. Second, the knocking of the Beloved could be heard on the battlefield. The small Israeli Defense Forces defeated the mighty armies of the Arab countries. Third, the Beloved began to knock as well on the door of the theological tent, and it may very well be that this was the strongest knock of all. The claims of Christian theologians that God deprived the Jewish people of its rights in the land of Israel have been publicly refuted by the establishment of the State of Israel and have been exposed as falsehoods, lacking all validity. Fourth, the Beloved was knocking in the hearts of the perplexed and assimilated youths. Many American Jews who had been semi-, demi-, or hemi-assimilated are now filled with fear and concern about the crisis overtaking the State of Israel, and they pray for its security and welfare, even though they are still far from being completely committed to it. The fifth knock of the Beloved was perhaps the most important of all. For the first time in the history of our exile, divine providence has surprised our enemies with the sensational discovery that Jewish blood is not free for the taking. The sixth knock, which we must not ignore, was heard when the gates of the land were opened. A Jew who flees from a hostile country now knows that he can find a secure refuge in the land of his ancestors.

(*Kol Dodi Dofek*)

אֵיכָכָה אֶלְבָּשֶׁנָּה רָחַצְתִּי אֶת רַגְלַי אֵיכָכָה אֲטַנְּפֵם. **ד** דּוֹדִי שָׁלַח יָדוֹ
מִן הַחֹר וּמֵעַי הָמוּ עָלָיו. **ה** קַמְתִּי אֲנִי לִפְתֹּחַ לְדוֹדִי וְיָדַי נָטְפוּ מוֹר
וְאֶצְבְּעֹתַי מוֹר עֹבֵר עַל כַּפּוֹת הַמַּנְעוּל. **ו** פָּתַחְתִּי אֲנִי לְדוֹדִי וְדוֹדִי
חָמַק עָבָר נַפְשִׁי יָצְאָה בְדַבְּרוֹ בִּקַּשְׁתִּיהוּ וְלֹא מְצָאתִיהוּ קְרָאתִיו וְלֹא
עָנָנִי. מְצָאֻנִי הַשֹּׁמְרִים הַסֹּבְבִים בָּעִיר הִכּוּנִי פְצָעוּנִי נָשְׂאוּ אֶת רְדִידִי
מֵעָלַי שֹׁמְרֵי הַחֹמוֹת. **ח** הִשְׁבַּעְתִּי אֶתְכֶם בְּנוֹת יְרוּשָׁלָם אִם תִּמְצְאוּ
אֶת דּוֹדִי מַה תַּגִּידוּ לוֹ שֶׁחוֹלַת אַהֲבָה אָנִי. **ט** מַה דּוֹדֵךְ מִדּוֹד הַיָּפָה
בַּנָּשִׁים מַה דּוֹדֵךְ מִדּוֹד שֶׁכָּכָה הִשְׁבַּעְתָּנוּ. **י** דּוֹדִי צַח וְאָדוֹם דָּגוּל
מֵרְבָבָה. **יא** רֹאשׁוֹ, כֶּתֶם פָּז קְוֻצּוֹתָיו תַּלְתַּלִּים שְׁחֹרוֹת כָּעוֹרֵב. **יב**
עֵינָיו כְּיוֹנִים עַל אֲפִיקֵי מָיִם רֹחֲצוֹת בֶּחָלָב יֹשְׁבוֹת עַל מִלֵּאת. **יג**
לְחָיָו כַּעֲרוּגַת הַבֹּשֶׂם מִגְדְּלוֹת מֶרְקָחִים שִׂפְתוֹתָיו שׁוֹשַׁנִּים נֹטְפוֹת
מוֹר עֹבֵר. **יד** יָדָיו גְּלִילֵי זָהָב מְמֻלָּאִים בַּתַּרְשִׁישׁ מֵעָיו עֶשֶׁת שֵׁן
מְעֻלֶּפֶת סַפִּירִים. **טו** שׁוֹקָיו עַמּוּדֵי שֵׁשׁ מְיֻסָּדִים עַל אַדְנֵי פָז מַרְאֵהוּ

רָחַצְתִּי אֶת רַגְלַי אֵיכָכָה אֲטַנְּפֵם *I have washed my feet; how can I defile them* The Jewish people searches for God but does not find Him. Once, He knocks on her door. "It is the voice of my beloved that knocks! Let me in, my sister, my beloved, my dove, my perfect one. My head is drenched with dew; my locks with the damp of the night." He is ready, but she was not. "I have taken off my robe; how shall I put it on? I have washed my feet; how shall I soil them?"

The Jew often has the opportunity to find the Master of the World. God quite often knocks upon the Jew's door and wants to share his abode with him. But somehow the Jew misses the opportunity. He does not have the courage to get out of bed and open the door. By the time we get up to open it, it is too late. We lose Him, and it is hard for us to find Him again. That is why the exile has lasted so long. The next time we find God it will be different, and we will not repeat the mistakes of the past. If we hear that knock on the door, even the softest knock, we answer, "The door is open; come in!" And once He enters our house, we will not allow Him to depart.

(*The Lord Is Righteous in All His Ways*)

וְדוֹדִי חָמַק עָבָר *But my beloved had turned away and was gone* Judaism also knows that the cosmic encounter, despite its importance, greatness, and force, is insufficient. God reveals Himself to His creation, but also eludes it. He is close to us, and the splendor of His majesty breaks forth from every blossoming lily and every ray of light, from the shadows of twilight and the peacefulness of a clear evening filled with expectation and suspense, from the soft breezes of spring and the howling of a storm on a dreary winter night, from the silence

כַּלְּבָנוֹן בָּחוּר כָּאֲרָזִים. **טז** חִכּוֹ מַמְתַקִּים וְכֻלּוֹ מַחֲמַדִּים זֶה דוֹדִי וְזֶה
רֵעִי בְּנוֹת יְרוּשָׁלָםִ.

פרק ו

א אָנָה הָלַךְ דּוֹדֵךְ הַיָּפָה בַּנָּשִׁים אָנָה פָּנָה דוֹדֵךְ וּנְבַקְשֶׁנּוּ עִמָּךְ. **ב** דּוֹדִי
יָרַד לְגַנּוֹ לַעֲרֻגוֹת הַבֹּשֶׂם לִרְעוֹת בַּגַּנִּים וְלִלְקֹט שׁוֹשַׁנִּים. **ג** אֲנִי לְדוֹדִי
וְדוֹדִי לִי הָרֹעֶה בַּשּׁוֹשַׁנִּים. **ד** יָפָה אַתְּ רַעְיָתִי כְּתִרְצָה נָאוָה כִּירוּשָׁלָםִ
אֲיֻמָּה כַּנִּדְגָּלוֹת. **ה** הָסֵבִּי עֵינַיִךְ מִנֶּגְדִּי שֶׁהֵם הִרְהִיבֻנִי שַׂעְרֵךְ כְּעֵדֶר
הָעִזִּים שֶׁגָּלְשׁוּ מִן הַגִּלְעָד. **ו** שִׁנַּיִךְ כְּעֵדֶר הָרְחֵלִים שֶׁעָלוּ מִן הָרַחְצָה
שֶׁכֻּלָּם מַתְאִימוֹת וְשַׁכֻּלָה אֵין בָּהֶם. **ז** כְּפֶלַח הָרִמּוֹן רַקָּתֵךְ מִבַּעַד
לְצַמָּתֵךְ. **ח** שִׁשִּׁים הֵמָּה מְלָכוֹת וּשְׁמֹנִים פִּילַגְשִׁים וַעֲלָמוֹת אֵין
מִסְפָּר. **ט** אַחַת הִיא יוֹנָתִי תַמָּתִי אַחַת הִיא לְאִמָּהּ בָּרָה הִיא
לְיוֹלַדְתָּהּ רָאוּהָ בָנוֹת וַיְאַשְּׁרוּהָ מְלָכוֹת וּפִילַגְשִׁים וַיְהַלְלוּהָ. **י** מִי

---

of the hills and the quietness of the plain, from the beating of the heart and the rhythmic movements of breathing, from the tumult of the masses and the loneliness of the individual, from the joy of youth and the melancholy of old age. But despite His closeness to us, He is boundlessly far from us. He wraps Himself in a cloud and retires to the recesses of eternity. He lives here with us and also at the "edges" of infinity. Now we see Him, and yet in a moment He rises above us.

(*From There You Shall Seek*)

אֲנִי לְדוֹדִי וְדוֹדִי לִי *I am my beloved's and my beloved is mine* When a Jew begins to pray the silent *Amidah* prayer, he turns to God as "the God *of* Abraham, the God *of* Isaac, and the God *of* Jacob." The Patriarchs belong to God, and, so to speak, God belongs to the Patriarchs. They searched for Him in an age when the entire world mocked them and the strange quest in which they persisted. Through the fact that they searched for Him and found Him, they acquired Him. They possessed the Eternal and He is their possession.

This mysterious relationship between God and the creations of His hands, between the Lord of Israel and the community of Israel, comes to expression in an extraordinary statement by the Sages of the Talmud that God, too, puts on *tefillin* (*Berakhot* 6a). We in our *tefillin* affirm the belonging of God to the Children of Israel: "Hear, O Israel, the Lord our God, the Lord is One"; and in the *tefillin* of the Eternal One, as it were, is expressed the possessory rights we have in Him: "I am my beloved's and my beloved is mine."

(*Hamesh Derashot*)

זֹאת הַנִּשְׁקָפָה כְּמוֹ שָׁחַר יָפָה כַלְּבָנָה בָּרָה כַּחַמָּה אֲיֻמָּה כַּנִּדְגָּלוֹת. **יא**
אֶל גִּנַּת אֱגוֹז יָרַדְתִּי לִרְאוֹת בְּאִבֵּי הַנָּחַל לִרְאוֹת הֲפָרְחָה הַגֶּפֶן הֵנֵצוּ
הָרִמֹּנִים. **יב** לֹא יָדַעְתִּי נַפְשִׁי שָׂמַתְנִי מַרְכְּבוֹת עַמִּי נָדִיב.

פרק ז

א שׁוּבִי שׁוּבִי הַשּׁוּלַמִּית שׁוּבִי שׁוּבִי וְנֶחֱזֶה בָּךְ מַה תֶּחֱזוּ בַּשּׁוּלַמִּית
כִּמְחֹלַת הַמַּחֲנָיִם. **ב** מַה יָּפוּ פְעָמַיִךְ בַּנְּעָלִים בַּת נָדִיב חַמּוּקֵי יְרֵכַיִךְ

בָּרָה כַּחַמָּה *Radiant as the sun* Religious experience is the outbreak of the wondrous force of the spontaneous metaphysical spirit in all its colorful variety and raging activity — a partnership in the act of creation. It leaps out of its restricted circle, aspires to the pinnacle of being with the enthusiasm of victory and sweeping triumph, viewing distant horizons reddening in the dawn of infinity. This sort of flourishing religiosity "shines through like the dawn" that drips on the mountaintops immersed in the morning dew; it is "beautiful as the moon" in the quiet night filled with serene breezes, and "radiant as the sun" in a transparently blue sky on a clear autumn day. The paramount principle is that man knows that religious life is an indivisible part of his essence; that the act is free, drawing its strength from his innermost being. All his spiritual directions — theoretical, ethical, and aesthetic — come together in a perfect variegated unity. The contents of his thought, will, and emotion are blended in the revelation of the religious sensibility. Man was created in God's image. A spark of the Creator was hidden in him. He desires creative freedom. The religious experience enables him to achieve this desire.

(*The Emergence of Ethical Man*)

לֹא יָדַעְתִּי *I have not been aware of myself* As a rule, *yada* and *da'at* apply not only to theoretical knowledge but also to awareness through the senses. "I have not been aware of myself; my soul set me amongst the chariots of a princely people." Hence the Tree of Knowledge, *eẓ ha-da'at tov va-ra,* corresponds to the aesthetic quality of the beautiful and the ugly. God forbade man the orgiastic aesthetic experience, the acquisition of the pleasure-impulse; he was not allowed to overemphasize the moment of wantonness, making the beauty ideal the fascinating force in human life.

(*The Emergence of Ethical Man*)

שׁוּבִי שׁוּבִי הַשּׁוּלַמִּית *Return, return, O Shulamite* The Midrash (*Numbers Rabbah* 2:4) interpreted this strange dialogue between an anonymous interrogator and the love-intoxicated Shulamite as symbolic of the unique steadfastness, fidelity, and commitment exhibited by the charismatic community to God. Return, O Shulamite, from your absurd engagement to your beloved, since even the

כְּמוֹ חֲלָאִים מַעֲשֵׂה יְדֵי אָמָּן. **ג** שָׁרְרֵךְ אַגַּן הַסַּהַר אַל יֶחְסַר הַמָּזֶג
בִּטְנֵךְ עֲרֵמַת חִטִּים סוּגָה בַּשּׁוֹשַׁנִּים. **ד** שְׁנֵי שָׁדַיִךְ כִּשְׁנֵי עֳפָרִים
תָּאֳמֵי צְבִיָּה. **ה** צַוָּארֵךְ כְּמִגְדַּל הַשֵּׁן עֵינַיִךְ בְּרֵכוֹת בְּחֶשְׁבּוֹן עַל שַׁעַר
בַּת רַבִּים אַפֵּךְ כְּמִגְדַּל הַלְּבָנוֹן צוֹפֶה פְּנֵי דַמָּשֶׂק. **ו** רֹאשֵׁךְ עָלַיִךְ
כַּכַּרְמֶל וְדַלַּת רֹאשֵׁךְ כָּאַרְגָּמָן מֶלֶךְ אָסוּר בָּרְהָטִים. **ז** מַה יָּפִית
וּמַה נָּעַמְתְּ אַהֲבָה בַּתַּעֲנוּגִים. **ח** זֹאת קוֹמָתֵךְ דָּמְתָה לְתָמָר וְשָׁדַיִךְ

---

strongest of bonds is dissoluble. Times have changed. History marches on. The covenantal union is no longer beneficial. On the contrary, it has become a source of misery and distress. The interrogator suggests the termination of the old covenantal relationship binding the Shulamite to her beloved. The Shulamite in her answer does not attempt to rationalize her absolute loyalty and her unqualified dedication to her beloved. She admits that her loyalty and dedication are a mystery even to herself. All she says is that it is futile to debate or to analyze her unswerving loyalty because she acts like one who, under the sway of a great ecstatic experience, has plunged into a never-ending dance whose very rhythm is intoxicating. In short, the covenantal community is metahistorical as far as it takes up fixed positions amid ever-changing historical events.

(*Family Redeemed*)

בִּטְנֵךְ עֲרֵמַת חִטִּים סוּגָה בַּשּׁוֹשַׁנִּים *Your belly is like a heap of wheat encircled with lilies* The Midrash on this verse well describes the capacity of the Jew to act often against the limitless strength of his natural desires. The groom longs for the canopy and the joys of marriage. On his seeking to associate with her, she says to him "I have seen a speck of blood the size of a mustard seed." He turns his face to other side. No serpent bit him, nor did a scorpion sting him. Alas, "encircled with lilies." Who would blame him were he to sin? Who would know about it? This entire drama takes place in the innermost chamber, in the dead of night. No iron wall shuts him out, but a flowerbed of lilies. He has only to step on the flowerbed and trample the lilies. But the unique strength found in every Jew prevents him from acting rashly, from trampling fresh and beautiful flowers which cannot protect themselves and can complain to no one. This is silent heroism.

(*Hamesh Derashot*)

מֶלֶךְ אָסוּר בָּרְהָטִים *The king is held captive in the tresses* There are times when God has to mete out punishment, when the *midat ha-din,* the attribute of judgment, prevails, because even though He is merciful, kind, and gracious, He somehow binds His own mercy and permits the attribute of *din* to be

לְאַשְׁכֹּלוֹת. **ט** אָמַרְתִּי אֶעֱלֶה בְתָמָר אֹחֲזָה בְּסַנְסִנָּיו וְיִהְיוּ נָא שָׁדַיִךְ
כְּאֶשְׁכְּלוֹת הַגֶּפֶן וְרֵיחַ אַפֵּךְ כַּתַּפּוּחִים. **י** וְחִכֵּךְ כְּיֵין הַטּוֹב הוֹלֵךְ לְדוֹדִי
לְמֵישָׁרִים דּוֹבֵב שִׂפְתֵי יְשֵׁנִים. **יא** אֲנִי לְדוֹדִי וְעָלַי תְּשׁוּקָתוֹ. **יב**
לְכָה דוֹדִי נֵצֵא הַשָּׂדֶה נָלִינָה בַּכְּפָרִים. **יג** נַשְׁכִּימָה לַכְּרָמִים נִרְאֶה אִם
פָּרְחָה הַגֶּפֶן פִּתַּח הַסְּמָדַר הֵנֵצוּ הָרִמּוֹנִים שָׁם אֶתֵּן אֶת דֹּדַי לָךְ. **יד**
הַדּוּדָאִים נָתְנוּ רֵיחַ וְעַל פְּתָחֵינוּ כָּל מְגָדִים חֲדָשִׁים גַּם יְשָׁנִים דּוֹדִי
צָפַנְתִּי לָךְ. **א** מִי יִתֶּנְךָ כְּאָח לִי יוֹנֵק שְׁדֵי אִמִּי אֶמְצָאֲךָ בַחוּץ אֶשָּׁקְךָ
גַּם לֹא יָבֻזוּ לִי. **ב** אֶנְהָגְךָ אֲבִיאֲךָ אֶל בֵּית אִמִּי תְּלַמְּדֵנִי אַשְׁקְךָ מִיַּיִן
הָרֶקַח מֵעֲסִיס רִמֹּנִי. **ג** שְׂמֹאלוֹ תַּחַת רֹאשִׁי וִימִינוֹ תְּחַבְּקֵנִי. **ד**
הִשְׁבַּעְתִּי אֶתְכֶם בְּנוֹת יְרוּשָׁלָם מַה תָּעִירוּ וּמַה תְּעֹרְרוּ אֶת הָאַהֲבָה
עַד שֶׁתֶּחְפָּץ. **ה** מִי זֹאת עֹלָה מִן הַמִּדְבָּר מִתְרַפֶּקֶת עַל דּוֹדָהּ תַּחַת
הַתַּפּוּחַ עוֹרַרְתִּיךָ שָׁמָּה חִבְּלַתְךָ אִמֶּךָ שָׁמָּה חִבְּלָה יְלָדַתְךָ. **ו** שִׂימֵנִי

---

victorious. He is like a king who is in chains, as it were. Indeed, the Midrash (*Lamentations Rabbah, Petiḥta* 34) comments concisely on the phrase "chained in fetters" (Jeremiah 40:1), it is as if God Himself is in chains. This is what the Kabbalistic scholars mean when they speak of "the king is held captive in the tresses."

(*The Lord Is Righteous in All His Ways*)

נַשְׁכִּימָה לַכְּרָמִים *Let us get up early to the vineyards* God takes His friend along and leads him into the wilderness. The motif of the Song of Songs prevails throughout the narrative of the lives of the Patriarchs. "Come, my beloved, let us go forth into the field; let us lodge in the villages. Let us get up early to the vineyards." The girl wants to lead her beloved away from the city life, from the peering eyes of the crowds and multitudes, into the solitude of the field, into the quiet, still lodgings of the villages. Love asserts itself in the desire of both partners for privacy and isolation. Spying curiosity of the stranger desecrates the holiness of intimacy. Love, exposed to public view, becomes vulgar and coarse. The self-sufficiency of both lovers expresses itself in their flight from

כַחוֹתָם עַל לִבֶּךָ כַּחוֹתָם עַל זְרוֹעֶךָ כִּי עַזָּה כַמָּוֶת אַהֲבָה קָשָׁה כִשְׁאוֹל
קִנְאָה רְשָׁפֶיהָ רִשְׁפֵּי אֵשׁ שַׁלְהֶבֶתְיָה. **ז** מַיִם רַבִּים לֹא יוּכְלוּ לְכַבּוֹת
אֶת הָאַהֲבָה וּנְהָרוֹת לֹא יִשְׁטְפוּהָ אִם יִתֵּן אִישׁ אֶת כָּל הוֹן בֵּיתוֹ
בָּאַהֲבָה בּוֹז יָבוּזוּ לוֹ. אָחוֹת לָנוּ קְטַנָּה וְשָׁדַיִם אֵין לָהּ מַה נַּעֲשֶׂה
לַאֲחֹתֵנוּ בַּיּוֹם שֶׁיְּדֻבַּר בָּהּ. **ט** אִם חוֹמָה הִיא נִבְנֶה עָלֶיהָ טִירַת כָּסֶף
וְאִם דֶּלֶת הִיא נָצוּר עָלֶיהָ לוּחַ אָרֶז. **י** אֲנִי חוֹמָה וְשָׁדַי כַּמִּגְדָּלוֹת
אָז הָיִיתִי בְעֵינָיו כְּמוֹצְאֵת שָׁלוֹם. **יא** כֶּרֶם הָיָה לִשְׁלֹמֹה בְּבַעַל הָמוֹן
נָתַן אֶת הַכֶּרֶם לַנֹּטְרִים אִישׁ יָבִא בְּפִרְיוֹ אֶלֶף כָּסֶף. **יב** כַּרְמִי שֶׁלִּי
לְפָנָי הָאֶלֶף לְךָ שְׁלֹמֹה וּמָאתַיִם לְנֹטְרִים אֶת פִּרְיוֹ. **יג** הַיּוֹשֶׁבֶת בַּגַּנִּים
חֲבֵרִים מַקְשִׁיבִים לְקוֹלֵךְ הַשְׁמִיעִנִי. **יד** בְּרַח דּוֹדִי וּדְמֵה לְךָ לִצְבִי אוֹ
לְעֹפֶר הָאַיָּלִים עַל הָרֵי בְשָׂמִים.

---

the crowd. God and Abraham seek to escape the big cities of Mesopotamia into the pastures of Canaan.

(*The Emergence of Ethical Man*)

תַּחַת הַתַּפּוּחַ *Under the apple tree I awakened you* On the verse "And he made the laver of brass … of the mirrors of the serving women" (Exodus 38:8), Rashi quotes a beautiful Midrash: "The daughters of Israel had in their possession mirrors which they used when adorning themselves … but Moses rejected them because they were made for the evil inclination. Said the Holy One, Blessed be He, to him: 'Accept them, for these are more beloved by Me than anything else.'"

The woman who appreciates her beauty and was able in Egypt, in the dark and fearful exile, to comfort and strengthen her husband's spirit, and to educate a generation thirsting for redemption, that woman if she sins will utter her confession with hotter tears and greater distress and regret than another woman. Such a woman will remember what she contributed "under the apple tree," and the feeling of guilt will weigh heavier on her conscience.

(*Hamesh Derashot*)

WORKS BY RABBI SOLOVEITCHIK QUOTED IN THIS HAGGADAH

Abraham's Journey: Reflections on the Life of the Founding Patriarch, eds. David Shatz, Joel B. Wolowelsky and Reuven Ziegler (© Toras HoRav Foundation, 2008).

Days of Deliverance: Essays on Purim and Hanukkah, eds. Eli D. Clark, Joel B. Wolowelsky and Reuven Ziegler (© Toras HoRav Foundation, 2007).

Family Redeemed: Essays on Family Relationships, eds. David Shatz and Joel B. Wolowelsky (© Toras HoRav Foundation, 2000).

Fate and Destiny (*Kol Dodi Dofek*), trans. Lawrence Kaplan (© Rabbinical Council of America, 2000).

Festival of Freedom: Essays on Pesah and the Haggadah, eds. Joel B. Wolowelsky and Reuven Ziegler (© Toras HoRav Foundation, 2006).

Halakhic Man (*Ish ha-Halakhah*), trans. Lawrence Kaplan (© Jewish Publication Society, 1983).

Kovez̤ Ḥiddushei Torah.

Out of the Whirlwind: Essays on Mourning, Suffering and the Human Condition, eds. David Shatz, Joel B. Wolowelsky and Reuven Ziegler (© Toras HoRav Foundation, 2003).

"Redemption, Prayer, Talmud Torah," (© Rabbinical Council of America 1978).

"Sacred and Profane," *Gesher* (3:1, 1966).

Shi'urim le-Zekher Abba Mori.

Books of the Toras HoRav Foundation are published by Ktav Publishing House.

ABOUT THE EDITOR

The editor of *The Seder Night: An Exalted Evening* is Rabbi Menachem Genack, a devoted student of the Rav who received *semikha* (ordination) from him and remained in close contact with him over the years. Rabbi Genack is Chief Executive Officer of the Orthodox Union Kashrus Division and rabbi of Congregation Shomrei Emunah, Englewood, New Jersey. He is the editor of *Rabbi Joseph B. Soloveitchik: Man of Halacha, Man of Faith*, and co-editor of *Mesorah*, a journal dedicated to discussion and analysis of the Rav's writings and teachings. Rabbi Genack has authored numerous articles and books on *halakhic* and Talmudic subjects, many of them pertaining to matters discussed by the Rav in his *shi'urim*. He is General Editor of the OU Press.